Unread Herrings

Renaissance and Baroque
Studies and Texts

Eckhard Bernstein
General Editor

Vol. 11

PETER LANG
New York • San Francisco • Bern • Baltimore
Frankfurt am Main • Berlin • Wien • Paris

James Nielson

Unread Herrings

Thomas Nashe and the Prosaics of the Real

PETER LANG
New York • San Francisco • Bern • Baltimore
Frankfurt am Main • Berlin • Wien • Paris

Library of Congress Cataloging-in-Publication Data

Nielson, James.
　　Unread herrings : Thomas Nashe and the prosaics of the real / James
Nielson.
　　　　p.　　cm. — (Renaissance and Baroque studies and texts; vol. 11)
　　Includes bibliographical references.
　　1. Nashe, Thomas, 1567–1601—Criticism and interpretation.
　　2. Realism in literature.　I. Title.　II. Series.
　　PR2326.N3Z783　　　　1993　　　　828'.309—dc20　　　　93-31708
　　ISBN 0-8204-2254-1　　　　　　　　　　　　　　　　　　　　　　CIP
　　ISSN 0897-7836

Die Deutsche Bibliothek-CIP-Einheitsaufnahme

Nielson, James:
Unread herrings : Thomas Nashe and the prosaics of the real / James Nielson.
- New York; San Francisco; Bern; Baltimore; Frankfurt am Main; Berlin;
Wien; Paris: Lang, 1993
　　(Renaissance and baroque studies and texts; Vol. 11)
　　ISBN 0-8204-2254-1
NE: GT

Front cover illustration from *A Most Strange and Wonderfull
Herring* (London: John Wolfe, 1598). Reproduced courtesy of the
Syndics of the Cambridge University Library.

Cover design by James F. Brisson.

CONTENTS

To the Two
Radiant Lamps and *Ever-Renewing Founts*
of my Existence,
Shirley Andrues and **Jean Canell**,
my *Mother* and *Grandmother*,
I gratefully dedicate these dear-purchased lines.

We read in the Roman poet Virgil, incomparable matrons of my life and lines, how the child should *"risu cognoscere matrem,"* acknowledge its mother with a laugh. And so I shall. For laughter is the language of the real, a language that the fortunate learn at their mother's breast. Whatever Melancholie Klein or Jacques Lack-con may have to say upon the subject, I know that the ancient poet was right to suppose that anyone who can't pay homage to his mother with a laugh isn't likely to stand a chance, let alone be fit to sit at a god's board or lie in a goddess's bed:

> *qui non risere parenti,*
> *nec deus hunc mensa, dea nec dignata cubili est.*

At least that's how it reads in the authorized editions. But this reading only arose when Quintilian (9.3.8) tried (against grammatical sense) to make the (plural) verb go with the (singular) child, instead of (rightly) with the parents. In all the manuscripts we read "cui non risere parentes," i.e., he *on whom the parents do not smile* is not fit, and so on and so forth. The real reading, however, has been rejected by the scholars because, as one of the rascals puts it in his commentary, it "gives easy grammar but feeble sense; a mother's smile hardly characterizes her child as exceptional nor would the absence of it, however unnatural it seems, obviously disqualify him from future greatness" (Coleman 1977, 148). But no; I'm afraid I can't agree. Without that precious smile I might not be "here" today. Happy is the child that has been suckled upon motherly chuckles; for, as that siberial savant M.M. Bakhtin has so rightly re-marked, all a child's "values are shaped, as it were, by its mother's embraces" (Bakhtin 1979, 46). Yes, blest the infant babe, who can still

vii

stride the blast of that maternal cacchination, and is still able to laugh as
Thomas Nashe could so often laugh. For though it may be true that
Nashe wasn't much of a scholar,

> Yet this I say, that for a mother witt,
> Fewe men haue euer seene the like of it

as someone wrote shortly after his death (Leishman 1949, 245).

Now on, to acknowledge nurturing that has been more gently avuncular than unconditionally maternal. I must first thank Heidi Burns and
Eckhard Bernstein at Peter Lang. If Dr. Burns had not solicited my
manuscript and if Prof. Bernstein had not given it such a sympathetic and
considered reading, my more extravagant work on Nashe might never
have seen print. I particularly feel grateful to Prof. Bernstein for his
gracious and charmingly written reader's report and for his constant
belief in the book and willingness to go to bat for it. Kathy Iwasaki has
been patient through a long series of last minute mop-ups.

I would like thankfully to acknowledge the graciousness of the Syndics of Cambridge University Library for permission to reprint the text
of *A Most Strange and Wonderfull Herring* (1598), of which the library possesses the sole extant copy, and for permission to reproduce the illustration appearing on A4^v of that pamphlet on the cover and on page 186
of this book.

In the process of revising for publication I have had encouragement
and intellectual challenge from many quarters. In particular, I would like
to thank Harry Berger, Jr. and Random Clod for a couple of heartening
spurts of correspondence, and my colleagues in the English Department
at the University of British Columbia, including Judy Brown, Noel Chev-
alier, Jill Franks, Sheldon Goldfarb, Leah Jahn, David Jordan, Dorothy
Lane, Shawn Malley, Bill New, Linda Pashka, Keith Richards, Paul
Yachnin, and especially Mark Vessey for many intriguing and comforting
confabulations. Thanks are due to Branko Peric for printing assistance.

Most of the material in this book was originally produced while I
held a Mellon Fellowship in the Humanities at McGill University, and I
would like to thank Dr. Robert F. Goheen and all those at the Woodrow
Wilson National Fellowship Foundation for their generosity, help, and
discreetly surveillant interest in my progress. I am also very grateful to
the Society of the Friends of McGill for blessing me with a two year
fellowship during the early phases of my Ph.D. and to the Government
of Québec for two years of Differential Fee Awards. The Department of
English at McGill was very generous in providing me with teaching and
research assistantships as well as a sessional appointment when most it

was needed.

Both of the external readers of the original dissertation version displayed extraordinary charity in gracing such a refractory tractatus with sensitive and comprehending readings. I must thank Professor Margreta de Grazia, fellow lexiphanes and lexi-fan, for her indulgent, witty, and beautifully written response, lavish in its praises and blandishing in its blames. Professor Donald K. Hedrick devised a critique whose sinuosities and *chinoiseries* seemed orchestrated to help lead me out of the maze of my own topiary hedging. Both of these exceptionally perceptive and engaged readers gave me muchibus about which to thinkibus in revising for publication.

I also profited mightily from participating in the 1989 English Renaissance Prose Conference at Purdue University, and want to thank Jon Lawry, Seth Weiner, and all concerned for their encouragement and engagement during that far too brief weekend. Deborah Mintz of Columbia provided camaraderie and later some appreciated legwork. Roger Pooley of Keele College made valuable suggestions on the inebriatory quality of Nashean rhetoric, and I am sorry that we did not get around as we should have to discussing it further over a beer.

To my friends and former colleagues at McGill I owe thanks for support both in letter and spirit. In particular, David Williams and Kerry McSweeney went out of their way to keep the wolf from the door. I had more than one enlightening *Kaffeeklatsch* with Mette Hjort, and she, of course, was good enough to provide the Danish. Ken Borris made available both intellectual and financial support. The students in my "Some Versions of Sixteenth Century Realism" seminar, and particularly Clare Frock, Karen Valihora, and the absurdly gifted David Theodore brought any number of intriguing things to my attention. David Hensley has been a cherished friend and has provided a model of pedagogical perfection to which no one could possibly live up.

The members of my doctoral committee showed immense patience and forebearance in reading a dissertation that was twice as long and at least as froward as this book. I want to thank Maggie Kilgour for showing a genuine understanding and appreciation of what I have been up to; Capt. Garibaldi Wihlo (Ret.) for graciously lending his ear, his advice and his help on countless occasions; and Paisley Livingston, long a cherished advisor and critic, for being magnanimous and impetuous enough to volunteer to be among my examiners. I am particularly grateful to Prof. Livingston and to Prof. Marguerite Deslauriers of the Philosophy Department for the gentleness to which they both schooled their harrowingly trenchant minds before approaching such philosophically problematical material.

Finally, to my former supervisor, the indefatigable Michael D. Bristol, just about the only person whose new readings of old plays I still find constantly delightful and enlightening, I owe in many ways this whole book (and much more besides)—a debt whose promissory note can perhaps be discerned in its overall argument, which (read backwards "as Witches say their Pater-noster" [Nashe 1592c, D3ᵛ/1:361]) charts the course of my thinking on Nashe from my initial work on him for that seminar almost ten years ago now in which mickle Michael first introduced me to the pamphleteer right down to the problematics of interpretation with which we both remain so fundamentally concerned today. In the course of my collaboration with that right leftist literatus, he has been my advisor, supporter, and friend; and he has always allowed me the freedom, trust, and critical tolerance which only a "big time" soul can afford to vouchsafe. He is truly a tutelary spirit hovering over this work—and now and then rising up from out of the floorboards of it like a stage-spook in his own reading of *Faustus*.

Although the days of dactylograph better-halves have gone where they belong, I have had in the past and must acknowledge here the inestimable help and support of Susan Van Deventer, Wendy Crowley, and especially Barbara Kerr, the latter two of whom assisted me in proofreading some of the old-spelling quotations. I also greatly profited from many delightful discussions with the eminent neo-literalist critic Rob Holton. Jim and Christina Bogar, Jake Brown, Timmikins Cashion, Dominique Darmon, Jenny Day, Carricita Hintz, Mitch Hogg, Eva-Lynn Jagoe, Gary Jantz, Elizabeth Knox, Scott E. Dogg-MacKenzie, Joe Masrour, and David Thomson occasionally provided pertinent criticisms but mainly helped keep me—well, be fair—completely deranged. "The Friends"—Puff, Marvid, L.B.B., and Chirpy—also deserve a lot of the credit.

Obviously any errors that may have crept in and that still remain could very well have been at least partly the fault of some or all of the people just mentioned rather than entirely my own offense. But, as Gérard Genette has so justly observed, "paratextual mentions are more of the nature of juridic responsibility than of factual paternity: the author's name, where onymity is concerned, is the name of someone who takes putative responsibility, whatever his actual role in the production of the work, and any kind of attempt at verification is in no wise within the province of the paratextologist" (Genette 1987, 41). Beyond that, however, in this case I can verify that my actual role in the production of the work *has* been pretty well omnibus. Kater Murr's editor has rightly, if rather indiscreetly, observed that authors often owe their cleverest ideas and most exquisite turns of phrase to the careless hands of the typesetter; but in the present instance it must be acknowledged that any such felicitous *coquilles* are also quite legitimately to be put down to my own imperfect but nevertheless quite absurdly concerted exertions.

And now it really has come time to thank the missus. Though this book is dedicated to my mother and grandmother, I know they will not begrudge me a *risus cognoscens* in the direction of that syngenethliac individual, the vicensimatertiarily worthy Nyla Jean Matuk, Flower of the Nile, *Sagesse de l'orient*, and Brownie of the Buttery, a person I begin at last to know as sometimes harrowingly other in so many ways and yet still at times so close ("heads throbbing," as she once said, though only rarely now "in dithyrambic certainty") that—both in her own finally more courageous attempts to face honestly and in good faith the often soul-ravenous madness of academe (and the petty parisologies of the likes of Prof. Hump Gissum in particular), as in the nowise merely figurative efforts she has made during these last three years to remain real in spite of the prosaic thorniness of the task (could there still be a dark bloom lurking in this veprecose mess? I wonder: *"Mignonne, allons voir si la prose . . ."*)—she may certainly only most improperly now be compared

to my simile.

ironic isn't it (how
           long that distance can
lie pathetically against the feel
of prosy cheek and cheek, turned pacifist-tense, and
ver(s)ify resistance of the real
ever
        unless you) even (read my lips
yell across the tautness of the skin
or g(r)asp unread unwrithed unrhythmic hips
unknown unverbs) though (never
           really can
make the bourgeois e(r)go we know blink
you and i still think
        the less) (distance(s)
stain the sheets in our invisible ink)
we blear the real sarcasm of the sinces (
ere róse-ache unpeeling numb nearnesses of ear
enough! we know we love we laugh still) we're
the mingling of two hearts in a single tear

Café Puff, Vancouver, 23 April 1993

Since which time I retired my selfe among the merrie muses, and by the worke of my pen and inke, haue dezinkhorni- fistibulated a fantasticall Rapsody of dialogisme, to the end that I would not be found an idle drone among so many famous teachers and professors of noble languages, who are very busie dayly in deuising and setting forth new bookes . . . .

John Eliot, *Ortho-Epia Gallica: Eliots Frvits for the French* (1593)

COCKTAIL HERRINGS

The Feel of the Real

I was altogether terrestriall, or rather melancholicke, or rather sadnesse it self in the Abstract. A friend of mine perceiu'd it, and told me I was in my winding sheete, vnlesse I droue out one contrary by another.

> T. Tyro, *Tyros Roring Megge, Planted against the Walles of Melancholy* (1598)

The only vertue in effecte in the whole crissecrosse rowe, ether of morall or intellectuall vertures, that nowe Adayes karrieth meate in the mowthe. The rest in a manner ar owte of fasshion, and ouerstale for so queynte & queasie a world: your delicacy would haply haue delighted your selfe in ouerturninge the prouerbe vpsyedowne and terminge them more artificiallye, mowthe withoute meate.

> Gabriel Harvey, Sloane MS. 93, writing of oratory

A former colleague of mine, having recognized the trend whereby first chapters have come most usually to serve as entryways in which one puts one's theoretical cards on the salver, has gotten into the habit of simply skipping over such introductions because, as he puts it, he wants to get right to "the meat." He presumably sees any methodological considerations not as a series of whetting apéritifs, then, but as a sort of tray of dipsetic saltines standing between him and some solid sustenance. By "the meat," of course, he means the *readings*; he wants to get right down to the main course; and his sentiment might even more colloquially be rendered by the impatient inquisition: "Where's the beef?" For what he is after is something higher up in the textual food chain, something already once digested: read meat.

In the Elizabethan age, of course, "meat" meant any kind of nourishing food, of which, however, meat in our sense seems indeed to have been the preferred version among the English. Thomas Nashe more than once alludes to his fellows as those "fleshly minded *Belials*" ("*or rather belly-alls" in the margin; Nashe 1592b, G1/1:201), and in *Christs Teares ouer Ierusalem* (1593) he complains of the voraciousness of English *academics* in particular: "In all other things *English* men are the stoutest of all others, but beeing Schollers, and lyuing in their owne natiue soyle, theyr braines are so pesterd with full platters, that they haue no roome to bestirre them. . . . For shame bury not your spyrits in Biefe-pots" (1593, Q2ᵛ/2:122-23). This flesh-feeding, then, is a form of intemperance to which the English seem peculiarly predisposed, and in his "Complaint of Gluttony" in *Pierce Penilesse* (1592), Nashe had sympathetically acknowledged how "other Countreyes whome wee vpbrayd with Drunkennesse, call vs bursten-bellyed Gluttons: for we make our greedie paunches powdring tubs of beefe, and eate more meate at one meale, than the Spaniard or Italian in a month." These foreigners for their part are "[g]ood thriftie men" who know how to "drawe out a dinner with sallets" (1592b, F4ᵛ/1:200), while Nashe's countrymen are "such flesh-eating Saracens, that chast fish may not content vs, but we delight in the murder of innocent mutton, in the vnpluming of pullerie, and quartering of calues and oxen" (G1/1:201). Thus, if an unsavoury taste for flesh may be typical of the scholar, Nashe seems to have considered it even more the weakness of the English as a whole; and how quintessentially, then, one supposes, a foible of *English scholars*. He tells a story in *Pierce Penilesse* of a "supper on a fasting or fish night at least" at which "an outlandish Doctor" fell upon the "one ioynt of flesh on the table," and then excused himself "to his friend that brought him thether, *Profecto Domine, ego sum malissimus piscator*," to which Dr. Thomas Watson, who was also present, promptly rejoined: "*At tu es bonissimus carnifex*" (G1-G1ᵛ/1:202-03).[1] In our manner of reading, we have, I think, come more and more to resemble that outlandish carnivore; and English scholars are only now, at the end of the century, gradually beginning to see that their taste for read meat may be environmentally unsound and uneconomical, considered crude or even politically reprehensible in some circles, and, if nothing else, bad for their own hearts.

Now, I had another colleague in those salad days for whom, having

---

[1] Some sort of then current, now (at least for me) lost quip may be further involved here, seeing that in *The Vnfortunate Traueller* Nashe makes the pedant Vanderhulke enigmatically remark that "*Artifex* is a citizen or craftes man, as well as *Carnifex* a scholler or hangman" (1594d, E2/2:249).

acquired more continental and progressive tastes, "the meat" seemed to be a kind of uncouth hamburger stew that one whips up when one needs something in a hurry to appease a decidely oafish gathering. He was fond of consoling graduate students who were fretting over the completion of their theses by drawling, "Aw, don't worry; if you run out of time you can always do a few *readings.*" He's a merry knave to have at table with you, no question; and yet his wholeheartedly theoretical conviviality can sometimes leave one with the calculated frustration of Petruchio's still unsatisfied bride as he declines any proffered cates on the pretext that "'Tis burnt, and so is all the meate" (4.1; TLN 1793).

So while I am at pains here not to serve up more of the McReadings after which the English scholar still generally seems to hunger—indeed, on the contrary to throw into question the whole practice of reading for the reading—I am far from so repugning the real readability of my "primary texts" themselves as to offer for the board only what Nashe's arch adversary Gabriel Harvey once suggested calling (in an overeasy flip of the proverbial "meat in the mouth") "Mowthe withoute meate" (Harvey MS.a, 40ᵛ/73). A vegetarian in *reality*, I do nonetheless still find myself at times trying to *read* as a true *"bonissimus piscator,"* fishing sustenance out of the semiotic fluidity of the prosaic. I like to think that I am a bit like that landlubbing hugger of the coastline of the real incidentally insulted in a "censure vpon Varro" in *The Scholemaster,* where Ascham compares the Roman to "one caried in a small low vessell him selfe very nie the common shore, not much vnlike the fisher mē of Rye, and Hering men of Yarmouth. Who deserue by common mens opinion, small commendacion, for any cunning saling at all" (Ascham 1570, S3ᵛ; cf. Nashe 1599, E2ᵛ/3:181). Nashe—who himself, to swipe one of Kilgore Trout's puns, has a barque that is mete to the bight of his real—tackles Ascham's metaphor literally and littorally, defending the yare lowness of his own craft and averring that

> in the captious mystery of Mounsieur herring low vessels will not giue their heads for the washing [i.e. submit to insult], holding their owne pell-mell in all weathers as roughly as vaster timber men, though not so neere the shore, as through ignorance of the coast he [Ascham] soundeth, nor one man by himselfe alone to doe euery thing, which is the opinion of one man by himselfe alone, and not beleeu'd of any other. Fiue to one if he were aliue, I would beate against him, since one without fiue is as good as none, to gouerne the most egshell shallop that floateth, and spread her nets, and draw them in[.] (Nashe 1599, E2ᵛ-E3/3:181-82)

Ostensibly correcting Ascham's misconceptions about the fishing industry, Nashe in his dissent characteristically adduces the *realities* of the vehicle in the scholar's metaphorical setup (writer=fisherman), also bringing into the figurative argument the deferred concrete violence of a knuckle sandwich (Ascham's simply an asshole, "*un poing sait tout!*" to pull Réjean Ducharme's pun*ch*) in an image which carries with it an additional fortuitous (?) whiff of masterbAshem (sick: "*cinq contre un*" is a slang expression for onanism going back at least to the seventeenth century).

As close readers of this kind we secretly know that we are the fishers of men's souls, but too often the sole sole we can serve filetted is that of the smelly boot we have expiscated from our own standing pools of disengaged method. Maybe we should be content to be critical critics in the morning and fisherpeople in the afternoon, and make a virtue of the necessity that the footprints we find in the sand of the text are always our own. If these are my own tracks, if there is no Friday hiding on this island which no man is unto himself, so be it say I. I can live with the idea that my line is hooked on the back of my own trousers. But I refuse to go trawling with a theory net whose mesh is so big that the little things slip through, or one so fine that everything gets bundled up together in hideous suffocating pandemonium. Perhaps this book is really, then, a reaffirmation of the critical in the faceless face of the theoretical.

Or maybe all I'm trying to insist upon is that if we really want the "meat" in what we read, *we* must be prepared to dismember each figure *for ourselves* as best we can—make ourselves bone it and gut it and take it to pieces before we consume it. That certainly involves an unsqueamish confrontation with the violence at the heart of such reading for the meat—we murder to delect and all. Most people recognize but indeed have learned to ignore all that violence these days, and it has increasingly been our theories that have been doing the dirty work for us, I find. Of course, hardly anyone hunts and fishes for himorherself anymore. But perhaps that's another something that isn't clear enough in our minds as we imagine ourselves out there like the Old Man and the Sea. Nashe's netaphor forces us at least to remember the existence of a—what was it we used to call it?—an *interpretive community*, yes. Like the brave Yarmouth herringmen, writers (including the writers of readings) are never isolated adrift in a dinghy on the sea of consciousness, but are always really reliant—and of course also *parasitic*, old J. Hill Stuart Satanic Mill—upon *others* in their concrete productivity. "Style," goes the saw (rasping through the tuna's gillmuck or tailfin), "is the man"; but style, you may recall V.N. Vološinov responding, "is at least two persons [Vološinov himself of course seems to have been at least two persons:

himself and Bakhtin!], or more accurately, one person plus his social group in the form of its authoritative representative, the listener—the constant participant in a person's inner and outward speech" (Vološinov 1926, 114). Writers of readings are always doing their fishing *for somebody else*. No afternoon's leisure here. But the consensual community thus reassured helps obscure what I am *really* interested in in this book—the fact that the "five against one" in Nashe's portrait is *really* the five staunch anglers and netters against that one lone little herring. Writers of readings, then, even if they *are* singlehanded, should never consider themselves by themselves in that eggshell shallop of the text. They have always been reading for some "thing," and there will be somebody there who's wound up *read*, and dead in the hold. It's not the author I'm referring to; it's the bloody fish.

Both of my whilom either/oarsmen, then—the old-style new-critical anchorite and the newfangled factoryship theory-trawler—might be thought by some, as we near the end of the century, to be showing an all too taken-for-granted lack of sensitivity toward the "literal text," seeing it as something that can or should so readily be converted into "read meat" for consumption. Their attitudes reflect the essential alienation not just paraded now as part and parcel of the wasteful theoretical exploitation that is indifferent to primary texts except as sources of prime cuts with which to exhibit their culinary expertise, but also at the back of the more wholesale butchery carried on in the commodified name of a seemingly sacerdotal critical reverence for such texts, each of which is thereby turned into a sacrificially dismembered god that must die to the world of the real in order that it may live on as *truth* or *meaning*, packed in its own juice. Text consumption seems now inevitably to be suspended between the incorporative strategies that yet another of my ex-colleagues not so long ago characterized as "a desire for the most intimate possible identification with another and a desire for total autonomy and control over others who are treated therefore as food, so that all exchanges [including critical ones] are reduced to the alternatives of 'eat or be eaten'" (Kilgour 1990, 18). The inquisitional critic at the end of the century seems still for the most part to be looking for the text not where he eats, but where he is eaten; and the voraciousness of this would-be reader of already read meat, *malissimus carnifex*, seems to me to have become as unreflective as our larger cultural reliance on what Carol J. Adams—in another recent book that, like my ex-colleague's, has a chapter on the Word and the Flesh—preposterously, and yet crucially, calls "animalized protein" (Adams 1990, 80).

I do not feel so alone in my eggshell shallop as I used to, either stylistically or in my ever greater aversion to commodified readings

(readings that add up; readings that make cents): there are plenty of others who are fed up with the automated processing of read meat, and who do not look down their prominent noses at a less (as Adams says) "disassembly-line" oriented attitude toward texts. Some postmodernisms, some feminisms, and even certain brands of neo-philological textual scrupulousness support a less manufactured textuality that might now and again feel at home with the personal, local and incidental engagement to be found in my kind of *vene*real reading, which I hope does *not* result in another freezerful of read meat, but only in the delicate, hard-to-trace abature left by beings that have themselves managed to escape the springes of print. The forest floor of metaphor is thus here, there and everywhere littered with the literal in my quasi-(sometimes queasy-) theoretical "readings." So if it at first seems that I myself am too often beating around the bush, keep in mind that this is because of my madly metaphorical conviction that two tremulous lovebirds in there are worth one stiff one in the hand (a revisionary ratio at better odds than "five to one").

Reading for the literal is, as Carol J. Adams argues in her often silly and wrongheaded, yet staggeringly profound *The Sexual Politics of Meat*, what re-members the absent referent of what I keep calling "read meat"; for it is the shift of metaphor, as I read her "feminist-vegetarian critical theory," that covers over the bodies bruised in the patriarchal dismemberment of texts (under which I would include their industrialized moralization as well as their more autoptic deconstruction)—along with the systematic slaughter of animals (including people); the meant and the meat are complicit for Adams in a narrative line that has at last to be refused: "Stories have endings, meals have meat. Let us explore whether these statements are interchangeable—stories have meat, that is, meaning, and meals have endings" (Adams 1990, 92). They do indeed; but as Adams reads the meataphors that inform Western meataphy(sics), the "end" of the meal, its meaning, has tended to be precisely, as for Nashe's over-carnivorous English scholars, the meat itself; a trope which stands for *anything but* the literal dead animal. Given this sense of an ending, I think I rather wish that I *could* in my readings identify with the vegetarian aesthetics Adams would bizarrely hope to cultivate:

> Vegetarians see themselves as providing an alternative ending, veggie burgers instead of hamburgers, but they are actually eviscerating the entire narrative. From the dominant perspective, vegetarianism is not only about something that is inconsequential, which lacks "meat," and which fails to find closure through meat, but it is a story about the acceptance of passivity, of that

which has no meaning, of endorsing a "vegetable" way of living. In this it appears to be a feminist story that goes nowhere and accepts nothingness. (94)

I fear, howsomever, that I cannot really claim to have attained either the full "feminism"—if feminism it really is—or the mystic passivism of this vegetextuality: I still have my hankerings after meat from time to time, even if I never could keep myself from throwing back anything that I caught in that eggshell shallop of mine (note though how I have *man*-aged to take the albuminous place of the "feminized protein" in that fragile vehicle itself—*is* this all just a glairing big yolk, then? [seek]). I do think that I *am* therefore (leggo of my ego!) most sensitive to the ways metaphoral aggressivity can disguise oppression, and I am eager to combat that all-dumbfounding metaphorality with reliteralizations in ways that I think might finally find me partaking in the eradication of what Adams calls "the patriarchal texts of meat" as well.[2]

Of course, those who are accustomed to reading for the meant, in-cluding those who, like Adams herself, prize a humanist concept of spiritual wholeness, may well feel that my own dismemberment of the meant and my almost pomo mere dalliance even with the literal (let alone the "deeper meaning") are still more violent and less sensitive than the painstaking if backstairs dressing of read meat practised by its (in)cor-porate purveyors in most English departments. I am, if nothing else, too *experimental* (in the Nietzschean sense: *"Wir sind Experimente: wollen wir es auch sein!"*) to be the good vegetextualist described by Adams. I hope, though, that rather than vivisection, my examinations here suggest only a little veterinarian prodding to check for fractures; for I have to admit to being prone myself to the sort of superstition about the *corp*oreality of

---

[2] My colleagues and students have been aghast to see me give *The Sexual Politics of Meat* the time of day, but I seriously wonder if they are sufficiently aware of the lateness of the hour themselves. This would-be *dernier cri* of politically correct critical theory is admittedly ramshackle, goody-two-shoes, and full of mutually contradictory propositions and self-deconstructing interpretations, but in a world of global ecological crisis, gender panic, endlessly bureaucratically deferred responsibility, and the ever more mindless media glossing (in many ways this includes academic publishing) of what is possibly the most viciously and unreflectively and certainly the most wide-scale exploitative *culture* in the history of the modern world, Adams's reflections on the politics of metaphor and the imperative to remember absent referents, however funhouse in some ways these reflections may be, seem to me to be far more timely than much of the theory-infatuated saving of the appearances that passes for cultural criticism today.

the text, familiar enough in a different guise to readers of Barthes *et al.*, which Adams has embraced: "If, through the story of meat, the word and the flesh are united, we might further argue that the body equals a text, a text is a body. From this perspective, changing an animal from her original state into food parallels changing a text from its original state into something more palatable" (94). I really do imagine that a kind of hygiene or ethics is in order in a world in which texts effectively *are* seen as bodies and bodies as texts, but my own superstitions surrounding the textual "body" are more *literal* than spiritual; more like those of Joseph Ritson, the eighteenth-century "Scholar-at-arms" described by Adams as fusing his concern for the physical well-being of animals with philological sedulity:

> Besides refusing to view dead animals as meat he was devoted to issues of proper spelling, definition, and etymology of words and the overzealous critical treatment of texts. Just as the text was not editorial property that could be changed and altered according to the whims and tastes of the editor so animals were not human's [sic] property to be altered, castrated, or killed according to the whims and tastes of meat eaters. He became enraged at dismembered texts and dismembered animals. (100)

Disgust at the truculence of *pr*reditors (stet) has now for some time been part of cutting-edge textual politics, and in a certain sense I am only trying to extend Random Cloud's concern with "un-editing" texts here by way of a further project of "un-reading" them. I admit that a worry over dismembered texts (as opposed to one over dismembered animals) frankly seems to me, in my calmer moments at least, trivial and irrational,[3]

---

[3]What, after all, constitutes dismemberment? When I acknowledge Adams's questionable punctuation of "human's" in the passage just quoted by reproducing it *literatim*, do I "dismember" it by intruding into its organic form my "own" word "[sic]"? Antoine Compagnon, on the first page of his anatomy of citation, misquotes Hobbes to the effect that a quotation is the clove that ruins a dish (paraphrased in French, 1979, 9); as Maggie Kilgour has pointed out to me, what Hobbes actually said, as part of his apology for his own lack of classical gleanings, was that "it is many times with a fraudulent Designe that men stick their corrupt Doctrine with the Cloves of other mens Wit" (Hobbes 1651, 727)—thus for Hobbes quotation is brought in not to corrupt the dish, but to mask its corruption. Surely here it is my own word that sticks in the meant of Adam's text and may spoil its savor? Would I have better served its holistic survival as something other than "meat" by leaving out my "[sic]," or by silently correcting her text according to my own view of what would make it a "health-

but at the same time I have been up and down the two-way street of metaphor (*keineswegs eine Einbahnstraße*) enough times to know that our insensitive behavior in a trivial sphere may well be carried over into a not so trivial one. It is all too easy for a metaphor to be bled of its lived experience and become the catachresis that condones oppression. Yet in the spirit of Adams's own literalism, I would have to question her identification of textual body and animal (or human) body. The text is not literally a living body, and it cannot be "hurt" by the blazonesque or tendentious (though note the forked-tongue little row of incisors lurking in that qualifier) reading it may sometimes be given. So while Adams excitingly recognizes the complicity of metaphor with oppression, and the need to re-member literal "absent referents" in reading, she does not perhaps wholly admit to herself the metaphorical roots and berries of her own ethical system of "feminist-vegetarian" criticism (to whose literal content I am entirely sympathetic), and how it may only be through re-membering (adding new members to) metaphorical constituencies that the wounds of patriarchy or of any other oppressive scheme of tropes (if there is any other really) can be stopped.

My own "realism" and "literalism" often lead me in reading to reject the *spiritual* wholeness of the text, even while my ethical "sense" insists that I never intentionally do violence to its "body." To attempt to appropriate the inner *meaning* of that body as opposed to its outer form, however, would for me be to treat the text as meat, sacrificing the living form for some killed content. But such concern over the body as opposed to what's "inside" may well itself seem a disturbing textual politics to adopt, given the *sexual* politics that Adams believes to be equally bound up with the meat and the meant.[4]

---

ier" entity? Perhaps my "[sic]" is a clove meant herbally to restore the health of an ailing text, as perhaps the "meat" of Adams's text offers itself as a restorative through quotation to the soundness of my own. And then, would an actual physical dismemberment I might perfom (God forbid!) upon my copy of *The Sexual Politics of Meat* (or a photocopy of it) by cutting it into snippets to paste into my own rough draft typescript of this introduction be a more serious act of "violence to the text" than quoting a part of its "content" in the less physical sense "out of context"? But is it possible even for *her* to incorporate a text without turning it into meat? Compagnon sees quotation as a "surgical removal [*ablation*]." But isn't that just another metaphor, or meataphor, for gore? "In the same way, every quotation is itself—essentially or additionally?—a metaphor" (Compagnon 1979, 19).

[4]The ethical question becomes urgent if we accept the metaphorical equation (which I do think is widely operative among "men of letters") between text and human (or animal) body. To show so much attentiveness to the "body" of the text

To the extent that I do actually *glance* pretty compulsively, perhaps longingly, at the text as meant, even if I refuse to indulge wholehog, I find it useful to consider my "reading" here of Nashe to be not so much *criticism* as *commentary*. Since one kind of experiment I try to make along the way involves the testing of a neophilological attentiveness to meaning and matter at the *microtextual* level (an endeavor more usually associated with annotation or detailism of the miscellaneous *Notes and Queries* sort or the well-padded post-Victorian editorial comfiness of a Quiller-Couch or an Arnold Davenport), it may be useful to recall the distinction that Walter Benjamin made between criticism and commentary, presumably in response to runaway German philology at the end of the last century:

> Criticism seeks the truth content of a work of art, commentary its material content [*Sachgehalt*]. The relationship of the two determines that fundamental principle of writing whereby the more significant it is, the less manifestly and outwardly is the truth content of the work bound up with its material content. Consequently, if the work proves to be an enduring one, whose truth is most deeply imbedded in its material content, in the course of this enduring the real elements become more clearly evident to the contemplator in the work as they die out in the world. Yet at the same time, by all appearances, material content and truth content, which in the juvescence of the work are united, move apart as it endures, because the latter always remains more or less concealed where the former breaks through. (Benjamin 1924, 125)

If we accept this discrimination, I think I am safe in saying that I am not really interested in the "truth content" of the works I am discussing: I want to concentrate instead on those "real elements" that do perhaps become more manifest as the "truth" of the work becomes more delitescent. As the work grows old, it may be precisely the real incidentals in it that begin to stick out like sore thumbs, while its immaterial *"truth"*

---

as opposed to its "soul," as I tend to, does suggest a familiar form of sexual insensitivity or consumption. On the other hand, to treat the *meaning* of a text as a spiritual content capable of wholeness (and *appropriation*) equally suggests forms of interpersonal objectification, and forms whose lack of *realism*—as the opponents of the sovereign unified Cartesian e(r)go have been arguing for a while now—would also leave the door open for determinism, ideological falsification, co-optation, or downright oppression which, *mutatis mutandis*, would be ethically execrable in the treatment of those really ununified "texts" we call people.

becomes less and less imposing. Benjamin goes on to suggest that "if for the sake of a similitude one would regard the growing work as a burning stake, then the commentator stands before it as a chemist, the critic like an alchemist. Where only wood and ash remain the objects of the former's analysis, for the latter the flame alone harbors an enigma: that of the living. So the critic inquires into the truth, whose living flame burns on over the solid faggots of the past and the frail ash of the lived" (126). But if the life of *meaning* is in the flame, the *reality* of the lived is in the ashes. The average "commentator" on Elizabethan texts, naturally, cannot claim to be any sort of chemist, but at best a kind of Sherlock Holmes, sifting through the ashes to arrive at a deduction. I suppose that I must admit myself, however, to be more of an opportunistic artist, taking bits of the charcoal and making of them scribbets with which to limn caricatures that will allow positive but unincriminating identifications to be made (and economically using whatever briquettes are too big to barbeque up a mess of Frankfurters or Wieners for those who still insist on having their stake well done [so as to mask its real provenance, *s'entend*]).

Another cavil, perhaps. The theoretical assumptions I am working with may well for some people already have a decided air of the *rechauffé* about them. Am I not largely only sifting through the ash left by the already thoroughly incinerated post of poststructuralism? In a way: but I prefer to think that I have taken the manavilins—the orts, scraps, and fragments—left over from the last couple of decades of banketing, and thrown them back in to stew a bit longer; maybe they'll even be a bit tastier served up catchpot like this; they do often betray interesting new flavors when they have been tossed into a different tureen and allowed to stew there for a while with a few secret additional ingredients. Anyway, where its assimilation of the theoretical insights that have been disseminated during the past twenty years is concerned, as in so many institutional situations, Renaissance Studies largely remains the tardie apish Nation of English Literature as a discipline, and its belated experimentation with theories already played out elsewhere may still provide unexpected cognitive bonuses with regard to the further articulation of both "The English Renaissance" *and* "The Postmodern Turn."

By the middle of the book, however, it may seem that I am providing a lot of mouth and not much meat—or at least drawing out a pretty diddly dinner at times with an awful lot of theoretical roughage from the well-stocked pluralist salad-bar of our postmodernist dispensation, even given the more than generous sprinkling of critical croutons to add palatability for the meat and *peut-être* crowd (Nabby's joke about Rabby's going to seek a "great potato"). But part of the satisfyingness of my unreadings for me is precisely the way they have helped me to work through some of the poststructuralist theoretical assumptions I (sometimes grudgingly) take for granted; so if I take my time attempting exemplary "reading" (not readings) of methodological problems *through* microtextual commentaries, and sampling scholarly alternatives to the totalizing reconciliatory reading of a discrete text, it is plainly in conformity with my sincere poststructuralist sentiment that in the texts under discussion, and in all *texts* when viewed as ensembles of *meaning(s)* as opposed to bodies of being, "the parts," as Stanley Wells has said of Nashe's works, "are always greater than the whole" (Wells 1964, 20). Ultimately, I think, I am interested in trying to situate myself with regard to the textuality of poststructuralism in the most postructuralist way I know how—by reintroducing *differences* into what has become a far too homogenous settlement—better say colonization—in an attempt to complicate our now rather banal conception of the "textuality" of the prose of the world. (The final chapters on things, theoretically post-cenal, are meant to leave one feeling obliged as a reader to empty full receptacles of the frail ash of the lived after the brandy and cigars with which we have followed up what may really have been a kind of *Cena de la ceneri* all along.)

One differential contrast I have found it especially timely to introduce into my theorizing on "textuality" is that of *prose* itself. The end of the century saw a boom in this mode in texts which, since their Victorian re-emergence, have been cited for the prosaically realistic picture they give us of life in "Shakespeare's England." But these texts—the first full flowering maybe not of the novel, but at least of what by any other name would still be a prose (and prick the skin as dearly)—have never really been made the basis of theorizing on the categories of realism, textuality, or for that matter of "the Elizabethan world picture." Prose, in fact, is the overlooked other of an Elizabethan textuality that has both traditionally and more recently been strung between the tenters of the pragmatics of the theater and the poetics of the verse. Only at the end of the century are we starting to see a few investigators turn up the prosaic weft of the tight tapestry of an Elizabethan world that had its share of genuinely "subversive stitches" (not just mopey gents writing about their inability to escape the power-structures of their day); and only with postmodernism has it become fashionable to try on our prosaic old duds inside out—mostly of course still just as a kind of badge betokening the most recuperated of countercultures. Thus, Jonathan Crewe, in his more or less poststructuralist reading of Nashe, suggests how his works could unravel and snarl the constantly reknit versions of sublimated textuality at the end of the century:

Simply for the record, let us recall that Nashe's prose is not governed by a poetic, but rather, as *The Unfortunate Traveller* suggests, by an antipoetic (which seeks to establish the domain of "prose as prose"), and that his poetry is of an exemplary squareness. The decorum of his prose, moreover, is unassailably learned rather than vulgar, and his work is never less than a popular art. (Crewe 1982, 17-18)

Although I wrote this book largely to take exception to the way Crewe eschews vulgarity and the vulgar reading, it seems to me that he has been correct in discerning the sheer negativity of Nashe's relationship to high canonical models of textuality, and this is one of the reasons these texts now seem so interesting to me. The pamphlet from which I take one of the epigraphs to this little methodological prologue you are reading is called *Tyros Roring Megge, Planted against the Walles of Melancholy.* A "roaring Meg" was a piece of small ordnance, a little cannon; and I would like to think that the prosaic texts whose surface I have begun scratching here with Nashe can eventually serve as a little *canon*, as loudmouthed and independent as Long Meg of Westminster and as disturbing as Bruegel's *Dulle Griet* (I've been delighted to hear myself referred to as a "loose cannon" myself on more than one occasion), planted against the melancholy walls of the Renaissance canon as it has been poetically and theatrically raised up.

From a theoretical angle, I am aiming largely to make contributions to (or maybe already *problems for*) an emergent category of textual analysis: the "prosaic." This rather Hegelian term, *si je ne m'abuse (point, c'est quelqu'un d'autre qui le fera)*, has most recently been theorized in two fundamental ways, and my study can be said to navigate between the rock of the one theory and the hard place of the other, whenever it isn't just hugging the shore of the prose as such.

In one usage, that developed by Gary Saul Morson and Caryl Emerson out of their work on Mikhail Bakhtin (or "Baxtin," depending on your system of transcription), the "prosaic" could be said to determinate the neglected overall mundaneness of all "textuality"—its groundedness, humanness, specificity, embodiedness, reality, lived-ness:

This is prosaic in both senses of the term: both prose-like as opposed to poetical, and ordinary, that is, pertaining to and celebrating the mass of unmarked everyday decisions that require work of us precisely because we cannot ground them in general norms, principles, or the drama of clean-cut openings and closings. Baxtin is a singer of middle spaces. A "prosaic" approach to his work, therefore, might shed some light on what many consider to be the most problematical sides of Baxtinian poetics: its insistence on decentering and "openness" in the novel, and its presumption that this openness is essentially benign.

A quote from the early manuscripts will illustrate "prosaics" with a difficult but crucial Russian phrase. "We live," Baxtin writes, "in a world of exitless reality, not of random potential" ("K filosofii postupka," 115). Note that for Baxtin this "exitlessness" is a very good thing. Random potential, mere possibility, always splits me off from the world; it is, as Baxtin says, the "unbridled play of empty objectivity," an "infinity of cognition" that no one has yet signed (120). (Emerson 1988, 519)

The Sartrean ring of "exitless" is not an unhappy one, since Caryl Emerson is here quoting from one of the drafts from the phenomeno-logico-existentialist period which preceded Bakhtin's better-known 1929 book on Dostoevsky. The "prosaic" in this sense has to do in fact with the actually existent *economics* of textuality, or in other words the various prosaic limitations imposed by reality on boundless poesis, representation, or *écriture*—limitations which implicate us existentially as people. As opposed to a textual reality carious with "loopholes" (as Bakhtin called them in his reconsidered opinion in the Dostoevsky book), or inherently constructed as a nexus of "paths of escape" (as "a certain poststructuralism" likes to construe it), the conditions of writing and reading the prose of the world entail a good many material, social, and of course "literal" constraints which make of that world a largely "exitless reality."

The conception of the prosaic developed by Jeffrey Kittay and Wlad Godzich in *The Emergence of Prose: An Essay in Prosaics* (1986), on the other hand, made ephemerally plain how precisely the mundaneness of the prosaic allows it, and the subjects bound up in it, alibis and ways out (of existential implication) by constituting its textuality as a transparent, unproblematic banality: "Among all the discourses it contains, it takes the position that it is just holding them together, it is just what there is. The prose of the world" (Kittay and Godzich 1986, 116). Prose here starts to become interesting by virtue of its very unremarkableness, a model for the delitescent discursive order that underwrites and reproduces the reality of the most unquestioned aspects of "our" world.

As opposed to the evident symbolic stratification of the poetry and the obvious re-presentational self-consciousness of the play within the plays, the prose from the end of the century has often struck critics as exemplary in its transparency. Only in the last few years has this prose come under the scrutiny of a new, theoretically chary and often even prosaically gritty pen of lit critters, best thanked for their vaccinary pains by quoting one of Rabelais's inverted proverbs: *"Si n'estoient messieurs les bestes, nous vivrions comme clercs* [If it weren't for the beasts, we'd still be living like scholars]."

The last decade has especially espied a soughing resurgence of interest in this pellucid palimpsestuous prose of Thomas Nashe. A good baker's half-dozen of books which deal wholly or largely with Nashe appeared between 1980 and 1990 (Rhodes 1980, McGinn 1981, Crewe 1982, Nicholl 1984, Hilliard 1986, Demadre 1986, Hutson 1989)—and this was a field previously held together by R.B. McKerrow's apparatus in his still astonishing edition (Nashe 1958; originally 1904-10) and by G.R. Hibbard's sturdy little *Thomas Nashe* (1962). When my own work was first conceived, the last three of the studies from the eighties had not yet appeared, but their interventions—mouthwatering but with different fish to fry—have only occasionally served to sidetrack me from my initial aims. For, much as *Elizabethan Grotesque* (1980) seems, according to his preface, to have arisen out of the need Neil Rhodes felt to answer (albeit somewhat tardily) Hibbard's *Thomas Nashe*, this study originated in my dissatisfactions with the poststructuralist reading of Nashe in Jonathan Crewe's *Unredeemed Rhetoric*, dissatisfactions which were really only aggravated by Crewe's obvious wit and mercurial mentality.

What I find disgruntling about Crewe's book is that it sacrifices its own insights about the experience of *reading* Nashe to an overall *reading* (however fragmentary, de-centered, etc.). Crewe is actually an astute reader of Nashe, and he often arrives at formulations or insights with which I could be quite happy. The problem is that *he* can't be happy with them. This isn't, needless to say, entirely his fault; there are enormous institutional pressures on him to make the texts he has chosen to "read" *mean something*; and of course, something big, something intellectual, something crucial. Crewe even makes a point of beginning by recognizing that he is going to be "'using' Nashe, as he has been used in other con- texts, to make a point" (vii), and oddly attempts to justify any possible misrepresentation of which he has been guilty by suggesting that "in the case of so uncanonical an author the offense may be considered pardon- able" (viii-ix; is that supposed to be funny or something?). But Crewe is on Nashe's side, or so it would seem; he is out to "save the text." In academic circles there has been this "Nashe problem"—the problem that Nashe seems to be all style and no content, and hence is not recuperable to an Occidental capitalist-humanist-Christian exegetical tradition in which texts have exchange value because of the meaning they crucially carry—but Crewe has found a way of making the Nashe text pay. He re- cognizes that the "problem" may not actually be with Nashe but might really be created "by the act of reading as such, or by *a particular way of reading*" (1; emphasis added). Replace that old logocentric reading strategy with a new souped-up deconstructionist one, though, and hey presto! Nashe's text will make tea after all. Crewe can perfectly well see the vulgarity, sensuousness, and realism of what Nashe is up to—that he is engaged precisely in the "self-overcoming" of rhetoric (45) and attempting "a sophisticated return to a state of innocence, a 'romantic' possibility" (92); that Nashe has a concrete style and no particular interest in metaphysical quandaries. The problem is, he knows he is not allowed to stop there. All this must fit somehow into some bigtime, highbrow reading, something neatly packaged that can be traded for a job, tenure, fame, whatever. And so out rolls the *reading*: Nashe's texts disclose the parlous but spurious opposition between Logic and Rhetoric; there is the *pro forma* reference to Derrida, or rather to one of those well-combed translators' introductions (5), and poof! Nashe the deconstructionist. Nashe's own early abandoned "attempt to moralize his rhetoric" (45) will be fleshed out by Crewe's handy dressing of the read meat. Nashe has no themes to speak of, but that is precisely his theme: theme itself is actually to be regarded as "a rhetorical device, or as the merely conventional pretext (the 'red herring') that Nashe ultimately and self-consciously makes it" (2). His theme *is* rhetoric, and what better theme for a person trying to work his way out of the mystified faith in the logocentric delusion of θεμα that under-rites Western metaphysics? True, Nashe might seem to have not the least interest in philosophical concerns of this sort, whether metaphysical or anti-metaphysical; he's a lively, uncerebral stylist and has an earthy way with words. Crewe quotes the poet John Berryman, who had remarked on "how physical" Nashe's language is, and "how active": "It is a self-conscious style," Berryman had admitted, "but *alert*, not laboured" (Berryman 1960, 11; qtd in Crewe 1982, 13). But Crewe rushes to assure us of the proper interpretation of Berryman's words: "All of which goes to prove that Nashe engages us primarily as a stylist" (14).

Yes and no. If we are constrained to analyse his writing, *we* will become conscious of his stylishness; and if we must write *about* him in an academic setting we will probably find it damned embarrassing to write about the meaningfulness or seriousness or worthwhileness of his manifest content. How can we save him for humanistic study, then? Precisely by concentrating on his style, and on style itself as a crucial key to the human experience (how definitively "80s", eh?). We live in a world of *Unredeemed Rhetoric*, says Crewe: Nashe is useful in reminding us of the fact. See, he teaches us after all. There is a message in his madness. Indeed, he perfectly crystallizes for us what has actually been a central issue in humanism from the very start, but has only finally become transparent in our own time:

> If the traditional opposition between logic and rhetoric has never been superseded within the field of Renaissance studies, it is partly because it is fundamental to the intellectual life of the period under investigation, and because rhetoric emerges in a privileged position in humanist education. It is also, however, an opposition that has been revitalized and regrounded in deconstructive criticism, not without consequences for the study of Renaissance literature. (6)

What is at stake in this opposition is the λόγος, of course (not the ῥῆσις); and we are now all aware that what is lurking around in the shadows and fog out there—misshapen, uncertain, always perhaps ready to strike again—is: the "Truth." It is against any centralized Truth claim, trying to rely for its centrality on the pre-eminence of logic since the Renaissance that Crewe would like to level the Nashean rhetorical canon; but in setting up his construction of Nashe's practice in terms of this coordination between the poles of Rhetoric, Logic, and Truth (in typical nineteenth century Nietzschean rather than sixteenth century Nashean terms), Crewe ignores what seems to me to be the really crucial Nashean category: the *real*. If there is one thing that Nashe doesn't take as his theme it is *anything abstract*. Nashe just isn't *about* this kind of metaphysical mumbo-jumbo. He may well be a pre-eminently rhetorical writer; he certainly is thoroughly performative. But that's not what his text is *about*. Crewe rightly recognizes that there is an antagonism between "literary performance and 'reading'" and that this antagonism parallels the disparity between "rhetoric and truth" (100); but even as he produces his own literary performance he is constrained to produce that "truth" as well, that "reading." It's desperately sad, really—but it's part of *our* predicament, not Nashe's.[5] However rhetorical, however performative,

---

[5]Crewe isn't any dummy, needless to say, so his book, though ultimately still wrongheaded, I think, is by no means lacking in interesting insights. But I do think it is clear that he felt obliged to bolt his meal, and that this has had an adverse effect on the clarity with which he could see what it was that he was consuming. All this is, of course, when taken to its most desperate extremes, a most miserable commentary on the degree to which *no one* has time to *think* anymore in university. The students must take too many courses, the meaning of which very often eludes them, and they are frequently only coming here because they have to anyway; and the rest of us are for the most part running around like chickens with their heads cut off, trying to assimilate the exploded and inflated

Nashe has little interest in categories like Truth, Logic, or even Rhetoric. Nashe is writing to be *read*, not writing to be *read*. And sure, just like Crewe or myself, Nashe is on a discursive power trip: but again that's not what his texts are *about*—they simply aren't *about* themselves! And nor by the way is *this* text really only "about itself."

In setting his own book up as a contention between the claims of logic (Truth; the "reading") and rhetoric (performance; "writing"), Crewe ignores the claims of the *real* (the *read*), no doubt a category which he would feel the postmodern turn had definitively spun off. *This* book tries to call attention to those realities: the literal and local realities of Nashe's text, the phenomenological realities of reading as opposed to doing readings, the realities of the world at which Nashe's text consistently points and which it consistently celebrates. And what can I possibly mean, you may well tiredly demand, in trying to answer his book and its properly Truth-dismantling message by bringing in such an impertinent term as the *real* at the end of the century? How can I even—or especially—*skirt* any idea of the real at this late date?

To take a turn at this perhaps grotesquely transvestite skirting where it actually makes a difference (the epistemological problems are going to get short shrift right on through), it may well seem to us all that as a straight white middleclass man having written yet another study of white men writing about white men, I already have a fair bit of explaining to do. What separates me from all those half-baked *peut-être* decon readings that I was just besmirching the memory of, after all (for it isn't really the "singular"—to use an appropriately Nashean epithet—Crewe that I have it in for, a "one-man crew" back in '82 whose piloting in those deep-sea waters was ultimately of a not unadmirable kind, but rather, to quote Harvey in his attack on Greene, that whole "scribbling crew" altogether, that "carelesse crewe of his own associates" [Harvey 1592, A4^v/1:164/15;

body of knowledge which is daily augmented, teach sometimes gruellingly heavy loads, and race for Ph.D.s, publication, jobs, tenure. Even those who are securely tenured and famous seem to be so used to this mad capitalist scramble for epistemological loot and career advancement that they feel obliged to churn out a new book every couple of years whether it needs it or not. No one has the leisure to sit back and ponder anything, mull it over, create anything that will last beyond next year's MLA, develop a thesis satisfactorily, do the research that would really be requisite to substantiating their theories, or even poperly poofread their footnotes. It's been all that I could do to *unscare* myself long enough to *think straight* for a few minutes here and there, and I really don't know where I found the time to have a bit of fun along the way, or when I ever will again!

D2/1:189/40]: all of us who "read" for a living)? Just as with those ultimately "text-saving" decon-jobs, any old "author study" like mine, however stylistically and theoretically forward,[6] is coming more and more to seem inevitably like the dog returning to his vomit once again (another stunning proof that Milton provides us with the best possible information about how to read Milton—but the question is, of course, should we be reading Milton at all?). I don't know anymore whether or not this book is just more of the same (same difference, yukka yukka).

[6]My style is obviously meant partly as an extention of the prosaic Nashean "extemporall vayne" into theoretical discourse, but this dubious fallacy-of-imitation alibi may, I recognize, partly be by way of self-delusion. My colleague Mark Vessey has recently penetratingly compared my style for me to that of the pre-eminently self-deluded Frederick Rolfe, an obscure turn-of-the-century figure best-known for his fantasy novel *Hadrian VII*, the blurb on the Picador edition of which describes him as "Writer, blackmailer and con man, pauper and pederast." *The Reader's Encyclopedia* claims that Rolfe was "Brilliantly original, but unbalanced and somewhat of a charlatan." Auden, writing of Rolfe's *Desire and Pursuit of the Whole*, remarks that "Rolfe certainly expected that his readers would see life as Crabbe [the protagonist] sees it, that they would take his side, agree that he was the innocent genius victim of a gang of malicious boobies . . . . Thanks to Rolfe's remarkable talent, however, the reader has the very different and, for him, more interesting experience of knowing that he is looking at the world through the eyes of a homosexual paranoid . . . ." This should probably be a sobering lesson for anyone attempting, even in a footnote, to account for him- or her- (or whom?-) self, but I stubbornly if somewhat ironically want to believe that I know me well enough amusedly to observe some of the deeper affinities I might have with this venomous and megalomaniacal dilletante. In the Preface to his *Chronicles of the House of Borgia*, writing under the pseudonym of the Baron Corvo, Rolfe crows upstartedly and all too familiarly of himself: "In his manner of writing, he has endeavoured to rush from mood to mood, in consonance with the subject under consideration, with something of the breathless masterful versatility which Nature uses." I fear I may recognize in such lines as these the super-self-serious auto-mythologizing glibness which academia and its little artistic disappointments have only served to accentuate in me. Perhaps it would be a little sunnier and funnier, however, and less self-romanticizing to boot (though I hardly really imagine so, given that my chain of associations here has been rattled by recollections of the delusional *méconnaissances* in the "Book on Adler"; see Kierkegaard 1955) if by way of "excusing" my way with words I were simply to remind the reader somewhat more pertinently of what Kierkegaard was planning to say in drafts for his own doctoral dissertation on *The Concept of Irony*: "and should there happen to be, particularly in the first part of the essay, various things which one is otherwise unaccustomed to meet with in academic dissertations, then the reader will have to forgive me my gaiety, and that I sometimes sing as I work in order to lighten my task" (Kierkegaard 1968-70, 3:114). *Basta.*

But it didn't seem that way to me when I began. Then I felt I was fleeing the deadening abstractness of theory for the good old prosaic lived (and maybe even shared) reality of food and drink, feelings and laughter, pleasure and pain; and words as things about things, and words as *words*, and the way they feel on the inner ear. I was setting out for the territories, looking for an alien textual space that hadn't already been wholly overrun and de-realized by critical colonists, though I was not, of course, able to kid myself at this late date about the imperialistic undertones of such a perfervid search for *Lesensraum*. Indeed, I prided myself on the immense dense empire, wildly teeming with untapped life, that I was Aguirre-like going to lay claim to, and I also took a certain secret satisfaction in my meta-elitist conviction that I was going to "diss" some of my supremely serious theory-head colleagues by pulling on them a version of what Nietzsche had called "Kant's Joke": "Kant wanted to prove, in a way that would make 'the average Joe's' head spin, that 'the average Joe' was right—that was the private joke of his soul. He wrote against the learned in favor of common prejudice, but he wrote for the learned and not for the common people" (Nietzsche 1882, 104). We now know, though, what's wrong with this; and I've translated Nietzsche's *"alle Welt* [the whole world]" as "the average Joe" to show that I have been educated myself to recognize the problematical nature of any shared experience of any "common people." This collective nonentity has in fact largely been constructed out of the abstract universalism of the "average" plus the white male presuppositions of guys like Joe (whether Stalin, McCarthy, or my own good sad dear departed old man). Thus, to use the word "real" in one's title must today be accompanied by a conscious or rather quite *self*-conscious embarrassment regarding one's personal political pretensions quite apart from any philosophical quandaries. Who do you think you are? And you'd better know ahead of time, or you're just going to look like the kind of utopian critical critic who has taken his rod and his real and gone fishing for the afternoon once again. Out to lunch.

For the "real" has, in a strange way, been the final court of appeal for all countercultural academic claims in this century, whether as the hardheaded economic *Hinterfragen* of postmarxism, the supposed ethical "principle" underneath psychoanalysis (cf. Lacan 1986), the "hyperrealism" of poststructuralism, or the lived and livid lucidity of feminism, queer studies, or last but harumpf oh certainly not least of course, the interventions of people of color (still the real unread margin for most of us). A disabusing "realism" that left the false consciousness of other perspectives looking not just morally bankrupt or spiritually oppressive or epistemologically unsophisticated but downright *"unrealistic"* in the most prosaic sense has been the key to countercultural authority. But our intellectual realism itself has long since led us to recognize the partiality of *all* realism, its constructedness, its exclusions, its exploitations; its unrealistic aspects. The real can now only be real *for someone*, and one must take responsibility for that reality, and recognize it as a particular version of what there is.[7]

This I am more than willing to do, but it has now started to look as though, while all perspectives may be relative, some of them are more relative than others, and as though me and those bourgeois hetero male cronies of little color of mine really are in a peculiarly nasty fix when it comes to being realistic. After all, many of us seem to be stuck still *living* the ideology everybody else is busy dismantling. And the transparency of prose, which Kittay and Godzich connect with the impersonality of the state (see "Nashe's Presence" below), is doubtless really only the effect of an unreal hegemonic perspective to which I (oops, I'm giving the ending away), to an extent that makes it impossible for me to see it, have been assimilated. (Of course, we still have the leisure to lean back against the hood like Wayne and Garth or Bart Simpson and sough complacently: "Unreal, dude!") Thus, there may indeed be something unsalvageably reactionary—or, as I suspect, at least re*d*actionary—about my realisms,

---

[7]The problem here, though no doubt imminently clear to most readers, is nicely brought out in my friend Tim Cashion's unpublished thesis on Richard Rorty when the Timster tells how he considered replacing the cumbersome term "nonintellectuals" in his account with "'real people,' because it contrasts well with the poetic people that Rorty likes," but ultimately abandoned the epithet "because 'real' has been used in front of, for example, 'women' in a way that I find unpalatable" (Cashion 1991, 110 n. 1). By the way, one reason I occasionally will be quoting my currently unknown friends and other "real people" (a beautifully *inconsequential* form of nepotism or sycophancy) is because I would like this book from time to time to be "amateurish" in the best and most etymological sense. Amateur scholarship seems to have pretty much gone the way of all flesh (although I've been tickled by the fact that my research has already helped bring me into contact with dedicated and industrious extra-academic workers on both the anti-Stratfordian theories and the topic of Freemasonry and Rosicrucianism in the Renaissance); in any case, the professionalism by which amateur scholarship has essentially been superceded in our century seems to me to have no absolute claim to the badge of the real it often sports at MLA. A "real scholar" today is someone institutionally certifiable (so to speak); but what does this "real" really imply then in an age of radical institutional *inquisition* not to mention Baudrillardesque hyperrealism? Perhaps something not altogether uncreepy yet still almost parodically absurb, in the end. As my academically invested (and superb) friend Carrie Hintz put it, "I thought that the insects in *Naked Lunch* were real. The cockroaches lived in my kitchen and in my heart" (qtd in MacKenzie 1992, 49).

relying as they do upon "personalism" (if not "humanism"), "impressionism," and a kind of nostalgia for an undoubtedly oppressive print culture textuality that seems to be in the process of becoming extinct (to be replaced by something infinitely more subtle, of course: you can *see* the *press* in op*press*ion, but only the *vide* can be viewed in video). Well, yes, then, my approach does rely beneath it all upon feelings, hopes, desires, fears, and—finally—*aesthetics* that (however real to me) are probably part and parcel of a politically privileged, but thus morally and cognitively often underprivileged subject position.

I nowise want to defy this insight (as the stupid anti-pc backlash shysters are so eager to do), but I am still determined to continue to look for "realities" within my strategically de-realized purview—matters I at least don't *feel* can be so glibly consigned to the dustbin of a "privileged" false consciousness; and I revert as a kind of desperate bid to hold onto my reality (and thus to my privilege?—but enough of this liberal soul scorching: insult to injury? seeing's how the Wayne Booth chair doesn't sit much more comfortably anymore than the *Wayne's World* couch does) again and again to things that *feel* real to me. I realize that this finally makes me guilty of a form of reader response criticism that would charitably be rubricized "impressionistic," but I have not been able to forgo the view, perhaps indeed because of my ideologically privileged subject position, that reality does finally depend upon feelings, in spite of my equally *painful* awareness that this is the most philosophically as well as politically ramshackle construction I could choose to squat in. To the extent that my drift can be summarized, then, I suppose this is a study of how I think we might be more realistic about our experience of prosaic and print cultural textuality; why the "realities" of a few Elizabethan prose texts sometimes seem to defy theoretical norms; why they are *not* of course the ultimate real, and why, yet, they sometimes *feel* so real; and why, for me, simply reading them (not doing readings of them) has helped to counter a continued de-realization of the prose of the world that I nevertheless recognize may at times be politically imperative.

What I often feel has been *un*necessary (and *un*realistic) about literary theory and criticism in general, however, has been its lack of *effets de vécu*, effects of what your feminists and other oppressed resistance groups call "lived experience," an absence that has slowly begun to be made up for in the last decade or so. Perhaps this is not the aptest time for people in my position to be trying to reclaim reality for aspects of their own "lived experience"—even the repressed, prosaic aspects of it that may finally not be so specific to the privileged nature of the perspective, or so oppressive in and of themselves—but I *felt* I had to try, as much out of a sense of being *real* for a change, as to find a way of working myself out of the theoretical cynicism that sometimes seems to have appropriated the badge of "realism" to itself as a way of avoiding the genuine *feel* of the real. Remember *"le grain de la voix"*? Well, it's *"la voix du grain"* that I'm trying to remember the feel of here: the sparkling particular, the seeds of the storm, to wax a bit Serresian in my seaside-sold seashell imagery: "A flight of screaming birds, a school of herring tearing through the water like a silken sheet" (Serres 1982, 15). These are the kinds of things I want you to hear here; but hear precisely *not* as aggregates, theoretical entities. Remember what it was like to feel what you read?

It has seemed to me that in their incessant *conceptualization* and *intel-lectualization* of the pain as well as the *pleasure* of the texts in which we live, most structuralist types and many poststructuralists too have, to recall a quibble of Randall McLeod's in a different, but not entirely unre-lated context, provided materials not so much toward an aesthetics as toward anaesthetics. This constitutes a kind of obdormition which should now be causing us pain as our bodies are forced to wake up to the real by the movements of their oppressed members. But I hope that the return of feeling may include, along with the pins and needles (which after all aren't such an ordeal for us to have to go through, considering what our insensitivity can and does sanction), new sources of pleasure and a new appreciation for the possibilities of the real as written as well.

No, I don't feel that I know what is real, but I do know that I *feel* what is real. From an epistemological point of view, any contribution I might make here toward a *theory* of realism would, I can only suppose, be negative, still more alienating, the *other* of a consistent system that could be pointed to, like the comedic insight Northrop Frye described as a shift from *pistis* to *gnosis* arriving at the happy cognitive bonus that "[i]llusion is whatever is fixed or definable, and reality is best understood as its negation: whatever reality is, it's not *that*" (Frye 1957, 170). Re-member what Julia Kristeva used to say about "woman," in the good old bad old days? We all know now that whatever reality is, *ce n'est jamais ça*; for the tragedies of history obligingly re-enact themselves as epistemo-logical farces for us in literature, or at least in literary criticism: the prose of the world is always *somebody's* reality (or even *nobody's* reality), sure. But that doesn't stop the real from coming back through it. "Fate," says Nashe, "is a spaniel that you cannot beate from you; the more you thinke to crosse it, the more you blesse it, and further it" (Nashe 1599, G2/ 3:196). All right then, these are *my* herrings: *"Mes Harengs"* (and no doubt really my *harangues*, more than anything else)—though I still can hope that you will see them as not only that.[8] But even seeing them as *mine* is more realistic than seeing them as deconstruction's herrings, the herrings of patriarchy, whatever. For theoretical realism at the end of the century seems to me to be shaping up, more than anything else, in the face of a global "textuality" that nevertheless would of course be a joke outside of the academy and a few highbrow art circles, as a recognition of the difficulty of maintaining a "critical distance" through textuality from *some* personal realness or other, and so also a demand for the admission, maybe only as a first step, that there can be no such distance without violence to the real, and finally for a confession either that the people, places and things that are held together and kept apart by the prose of the world don't really matter because, after all, they don't even *really* exist, or else that, when all is said and done, in that vast text you are *not* neither here nor there; that *you* (even if only personally, locally, incidentally, momentarily, all too scarily)—that you too are there, and perhaps even: care.

[8]And in fact, they may be only *that* in a purely expropriational rather than a "subjective" sense. Given the strong attraction of the pre-modern for me precisely as an escape not only from the penuriously homogenous supposed heterogeneity of postmodern McCulture but also from the constrained horror of the still-paranoid-after-all-these-years bourgeois subject ("*L'enfer, c'est le moi*"), it would not do to ignore the blatant *not-mineness* of Nashe's herrings. My pal Scottiedog MacKenzie tells of how he went in search of the only two films his grandfather had reportedly ever viewed—the emotionally pictic *Tunes of Glory* and *Whisky Galore!*—supposedly in order to find out a bit about who *he*—Scottiedog MacKenzie—actually was: "Yet, this is a facile reading of a past I know nothing about; I now feel more than ever that in attempting to theorize the 'real' in the cinema, I am attempting to explain my own fascination with moving images by analyzing 'Others' who seem far easier to unpack than myself. This is an interesting coincidence, as I suggest that this is exactly what one does when one *goes* to the cinema: the viewer sees the world through images that are easier to live with than the real world" (1992, 136).

Reading against Readings

LITERAL READING—LOCAL READING
TOPICAL READING—READING IN DETAIL
INCIDENTAL READING—SURFACE READING
READING RED—FEMMILIAR READING
POLITERAL READING

> The issue of vegetarianism is a touchstone for the literal for
> it addresses the literal activities of meat eating by discussing
> what is literally consumed.
> Carol J. Adams, *The Sexual Politics of Meat*

Thomas Nashe was against interpretation—but what, one will immediately want to know, can I possibly *mean* by this? Nashe is constantly protesting against the "mice-eyed decipherers and calculaters vppon characters" (Nashe 1599, K2/3:218) that, he claims, habitually "wrest and peruert" (Nashe 1592a, ¢2^V/1:155) his homely and trivial matter to make it disclose a latent subversive political (dis)content, and nowhere is his crying out against this kind of reading more stridulous than in his last pamphlet, *Lenten Stuffe* (1599), a book which consistently insists that it really is about the virtues of the fishing town of Yarmouth and of that town's chief product and export, the red herring. Jonathan Crewe takes this "mock encomium" to be paradigmatic of the textual practice which has created the "Nashe problem": *Lenten Stuffe* would seem to have no message; but its message is precisely about the need we feel to invest language with a message, and about writing's unsuitability

27

for this sort of investment. Although Nashe's rhetoric enacts "a sophisticated return to a state of innocence," this return "does not fully liberate
rhetoric from its constitutive opposition to logic and even to truth; it even
exacerbates that opposition" (Crewe 1982, 92). Other recent readings of
Nashe's pamphlet have found themselves constrained to produce similar
meta-messages. Indeed, only Stephen Hilliard manages to give some
account of his *reading* of the text without offering a totalizing, moralizing
reading of it. Crewe believes that it is self-referential, not about Yarmouth
or the herrings, but about its own situation as unredeemed rhetoric. But
Hilliard, while he admits that the "*mockery* is self-referential, directed at
Nashe's pretensions as a poet and the excesses" of what Hilliard
amusingly spells "epideistic rhetoric," insists that "[a]t the same time
Nashe gives credit to the value of red herring as a staple, suggesting that
inexpensive food has an importance that puts humanity's more exalted
desires in proportion" (224, emphasis added; 230). Ultimately, though,
although he has actually read the herrings that so many readers have
only read something into, Hilliard cannot help but see Nashe's pamphlet
as "an admirable though relatively *insignificant* work" (230; emphasis
added); and even Hilliard, whose reading in both senses is arguably the
most sensitive and sensible to date, must then go on to demonstrate how
the pamphlet is in some ways really about the nature of interpretative
expectations themselves, and so on. But at least he never forgets the
actual prosy theme of the pamphlet:

> This outrageously puffed-up style is used to glorify prosaic salt
> fish in a parody of Renaissance literature of praise. At the same
> time the Elizabethan taste for allegory, particularly its propensity
> for topical allusions, is tempted with enigmatic passages. (235)

But it is not just an *Elizabethan* hermeneutical compulsion that is thus
clearly tempted. It takes a tremendous act of *Unlernen* for most of us to
go back to reading something like *Lenten Stuffe* without "reading" it. And
we may ultimately find ourselves obliged to make use of strategies that
are in fact always (all ready?) subjected to the overall institutional imperatives by which we do our reading: reading in detail (for *effets de réel*,
structuralism), reading literally (for *écriture*, poststructuralism), reading
locally (for pockets of resistance, postmarxism), etc. None of these is
really good old reading reading. Hillard does his best, but he is up
against insuperable institutional odds.

All other recent *readings* of Nashe's "Prayse of the Red Herring"
have, on the other hand, been concerned to show that it is actually about
something other than the red herring: in fact, it is usually read as being

essentially about the predicament of interpretation itself, the very act that Nashe seems to be writing against. I can go right ahead and insist for my part that Nashe's red herrings are meant to fly in the face of all allegorizing interpretation (whether Early Modern or Postmodern), but yes, I am aware that in order even to argue that Nashe was writing against interpretation it is already necessary to have *read* beyond the literal or the local or the detail or the real. It would seem that all critics have gloomily accepted this institutional compromise, even if increasingly they have resentfully made *it* the butt of their readings. Thus, Lorna Hutson, in her dazzling state-of-the-art account of *Lenten Stuffe* as text "indigestible" and "intractable to any impulse to interpret as well as experience its linguistic plenitude" (Hutson 1989, 245), eventually knocks up the spiciest—but thus all the more "indigestible"—interpretation, one whereby Nashe's genuine "non-sense" (248) is meant to ridicule and undo the Elizabethan practice of moralizing interpretation itself, ironically criticizing, by consistently baffling, the expectation that his work has anything to do with the "very activity" of producing language with delitescent reference:

> The very suggestion that a subversive significance might be teased out of Nashe's ironic comparisons by someone in the know is a mockery; the paradoxes are impenetrable as they are suggestive. Ingeniously conforming to the sophisticated rules of the ironic encomium, their substitution of mockery where praise is expected and vice versa is designed to frustrate the politic reader and to lead him nowhere at all. (Hutson 1989, 248-149)

Nowhere else, in other words, but to Hutson's own moral that this form of "reading" is itself alienating, manipulative and tied to the commodification of both words and things. In a world in which "there are no facts, but only interpretations," and where even a stand "against interpretation" can only be codified as the core of a unifying reading that will allow us to "start considering the way in which an apparent shapelessness, a lack of continuity and coherence, might function as a politically and morally significant aesthetic in its own right" (5), even "reading literally," even the literal act of reading, becomes the phantomatic double of the always already read, the unquiet sleeper in the good earth of the recently *inter*preted.

≈≈≈≈≈≈≈≈≈≈

Hutson's recourse to an *interpretation* to disclose Nashe's "political" resistance to interpretation seems to invite its own instant allegorization as concealing an ironic level of counter-institutional critique. Indeed, I think that her reading positively *demands* of its own astute reader that it be *read* as yet another desperate commentary on the capitalist-humanist proliferation of "readings" that continue to glut the scholarly market. At least that's how I read it. For even if I can agree with nothing that Richard Levin has *literally* written in his provocative critique of the constantly redoubled "new readings" of "old plays" at the end of the century (Levin 1979), I *can* sympathize with the underlying distaste with which he contemplates the relentless recourse to this brand of scholarship and intervention in the institutional settlement we have inherited. But against these endless "readings," Levin can only propose attention to the text "as read"; not the text as it actually *is* read, of course, but the text as it *has been*, or *should be* read. "Readings" always refer to the text "as read," not the text as actually experienced in reading: the text of the reading is always all read (to mildly pun). Thus, Michael D. Bristol's account of Levin's position, subheaded "Against Reading," might more realistically have been rubricized as "Against Readings," for it is not the act of reading to which Levin has objected, but the act of *writing* readings. To be against "reading" in this sense, however, entails for Bristol an unsavoury metaphysics of sense or sensibility. He suggests how those of us who are "against interpretation" seem invariably to be committed to the artwork either "as a priceless aesthetic value" or as "the sedimented expressivity of an individual artist," and thus to a "counternormative agenda" that views vying readings as substitutes for or betrayals of "'the real thing'" (Bristol 1989, 197-99). It is certainly out of a most suspicious sense of realism, I think, that both Levin and Susan Sontag herself have in their separate ways argued for their "manifest surfaces" and "apparent meanings"; but I wonder if there could not be some form of "literal reading" whose reality would not be so easily consignable back to the false idealism of hermeneuticist culture. Clearly, whatever her own illusions, Sontag felt that the effect of interpretation was henceforth always one of a mystification that added to the continued derealization of a bourgeois *Lebenswelt* at large:

> The aim of all commentary on art now should be to make works of art—and, by analogy, our own experience—more, rather than less, real to us. The function of criticism should be to show *how it is what it is*, even *that it is what it is*, rather than to show *what it means*. (Sontag 1964, 14)

Well, "more real to us" is hardly the sort of phrase most of us would use to describe how the average reading leads us to experience the text read. More meaningful, perhaps; more politically useful, more consoling, maybe more disturbing, more interesting, but not "more real." *Reality* demands the feeling of immediacy which interpretation is there to debunk and supplement, a feeling of surface truth, unproblematical apparent meaning—above all that most anathema of critical categories: a *feeling*. Read*ings* repress this feel and this real: they themselves are "against reading," they are the "supplement" of reading, reading's other. The gerund of our descriptive term is misleading, for our exegeses necessarily take the text as *read* and have little to do with the *real* experience of read*ing* at all. They should—and I suspect Levin would be in agreement here (look at the homophonic possibilities)—be called not "readings" but "reads."

≈≈≈≈≈≈≈≈≈≈

Nashe's aversion to interpretation—like that of Sontag or even that of Levin—asks for a political reading, but not necessarily the one that it gets. Sontag, for all her bourgeois romanticism, can still be seen to have really been taking a stand against the commodification of artistic values in the institutional reification of their substantial and sensual qualities into commensurable meaning-values that could then be traded within a conservative settlement of humanist affirmative culture. Levin, on the other hand, reacts to the runaway inflation of late hermeneuticist readings of historically remote texts, readings, however, ineluctably made, as we now know, and as people like Catherine Belsey are frequently fond of patently stating, "from the present" (Belsey 1985, 2), and readings which have in fact come, within the institutional dispensation, increasingly to tend toward disclosure of subversive or symptomatically uncomfortable political contents in texts whose "apparent meaning" (read previously prevailing reading) supposedly conformed to the positions propagated in some increasingly caricatural "official discourse."

The political context of Nashe's aversion to interpretation will thus in vain proclaim itself on the surface to be far more idiosyncratic than ideological. He plainly *says* that he doesn't want to be held responsible for latent political content, and his protestations will only be shown themselves to have a more articulated political intent by refusing, as Hutson among others does, to read them in any sense *literally*. Read literally (perhaps here this means, read as sincere), Nashe's text disowns the seditious intentions that are with greater or lesser ingenuity assigned to it. While it would not do to disregard Bristol's crucial observation to patentists like Levin that, as Annabel Patterson (1984) has demonstrated, given the conditions of censorship operating in Elizabethan England, "it is by no means reasonable to assume that authors want to be understood," it is worth looking below the surface of Bristol's throwaway line a little further on: "Even under the relatively more pleasant conditions of liberal society, guile and perversity may figure in any account of an author's desire" (Bristol 1989, 200-01). If the New Historicism has made any kind of "advance" upon the Old, it is, as Louis Montrose blurted out one time, in the suspicion that the readings of both schools may say more about the political unconscious of the critics than that of the producers of the texts being read. Indeed, no one should be particularly surprised to learn that the only real examples we have of those uncalled-for readings by the "lawyers, and selfe-conceited misinterpreters" about whom Nashe was so wont to complain (1599, I4^v/3:216), come to us from *our own* century. Thus, the "allegory of the bear and the fox" from *Pierce Penilesse*, which supposedly proved such a dangerous embarrassment to Nashe in the early 1590s, was fairly convincingly commuted to a bit of topical critique of Leicester and a couple of already officially demonized Puritans by Donald J. McGinn in 1946. Note too that this reading doesn't simply reduce a bit of caveat for the general, as Nashe insisted, into an overly particularlized example of getting personal, it also agglomerates Nashe's satirical or subversive reserve to a basically party-line bit of affirmative culture pillow fight. This was still the days of the Old Historicism, when, although Nashe may have had a political intent, it could hardly have been considered "subversive," since the idea of genuine subversion didn't exist as an institutional good.

Heard from the end of a century of Old and New Historicism, Nashe's misgivings ring with an uncanny sense of the proleptic: "I know," he repines at the beginning of *Strange Newes*, "there want not welwillers to my disgrace, who say my onely Muse is contention; and other, that with *Tiberius Cæsar* pretending to see in the darke, talke of strange obiectes by them discouered in the night, when in truth they are nothing else but the glimmering of their eies" (Nashe 1592c, A4^v/1:259). Indeed, readers have come to take Nashe's strongest objections to the allegorical interpretive strategies of his day precisely as the most salient clues to the correct road to the real meaning of his texts. At the end of *Lenten Stuffe*, he bemoans: "Talke I of a beare, O it is such a man that emblazens him in his armes [precisely McGinn's evidence for Leicester (McGinn 1946, 435, following McKerrow 1908, 4:139)], or of a woolfe, a fox, or a camelion, any lording whom they do not affect, it is meant by" (Nashe 1599 I3^v/3:214). And overleaf he introduces a pair of red herring riddles (which he claims have no more latent content than some empty Jamesian "amusette" would today) with a self-fulfilling prophecy about the resourcefulness of the interpretive when it comes to reappropriating the literal: "though there be neither rime nor reason in it, (as by my good will there shal not) they according to their accustomed gentle fauors, whether I wil or no, shall supply it with either, and runne ouer al the peeres of the land in peeuish moralizing and anatomizing it" (I4^V-K1/3:216). Almost unbearably, Alice Lyle Scoufos was content, in 1968, to read the entire "praise of the red herring" from which these riddles come as a satire, via "herringcobs," on Lord Cobham and his family, the peers who had been upset by the abuse of their ancestor Oldcastle in the *Ur*-versions of Shakespeare's second Henriad, and the supposed targets of Jonson and Nashe's lost *Isle of Dogs* play (Scoufos 1968).

I agree with Lorna Hutson's assessment of this latter reading: "Although the supporting evidence makes this explanation seem plausible enough, it is curiously belied in the experience of *reading Lenten Stuffe*" (Hutson 1989, 246, emphasis added). I am personally sympathetic with Hutson's hypothesis that by the time he wrote *Lenten Stuffe*, Nashe really was against interpretation *on principle*, and averse to the allegorical practice of writing that facilitates interpretation. But I am not then entirely willing to follow her on her own all but crypto-deconstructionist hermeneutical recuperation whereby "it is this very activity—the activity of inventing language in such a way as to create such references—that is, if anything, the satiric focus" of Nashe's ultimate text (Ibid.). This is a version of the negative bonus in that de Manic depressive epistemophile hermeneutic which insists that texts are now "about" their own readings, a position most eloquently defended, perhaps, by Naomi Schor in *Reading in Detail*:

> If, as I am suggesting, interpretation is viewed not as something that is done *to* fiction but rather something that is done *in* fiction, then to be against interpretation becomes an untenable position, for it is tantamount to rejecting a considerable body of (modern) fiction that is explicitly, indeed insistently, concerned with interpretation: its scope and its limits, its necessity and its frustration. (Schor 1987, 121)

≈≈≈≈≈≈≈≈≈

No *position* "against interpretation" seems any longer to be *"tenable,"* then, and the absence of such a position brings the problem of literal reading further onto the black ice of what I will sometimes be calling, following Leah Marcus but further pinpointing the coordinates, "local reading." The reading "in detail" which might stall hermeneutic closure—the "non-position" against interpretation—would presumably demand greater attention to those "bizarre, local effects" in whose interest Neil Rhodes, in *Elizabethan Grotesque*, suggested the Nashean narrative gets "distended" (Rhodes 1980, 31). But Hutson has since argued that while Rhodes, along with John Carey (1970), quite helpfully has "encouraged readers to be more attentive to local effects and ambiguities in Nashe's writing," this ultimately betrays a "determination not to read the pamphlets as entities" and thus "leaves scholarship and reading somewhat at a standstill" (Hutson 1989, 4). "Entities"? It would seem that this "standstill" Hutson worries about is what, paradoxically, is now perceived as an "untenable position." Yet "local reading" like Rhodes's and reading "in detail" like Hutson's are eventually (just like "dialectical materialism") none of the above: neither local, nor in detail, nor above all *reading*—"Neither flesh nor fish, nor good red herring" (Nashe 1599, K4/ 3:222).

This doesn't mean that such readings may not be interesting, institutionally marketable, politically useful, loads of fun, or just plain comforting—undoubtedly: a reading is, after all, a kind of existential reconciliation and making peace with the text—but it *does* mean that they go on avoiding the reality of reading. If Nashe's last pamphlet could really be read in detail (I'll be trying here and there)—that is, if the moment-by-moment reading along from detail to detail could be somehow represented without turning it into an articulated *single* utterance "about" the temporarity of meaning or the falseness of interpretive commodification or whatever, then I could agree wholeheartedly with Hutson that "the proverbially based, nourishing wordplay of *Lenten Stuffe* and the uncomfortable, disorienting puns of *The Unfortunate Traveller* serve different aesthetic and polemical ends" (Hutson 1989, 3). But Hutson's reading, for all its finesse, still winds us up back at a totalizing aesthetico-polemical focus from which the details themselves must fall away. It's not so much that *Lenten Stuffe* is really about herrings and that *The Unfortunate Traveller* is really about metaphor, or narrative, or what have you. It's that what those pamphlets are really *about* is so incidental that no "reading" can take account of it. It doesn't seem to be possible for the *incidental* to become the "focus" of a "unified work of art" (i.e., of a unified reading) without a re-commodification of it in terms of what Hutson herself might call "epistemological capital." It falls to the metaphysics not of reading *per se*, then, but of read*ings* for the necessity of "unnecessary details," the significance of the "insignificant," to impose themselves. Thus, after having argued that "Balzacian detailism" arose from a movement which had as its program "to demonstrate that the neo-classical opposition of particularity and the Sublime was not insuperable," Naomi Schor goes on to prove by the usual abracadabra that the metaphysic is nevertheless "reinscribed" in such detailism "by sublimating the prose of the world" itself (Schor 1987, 146; 147). The details *add up*, and of course *heben auf*.

But it is this prose of the world that Nashe had at last come to write *down*, and his herring does demand to be "read" *in de tail*. Any connections of an Oldcastle sort would better be explored in terms of J.B. Steane's winningly literalist asseveration:

> In its Falstaffian way ("Banish plump Jack and banish all the world") [*Lenten Stuffe*] gives us the world. We are creatures who want food and love food (the actual physical stuff that goes into our stomachs and keeps us alive): so praise the red herring. We spend our strength and our skill getting it: so praise the fishermen of East Anglia. (Steane 1972, 43)

Steane rightly points out the fleeting seductiveness of the incidental in reading, and suggests that it is in incidentals as such that Nashe's value is really to be found. For Steane, Nashe is a kind of Elizabethan version of Orwell's Dickens, master detailist, king of the "thumbnail" character sketch: "The Dickensian touch is there in the specificity" (39; cf. 25; 38; 40). But this Dickensian detailism cannot become the subject of a *reading* without being recouped yet again to some systematic transcendental signified, whether, as with the "unnecessary details" in Barthes's "*effet de réel*," a connotatory pseudo-empirical one: "we are reality" (cf. Barthes 1966b, 174), or, as with the politically underwritten carnivalesque of Hutson's reading, some now institutionally authorized version of the second order epistemological bonus that self-satisfiedly sighs: "cognitive clout's come home again." Neither "reading" of Nashe's incidental matter can have anything to do with the experience of actually *reading* such "details." As Gérard Genette has pointed out, effects of verisimilar unnecessity à la Barthes can hardly be the upshot of reading, but only of *a reading*, since an "unnecessary detail" is only unnecessary to some unifying agenda: "Its role as an agent of mimesis can thus only be retroactive, on a second reading or on thinking back about it afterwards, which is scarcely compatible with the effect of immediacy it is supposed to be aiming for" (Genette 1983, 33). The "reality" of Nashean detail, then, does not reside in its "lack of necessity," and we would be misled if we attempted to "read" Nashe's text with an eye to somehow putting its local detail on some map of misreading according to a counter-sublimation of immediacy. Not that immediacy isn't one of the effects of actually *reading* the text, at least for me. But it is impossible to derive a "unified" reading of Nashe's text from the local effects one experiences in reading, and such interpretation is bound instead to revert to the sort of tendentious "reading" Nashe was most nervous about, the dilletantism of "the silliest millers thombe or contemptible stickle-banck . . . busie nibbling about my fame, as if I were a deade man throwne amongest them to feede vpon" (1599, B1/3:153). So he is, of course; and we must look forward to a new generation of wellwillers to his discredit and self-conceited misinterpreters practising readings so de Manically close that we may say of them with Marx: "If I hold you any closer, I'll be in back of you" (*A Day at the Races*, MGM, 1937). Such reading may really get closer and closer to the recessive political unconscious of language itself, but it has less and less to do with the feeling of closeness that the real incidence of reading allows, the transient presence of relative immediacy which in a "reading" winds up troped away by some rhetoric of temporarity. The literal, the local, the incidental, the detail cannot be *used* to defy this spacing in "reading," this remove. Yet they *do defy it*, simply by being there.

≈≈≈≈≈≈≈≈≈

Hutson's attempt to "read literally" fans the sensuous materiality of the signifier's luculent literality—uh huh. But even this literality cannot really be *read*, glowing coal-like to smoke a brace of herrings as it is, as some programmatic critique of the commodification of sense or of mystificatorally thuribular in-sense. It is only Hutson's *interpretation* that allows Nashe's material an *allegorical* figurativeness, the "auricular" figurality (in Puttenham's sense) of his language slyly being used by her as a synecdochic representative for the infinite interpretability of the figurative in its "sensible" or "sententious" capacities. But Nashe's genius is in making *sense*, not in making sense. Nashean figurality is in the main (as *The Times* crossword compiler might put it) not sense-oriented, but *sensual*: it skates over the surface of the prose of the world; it is anti-allegorical, anti-symbolic, it plashes in the tympanic shallows of the pseudotic, of "read hearing"; and it is on that dime of insight that Hutson's reading should perhaps have come to its own standstill. For Nashe's material language can doubtless be *read* as part of an allegory of the valueless exploitability of material resources by those out to make read sense, but this is no longer reading, just grasping at the hollow reeds of a dignified signified, and Hutson herself is ready enough to quote Nashe's sarcastic remark about the infinite political utilizability of the herring-slippery quasi-auricular signifier: "an infant squib of the Innes of Court, that hath not halfe greased his dining cappe . . . catcheth hold of a rush, and absolutely concludeth, it is meant of the Emperour of Ruscia, and that it will vtterly marre the traffike into that country if all the Pamphlets bee not called in and suppressed, wherein that libelling word is mentioned" (1599, I3/ 3:213). Hutson comments:

> What is so ingenious about this caricature is the way in which the revitalization of the proverb has made 'superficial' linguistic activity (the unexpected transition from 'rush' to 'Russia') seem so satisfying and rich as to preclude the reader's desire for any further 'depth' of significance. Indeed the search for a 'deeper' meaning emerges by comparison as a superficial activity, mocked by the material density of the linguistic surface itself. This tendency to 'palpabrize' linguistic activity, a tendency evident throughout Nashe's writing, is here in *Lenten Stuffe* most fully realized for this very purpose. (Hutson 1989, 247)

For this very purpose. To bring home again the depth of meaning in surfaces and the superficiality of looking for meaning beneath them. I'm not trying to make fun of Hutson, who in any case is well aware of the ironies: her dilemma is the same as the rest of us face—we are *wörtlich betäubt*, literally anaesthetized. At some point in her daredevil drive over the thin ice of the literal she is bound to wind up idling at that fatal standstill over what is, *on the surface*, an "idle text." It is the idleness which cannot fully be accounted for, the literal thereness which stands "against interpretation"; and, it goes without *seing* (*qui tombe*), the institutional imperatives of late hermeneuticist affirmative culture even now balk at that idleness: "*Sed caueat emptor*, Let the interpreter beware; for none euer heard me make *Allegories* of an idle text" (Nashe 1592a, ₵2ᵛ/ 1:155; emphasis added).

As Hutson crucially recognizes, however (ready with that sigh?), Nashe's text is not *really* idle, but busy about making our everyday experience more real to us. Yet she insists on making a submarine sandwich out of Carey's statement to this effect, surrounding it with her own thick shives of figurative polysemy and the anxiety of interpretation:

> Throughout *Lenten Stuffe* this kind of metaphoric density challenges the inventive capacity of the reader just to keep making sense of it all. John Carey puts this best when he writes of *Lenten Stuffe* that Nashe's 'loving cultivation of the commonplace renovates experience for us'. But this renovation of experience through language has its own polemic purpose. It pleads on behalf of the figurative power of the English language, that

it may be developed by contemporary poets, without being interpreted or expounded out of existence. (Hutson 1989, 248; cf.
Carey 1970, 376-77)

Again and again the bizarre local effects and the loving cultivation of the
commonplace are provided with institutional alibis in the form of readings behind. Hutson's inability to keep from interpreting or expounding
into the ground the concrete experience of actually reading Nashe's text
once more testifies to the incapacity of what she equivocally calls the
"reader" to take up a position against interpretation. One can't even read
on the surface without *a reading*.

≋≋≋≋≋≋≋≋≋

I myself do *read* Nashe's works, as anti-allegories of surfacing *de profundis* (*de quibus* "*natus est fex* [i.e., *faex*]," not "*rex*," as the herring-
whiffing cardinal in *Lenten Stuffe* ungrammatically suggests [1599, H4^V/
3:209]), texts about which could be said, with Montaigne, "that, which
Crates said of *Heraclitus* his compositions, that they needed a Reader, who
should bee a cunning swimmer, lest the depth and weight of his learning
should drowne and swallow him vp" (Montaigne 1588, 2:520; Florio's
translation). Old and new allegorizers are no such natators, but rather
good epistemological capitalists, plowing in with their jumbo tankers,
setting up their oil rigs, plunging for profit, and leaving the surface
splayed with bellyups. Nashe could already at the end of his century
complain of the profound shallowness of "a number of Gods fooles, that
for their wealth might be deep wise men, and so foorth (as now a daies
in the opinion of the best lawyers of England there is no wisedome without wealth, alleadge what you can to the contrarie of all the beggarly
sages of greece)" who, "out of some discourses of mine, which were a
mingle mangle cum purre, and I knew not what to make of my selfe,
haue fisht out such a deepe politique state meaning as if I had al the
secrets of court or common-wealth at my fingers endes" (Nashe 1599,
I3^V/3:213-214). The industry of interpretation demands those deep-
trawling, overfishing factory ships of reading that have fished out the
political unconscious of the plays of the period so that not a fin is left to
cry *finuto* to them. But Nashe's texts all prosaically protest, with the
Prologue to *Summers Last Will and Testament*, that they be made a square
meal of, not repackaged and sold for prophet:

Deepe reaching wits, heere is no deepe streame for you to angle
in. Moralizers, you that wrest a neuer meant meaning out of

euerie thing, applying all things to the present time, keepe youre attention for the common Stage: for here are no quips in Characters for you to reade. Vayne glozers, gather what you will. Spite, spell backwards what thou canst. As the *Parthians* fight, flying away, so will wee prate and talke, but stand to nothing that we say. (Nashe 1600, B1^V-B2/3:235)

All such protestations are now habitually depth-read as ironic disclaimers, reader-baiting, ass-covering, or even self-delusion. Latent meaning cannot be escaped; and the task of reading literally demands that the issue finally be thrown back, the bootless boot it has always been. The point is not that Nashe has no subtext, no submerged text, but that, *whether he has one or not*, he is terribly artful at eking out the sense of reality on the slippery, transparent, often thin ice of the literal. I think of one of Nietzsche's absurdly misogynistic "little maxims for women" here: "*Kurze Rede, langer Sinn — Glatteis für die Eselin!*": short on talk and long on sense — slippery ice for the she-ass (1886, 180). For the shrewd and shrewish she-Nashe, as well: for he *is* all talk, "a mingle mangle cum purre" (hogwash) of "prating and talking," a rhetoric of tempting orality which you will lose in the middle of the river if you open your mouth to try to start talking about it yourself. There is no point at the end of *Lenten Stuffe* in asking for "*der langen Rede kurzer Sinn,*" as Schiller's line originally had it, the "short meaning of this long harangue" in Coleridge's translation. In my "reading," it is the ability to stop reading for this short meaning that Nashe's text can be useful in re-teaching. Perhaps the critic who has come closest to realizing *this* reading is Kiernan Ryan, in his attempt to recuperate Nashe for a "socialist criticism" and interpret the text as a lesson in the reading of a herring that is decidedly red:

> The subtitle of *Lenten Stuff* warns us openly that to read the narrative in the hope of reeling in an authoritative statement or message is indeed to chase in vain the 'red herring' of which it purports to offer an encomium (III, 146).
>
> What the reader is being re-educated to expect instead is a 'senseles discourse' (*PP*: I, 239) which displays 'neither rime nor reason' (*LS*: III, 216) and is thus 'bequeathed for wast paper here amongst you' (*UT*: II, 207). Nashe has no predefined didactic motive. He is simply 'playing with a shettlecocke, or tossing empty bladders in the ayre' (*LS*: III, 225). The playing is pointless in that the narration is governed by no subsuming teleological design and defies reduction to a stable vision or conclusive summation. The discourse is 'senseles' only inasmuch as it re-

fuses to make conventional sense by confirming the semantic authority of what counts as accepted wisdom. In response to a fast-flowing Renaissance reality, deprived of any sure epistemological or ethical anchorage, Nashe initiates his readers into a new kind of narration whose meaning is always correspondingly provisional, calculated to survive within the fleeting context of its utterance alone, resisting all attempts to freeze its flow at any point. Nashe's writing changes the way we read in order to change the way we see the world. (Ryan 1985, 48)

But if Nashe's flow can only be periodically frozen, the prosa-iciness of the surface is broken up again in that unheroic manner in which the laketop breaks up in Eisenstein's *Alexander Nevsky*, glugging down the warring factions with an antisublime sax glissando courtesy of Prokofiev. As there is nothing much Russian about rushes, so there is nothing all that "red" about the red herring. The Slavic materialism in Nashe's view of writer/reader rapport is better uttered by Nashe himself: "*In* Ruscia *there are no presents but of meate or drinke; I present you with meate, and you in honourable courtesie to requite mee, can do no lesse then present mee with the best mornings draught of merry-go-downe in your quarters* . . ." (1599, A3^V/3:150). The *faex* brought up *de profundis nassa texta* (*sc. Nashio texto*) is not the popular wisdom of the "scum of society" (*faex populi*), nor the wine-dreg comic re-surfacing of representational disguise (cf., e.g., *Ars poetica* 277), but the solids that settle at the bottom of the semiotic, the literal that litters the floor of metaphor, the crumby old *faex foculorum*, those linguistic lees from the kitchen of the real. Nashe's big trap of a text (the world really runs on such ramshackle weels) may, just as Ryan would like to think, manage in its local moments to get beneath the frozen surface of the prosaic and re-train our capitalist expectations of exploitation along the lines of an emancipatory underground railway; and Hutson is also right to point out his use of a merrily blazing signifier to melt through that isotopicity of superficial figural skating so he can drop his fishtrap in. But his work is not epideictic (or certainly epi*deistic*). The weel wasn't woven for show. Of course from it *can* readily be culled a clutch of protest signs for countercultural *demonstrations*, just as Nashe insists that, like the knitters that Norwich had gotten to put on a needle-work demonstration for the queen in procession, Yarmouth, his haven and the object of his praise, "could clap vp as good a shewe of net-brayders, or those that haue no clothes to wrappe their hides in or breade to put in their mouthes but what they earne and get by brayding of nets" (1599, D1/3:169). But Hutson is wrong to cite this passage as *merely* another exemplum of Nashean "*textual*" resourcefulness: "The profits of the net-weaving industry come alive in the verbal relationships generated by image and assonance; nets appear to transform themselves into clothes as *braiding* miraculously produces *bread*" (Hutson 1989, 263-64). Such exchanges no doubt do partly inaugurate the commodification of sense, and it is true that thanks to such exploitation we have now grown rich enough, as Nietzsche liked to put it, to get our meat—food, not flesh— without a raid upon the submerged realm of the real, without having to exchange the labor of our braiding for the funereally baked *cold meat* of the *brrr*read. Still it is the *bread* of the text, not its braiding, that it is *about*. Fishes and loaves; that's what it's really *about*. ("Let me but name bread," Nashe complains of his readers-into, "they will interpret it to be the town of Bredan in the lowe countryes; if of a beere he talkes, then straight he mocks the County Beroune in France" [1594b, **1^V/2:182].) There is no latent *lesson* down there under the surface of *Lenten Stuffe*, only latent *stuff*. And there is only one short meaning, the obvious one, the literal one: the meaty present. Nashe only stops long enough on the prosaic ice to punch a hole in it and guddle up a gowpenful of what's right near the surface, what really exists and really matters. His text isn't about the gaping hole, or about some texty trap, or about the slipperiness of the ice. As Hutson at one point perfectly expresses it: "the moral kernal of every fable, concealed under every leaf, shadowed in every trope, is none other than a red herring" (Hutson 1989, 248). But not a red herring in the irresistible but anachronistic sense of a "false lead," a hermeneutical dodge, a deferral of meaning that can be interpreted as a meta-message about meaning; not a *read* herring—no; the true, frolicking, fatally nourishing, unspeakably real substance of a *real* red herring.

But what kind of a radical new political re-reading of Nashe is that going to be any good for? What about Queer Tom Nashe, "Post-colonialism: The Sodometrics of Nashionalism," "'A tall man under Ajax shield': Nashorty and the Limits of 'High' Culture" (Nashe was notably— er—vertically-challenged)—or at least how about that "she-Nashe" you were just mentioning? Well, it's actually true that Nashe was seen by Harvey and has even been considered by one modern critic as the froward wielder of "kitchen-stuff rhetoric" (Nicholl 1984, 43). So just to see if I can't get myself into a little more hot water, perhaps I *can* here argue the writeability (however wrong) of a reading that would involve an even more improbable institutional recuperation than that of the postmarxists.

To suggest that there is something "feminine" in the concoction of "nourishing wordplay" whipped up in this final work of a writer who, in his first work, *The Anatomie of Absurditie* (1589), "announces he has turned misogynist" (Woodbridge 1986, 62) should, of course, strike readers as approximately as grotesque as Derrida's efforts to read

Nietzsche's recurrently gynophobe texts as uh really kinda the writing of (a) "woman" themselves in a way: a she-Nietzsche, or Nietz-she. It *could* conceivably be argued, however (the impossible just takes us a little bit longer), that Nashe's constant recurrence to the most homely of bottom lines—the affairs of the kitchen, food and a warm hearth, clothing—made him somehow more genuinely epicene than the so-called "effeminate" gents of his day.

But this is not really where "the feminine" would enter into the matter for me. Rather, I would be reminded of the unsung womanliness of the everyday in the very substance of Nashe's subject: the little red herring would be part of the little read history or herstory (itstory, really) of what Hélène Cixous, in her writing on the thingful, sensual, post-phenomenological realism of Clarice Lispector, once called the *"femmilier"* (Cixous 1979, 419). In reading such writing it is no longer that one must be made—politically or epistemologically—to *see* things: "Seeing? Isn't that always already having seen?" (414). Refemmiliarization reminds us that a phenomenology of reading is as impossible as the phenomenology of writing (*"Voir," c'est toujours déjà avoir vu; "lire," c'est sans doute toujours déjà avoir lu*). Or rather, perhaps, the point is that that phenomenology *is* as possible—while the real of read*ing*, on the other hand, is, as Lacan used to say (forced to see a sardine can that couldn't be forced to see him) *the impossible*. Real reading would then demand that supposed re-femmiliarization that would force us to *stop* forcing ourselves to *see*. Rather than being made to see some point by Nashe's text, we should allow ourselves to listen to its punctual content and its contrapuntal discontent—and, who knows, maybe this could indeed be hooked in somehow to the background noise of "the feminine" in patriarchal culture; the *her*ring of Nashe's text would thus demand a hearing—just as Cixous asks us to harken to the texts of Lispector,

> so that the things that have always been presented as mute come to be heard. There is no silence. The musics of things are ever resounding, waiting for us to hear them faithfully, with our ears, our skin, our nostrils, and especially with our breasts.
> Preferably our attentions will move like fish in slowness.
> (415)

The femmiliar reading of Nashe's text would finally attend to that red herring that is part of what has been there, unread, left dead, on the surface of the prose of the world, and which (like the ermine stole that infamously graces Cixous's own shoulders) we have tended to ignore to our cost and to its. So, be fair: maybe by someone determined to read (c)literally or whatever, Nashe's *her*ring could briefly become her no longer fashionably jangling ear-ring, *could* be read as an allegory of "the feminine," or vice versa, at least for a spell, provisionally, just as I hesitated in reading some lines from Rilke quoted by Cixous: "*Abelone war immer da. Das tat ihr großen Eintrag. . . . Abelone war da, und man nutze sie ab wie man eben konnte*" (Rilke 1910, 824; Cixous 1980, 416). For a moment, I wanted this to refer to the seafood: "There had always been abelone; it had always been there, and that had cost it dearly. . . . Abelone had been there, and it had been consumed as well as it could be." But when I looked in *Malte*, I found that, just as I had creepingly supposed, "Abelone" was a woman, of course, like the women Cixous claims have been too much there to be written or read.

I assume that even the most irenic of cultural feminists will by now, however, be guffawing "Ah baloney!" (if they are feeling charitable) at this all too fishy attempt at co-op shoplifting or passing for quasi-"correct" (piscatorial vegetarian-feminism; not even ovo-lacto!) what would arguably just be more unsavoury sausage from the factories of read meat to which so many of us have so long been addicted, and for the most part still are (even some of the more hard-minded feminists). Yet despite its patent *unreal*ness, we all know that this reading might well hold water, at least long enough to get into print. And, what the hell, Queer Thomas Nashe, too.

The literal reality, however, would seem to be that Nashe is a noted misogynist and (if there was such a thing, and I still think that there may have been, the Elizabethan equivalent of a) homophobe. His works say little, whether literally or clitorally, that could be of an empowering nature to oppressed groups—or frankly that is very illuminating when it comes to dismantling any hegemonic ideology from inside either, even the luxury anti-politic of the modern bourgeois liberal ironist with whom he might by some be confused. Nashe's politics are all grossly but unremarkably wrong. The usual kind of political reading seems a thankless task. Indeed, it mayn't even be all that long before his very valorization of the red herring *through a celebration of its unappreciated edibility* will be looked on as grotesque beyond readability as well. And then no one will much care anymore about all the hers or reds or Derridean errings that the literal red herring has been mangled into standing for—they'll recognize the *literal* atrocity of Nashe's carnivoresque freeplay, the painful prosaics of the reel. The still smouldering punk of the "absent referent" might well ultimately be responsible for exploding Nashe and much else now firmly tamped into the canon or the noncanon. Consciousness seems to be raised in a rather "Hegelian" manner (with a lot of cancellation). As Carol J. Adams reads the self-alienation of Atwood's *Edible Woman* herself in *The Sexual Politics of Meat,* "Both meat eating and first-person narration are suspended once Marian intuits her link to other animals, suggesting that a challenge to meat eating is linked to an attack on the sovereign individual subject. The fluid, merged subjectivity of the middle part of the book finds mystical identity with things, especially animals, that are consumed." But, then, as Adams goes on to recognize, "Marian returns to eating meat once she is able to think again in the first person" (Adams 1990, 131; 140)—a hermeneuticist cautionary tale for feminist literary critics and for anyone else whose metaphoral fixations are not absolutely bound by the lets and letters and literally *literal* fetters of the prose of the world.

No, Nashe cannot plausibly be salvaged for any politically correct strategic reading with which I am familiar or even femmiliar today. Neil Rhodes rightly reminds us that "[i]t is clearly a mistake to consider verbal excess and rhetorical flamboyance as indicators of radical intention in the writing of this period" (he means the Renaissance, but it is true today as well, obviously), and that "[i]t is therefore very difficult to see how a connection can be made between a 'subversive' literary style (i.e. rhetorical excess, rhetoric as play) and radical political and social ideas" (Rhodes 1985, 31, 27). — So what *good* is he to me? I know what side my b*read* is—er—vetted on, after all.

Well, none. But wait. Before those who prefer their stakes red, their meat on the genderized side, their butchery bloody, and so on, get up in a snuff to join all those who just wanted their "knowledge nicely browned" and, even worse, those who only sat down to begin with in hopes of picking up a few new recipes, and have thus already left the table, I would ask you all at least to consider briefly if you scent nothing heartbreakingly familiar, as pangful as a long forgotten aroma of home-cooking (even if you never had that home or that cooking: "He had never had an old gang, old sweethearts and pals, but he missed one anyway, as the quartet made slow, agonized experiments with chords—chords intentionally sour, sourer still, unbearably sour, and then a chord that was suffocatingly sweet, and then some sour ones again" [Vonnegut 1968, 172-73])—is there not something that strikes an all too familiar, all too bittersweet chord in the *politeral* content of that patent emotional whitemale at one point proffered by Atwood's roving doctoral candidate, the ne'er unguarded Duncan: "And besides that, everything's being done, it's been done already, fished out, and you yourself wallowing around in the dregs at the bottom of the barrell . . ." (Atwood 1969, 96).[1] Read

---

[1]". . . one of those ninth-year graduate students, poor bastards, scrabbling through manuscripts for new material or slaving away on the definitive edition

politerally within an increasingly derealized institution of interpretation, Nashe's text can be recognized as the writing down of those dregs, the bringing up of those dregs; the real that is left over from the banquet of sense; what is too much *there* for us, getting in the way of all of our latest efforts at textploitation. The domestic, the everyday, the overlooked. Food, drink, shelter, clothing; things that are actually around and that really matter. The real; and even if "the real is the impossible," it is time to admit that there are indeed more things in your philosophy, melancholy Jacques, than are dreamed of in heaven or earth, but that there is more that should *matter* in that can of tuna than in Kant's whole *Critique of Puréed Reason*. Only the tuna is too much with us; it defies aggrandizement or even subversion—it defies serious mention. I'm overfond of boring people with an anecdote from over a decade ago now: one day on a bus, before I had been to university, when I suddenly caught in my nostrils the smell of the tuna sandwich I had packed for my lunch: the illegible epiphanic *reality* of that smell. That is what Nashe's multilayered texts at bottom are *about* for me: "*de profundis natus est fex.*" But, yes, it's true, the phenomenological fumes even of that homely epoch are now too becoming *unheimlich* noxious for me, and a damn good thing, of course. I don't eat tuna anymore, either—*es war immer da*, but it is no longer possible for me to ignore; and I've never had herring and now never will. What the oppressive forces of metaphor cannot stand (Carol J. Adams is perfectly right about this; and so, to the extent that they concentrate on the abuse of the literal, are all politically inclined critics, even derivative and semi-sincere bandwagon careerists such as I've just been sort of jadedly anticipating) is the sight of the literally read.[2] And just perhaps, at most—locally, incidentally, detailedly—Nashe does write—and deserve

---

of Ruskin's dinner-invitations or theatre-stubs or trying to squeeze the last pimple of significance out of some fraudulent literary nonentity they dug up somewhere" (96-97).

[2]Nashe's vulgar intractability to late hermeneuticist recuperation is thus for me a bizarre twist on the parable of the unconsummability of highbrow culture which opens Bristol's book on the reception of Shakespeare: the "strange case [a packing case?] of Charlie the Tuna": "It is Charlie's desire to be recruited by a certain Tuna company, and so he proposes to 'do Shakespeare' to show that he has good taste. To do Shakespeare, Charlie explains, 'I beat guys wit' 'dis sword whilst hollering poetry'. Alas, the tuna company is unimpressed by good taste; it only wants tuna that tastes good. 'Sorry Charlie!' He never understands the distinction between 'good taste' and 'tasting good' or between doing Shakespeare and getting processed into canned tuna. Because of this, he will remain a 'lovable loser' whose inadequacies keep him outside the dispensation of the industrial corporation, though marginally serviceable to its interests" (Bristol 1989, 15).

to be read—*politerally*.

I've already spent too long here incidentally reading readings, feeling I must lap a little while wave-like against the monolithic hermeneutic presuppositions we have come to take for granite. For I can't help feeling that at the end of the century the "fear of fish" that haunts so many of our readings is no longer an aversion to the supposed ichtheological subjectivism of another-fine-mess Stanley (a pool of puns which in contradistinction to the Cardinal's fishpond in *The Duchess of Malfi* [5.5.5] reflects a rake with a figure; cf. Fish 1984), but a representational d*read* of the *herring itself* (*das Ding an* sic). Not even the herring is safe reading anymore, if it ever was—overplain, politically disturbing or anyway annoying, too much there. So to those whose swampingly dense reads I have thus rushed through, or whose readings I have so far ignored altogether, I can still only object with Nashe, that "[i]f idle wittes will needes tye knottes on smooth bulrushes with their tongues, faith the worlde might thinke I had little to attend, if I should goe about to vnloose them with my penne" (1592c, A4ᵛ/1:259). This seems enough by way of the temporization whereby we sportsmanlike play out the real, suspending a little while longer the inevitable catch from our own heavily seeded waters. Enough in the way of a grace, then: Good food, good meat, good God, let's eat! "I stand lawing heere," runs Nashe's rasher complaint, "what with these lawyers, and selfe-conceited misinterpreters so long, that my redde herring which was hot broyling on the coles, is waxt starke cold for want of blowing" (1599, I4ᵛ/3:216). I can only beg my own interpreters—both of you, please!—to try to *read* me herringwise, not to join with those who "persecute Art (as the Alcumists are said to persecute Nature)" and "hauing founde that which is blacke, . . . seeke for a substance that is blacker than black, or angle for frogs in a cleare fountaine" (1592c, B1ᵛ/1:261). Rather, if you are for me, help me melt through the prosaic surface of the literal with that flint-sprung signifier: "ignem faciens ex lapide nigro (*which* Munster *in his Cosmography alledgeth for the greatest wonder of* England) *that is, wresting delight out of anie thing*" (1596, D2ᵛ-D3/3:22-23).

NASHE'S PRESENCE IN
A PROSAIC CONTEXT

Disturbing Prosaic Assumptions

Narren, die den Verfall der Kritik beklagen. Denn deren Stunde
ist längst abgelaufen. Kritik ist eine Sache des rechten Abstands.
Sie ist in einer Welt zu Hause, wo es auf Perspektiven und
Prospekte ankommt und einen Standpunkt einzunehmen noch
möglich war. Die Dinge sind indessen viel zu brennend der
menschlichen Gesellschaft auf den Leib gerückt.

        Walter Benjamin, "Diese Flächen sind zu vermieten,"
Einbahnstrasse

The textual question of the hour as we near the end of the century
would seem to be no longer *qui parle?*, but *où en sommes nous*? Still, from
where I sit, broken-hearted, etc., it seems to me that "positionality" is one
of the real-world or lived-experience effects that prosaic textuality almost
inevitably serves to obscure ("I am sitting here in the smallest room of
the house with your book before me; soon it will be behind me"—to
paraphrase, who was it? A.M. Klein?).

Of course even before it became politically territorial, the "printer-
textuality" of which I would make "the prosaic" the synechdochic center
got used to pervasively figuring itself through *topicalities*, and vice-versa.
We now further acknowledge that beyond this metaphorical identification
of textual and real space there is a more obvious metonymic one whereby
any written utterance is "said" to be made in a certain social situation
and from a certain "subject position." The text's attempted claim to an
extensionality metaphorically related to real space is now generally
exposed by those who recognize its actual metonymic inclusion *within*
space as it has been sociopolitically articulated; so that there is an
unexpected punctualtity in—what seemed an act of pure "illocation," as
we might say—Paul de Man's pronouncement almost a generation ago

to the effect that the exposure of the actual metonymical uniplanarity of metaphorical transcendencies "will in fact be the task of literary criticism in the coming years" (de Man 1979a, 17).

The insistence on the situatedness of text has had ramifications for cultural criticism that do not stop with its constitution of its objects of study. Textual situatedness has become a self-conscious topicality in itself. Although it is still considered inappropriate in most circles, thus, to tamper with the prosaic neutrality of academic discourse in such a way as to create effects of idiosyncratic *person*ality in one's texts, one is now urged to acknowledge and represent the *position*ality on which such personality is recognized to depend, and to attempt to take it into account in one's construals of other positions. A recognition of the situatedness of a grounded subject and object is henceforth taken as the first step in any cultural criticism. The methodological hygiene subscribed to by those who assume *this* position has been given excellent articulation for critics of the Renaissance by Leah S. Marcus in her endorsement of "local reading":

> "Localization" is an idea we need to apply to ourselves as readers as well as to what we read. In the same way that we have begun to explore the "local" circumstances that have shaped past critical efforts (like John Dover Wilson's encounter with a fragmented *Hamlet* during the First World War, for example, or E.M. Tillyard's construction of an ordered "world picture" during the Second), we need to locate our own attempts at reading, or at least never lose our awareness that our activity has local coordinates of its own. (Marcus 1988, 36)

This, however, may well be easier said than done; or perhaps easier done than "said" (*mis en texte*). According to the earliest and still most radical version of a Bakhtinian prosaics, in order to be able to "place" someone, one must be in a position of outsideness with regard to that person; meanwhile the prosaics of textuality as put forward by Jeffrey Kittay and Wlad Godzich is such a matter of simultaneous privation and provision that it inevitably does contain *other* positions from its own position of "withoutness." Locating *oneself* in either of these prosaics would thus be a theoretically impossible gesture, one indeed potentially politically shifty, inasmuch, to take the Bakhtinian tack first (and place it in the seat into which you are just about to settle), as it would usurp that privileged alterity of other people and try to include (contain) what Bakhtin refers to as their necessarily "transgredient" positions vis-à-vis oneself in one's own self-accounting.

By "transgredient" Bakhtin would refer to elements of consciousness which though external to it are still necessary to its completion—in other words, aspects of personality which can only be supplied by *another person*. According to these early theories, the individual or the person can in any case only be an *aesthetically satisfying whole* when contemplated from a position of what Bakhtin called "outsideness" [внена-ходимость], that is, from the perceptual, semantic and valuational *vantage point* which belongs to an other. One's personality is not simply generated from within, but in fact exists in any kind of unified way (and thus really exists at all) only from outside, from the external spatial and temporal perspective of another point of view. Most radically: "This personality will not exist if another does not create it" (Bakhtin 1979, 34). From within consciousness, the self is always open onto an horizon, always active and evolving toward a future. But *another* consciousness can perceive the self as a spatial whole, lodged within surroundings and a context which complete the meaning of the personality. More importantly still, *only* another can see the self as a finalized *temporal* whole, *after* the end. The self can never get any complete sense of its meaning and value because it can never contemplate itself as something *over*; one can thus never really be the author of one's own identity or one's own life— precisely in attempting to be both subject and object one *fails to coincide with oneself*, and fails to achieve integrity or know oneself as a whole. One can never have the last word on oneself, or even know what that last word will be: "In this sense we may say that death is a form of aesthetic completion of a personality" (115).

My interest in Bakhtinian "personalism" has brought me back time and again to Bakhtin's ideas in this early corpus (published, appropriately, only posthumously). There, in contradiction to his later, more other-shy version of the self-other interface in his book on Dostoevsky, Bakhtin saw the inter-authoring of self by other and other by self as, not exactly innocent, but in any case mutually beneficent. The other as author inevitably appears as a loving donor to my self of the completion and unification which it could never achieve alone: "From within, life can express itself in an act, a confession, a cry—but absolution and bliss [благодать] descend from the Author" (Bakhtin 1979, 71). Late in his life Bakhtin was to see this "outsideness" as an integral part of cultural and historical understanding as well. No one can ever comprehend his or her own cultural or historical position as a whole—that must be left to other "authors":

There exists a very strong, but one-sided and thus untrust-worthy, idea that in order better to understand a foreign culture, one must enter into it, forgetting one's own, and view the world through the eyes of this foreign culture. The idea, as I said, is one-sided. Of course, a certain entry as a living being into a foreign culture, the possibility of seeing the world through its eyes, is a necessary part of the process of understanding it; but if this were the only aspect of this understanding, it would merely be duplication and would not entail anything new or enriching. *Creative* understanding does not renounce itself, its own place in time, its own culture; and it forgets nothing. In order to understand, it is immensely important for the person who understands to be *located outside* the object of his or her creative understanding—in time, in space, in culture. For one cannot really see one's own exterior and comprehend it as a whole, and no mirrors or photographs can help; our real exterior can be seen and understood only by other people, because they are located outside us in space and because they are *others*. (Bakhtin 1986, 6-7)

Self-situation would be an attempt to get outside of one's own position and would thus always again constitute a further "one-sided" position which the self-situator could not finally determine for him- or herself. *Self*-anything is always pre-emptive, always would-be transcendent, always a view presupposing an impossible outsideness with regard to the self's positionality. And literal prose might seem now on the one hand to be the all-too-amenable vehicle for such a reassumption of the *illusion* of totalizing self-outsideness. Indeed, it seems possible to me that the self-containment of the prosaic might well *force* a position, or rather a-position, of always being "out of it"—a-position which can only sporadically be abandoned through artificial creations of localizing effects. In his prose, Thomas Nashe attempts to effect such localized anti-prosaic disturbances; but he cannot perhaps in the long run take up a position there other than that non-position which prose has already prepared for him.

Near the end of *Lenten Stuffe*, Nashe interrupts his encomium to the red herring with one of his frequent objections to the prying of "mice-eyed decipherers and calculaters vppon characters" (Nashe 1599, K2/ 3:218) who read more into his texts than is there. At the finish of this digression he has a start: "Stay, let me looke about, where am I? in my text, or out of it? not out, for a groate: out, for an angell: nay, I'le lay no wagers for nowe I preponder more sadlie vppon it, I thinke I am out indeede" (K2ᵛ/3:219). "Out of it?" we may grunt with the academic contemplating Anthony Burgess's dreadful (yet dreadfully clever) dead sexist racist homophobe writer Enderby: "Do not think that anyone can escape it merely by—I will not utter the word: it is quite irrelevant. Out of it, indeed; he is not out of it at all" (Burgess 1973, 161).

According to Bakhtin, the soul is "spirit as it looks in another from *outside*" (Bakhtin 1979, 89). From within the self, inside my own text, "I am only bound to lose my self; it can be saved [убережена] only by powers that are not my own" (90), since the true soul "is the self-coincident, self-equivalent, closed whole of an inner life, which presupposes the outsided loving activity of another. The soul is my own spirit's gift to *someone else*" (116). "Nashe" is only in there, then, because *we* are out here, only in there *as long as* we are out here. But precisely because this is so, I am unable to give up this feeling that he really *is in there* somewhere. *Is* it somehow true, though, that Nashe is still in there somewhere as long as we are out here—that we put him in there our-selves? Might it not in fact be much more prosaically *the other way around*? The intermittence of this old *in-out in-out* used to lubricate critical debate on authorial-lectorial relationships; but we are all too chary in this age of "safe text" to assume any *personal* position at all any more. And we seem to be convinced that there can be no way out of this grossly *textual* mess. But an examination of the emergent *prosaic* context in which Nashe would seem to be such an exceptional presence may initially throw into question the *topos* of a "positional" articulation of *Realpolitik* itself. How can we help in this prosaic state, it might well be asked, but be neither here nor there?

In their account of prosaic textuality in *The Emergence of Prose*, Kittay and Godzich begin articulating a prosaics that would place in question the metaphorical topicalization of a Bakhtinian "outsideness" to our prosaic existence *tout court* and instead posit an always purely provisional "positionality" to what they call "prose *literacy*." The prosaic itself, as they see it, *is* always neutral in terms of positionality. *It* does not "take place" in any obviously appropriating sense or take up a transcendent stance in a clearly distancing manner, but rather quietly constitutes itself as a pervasive circulation through coordinated positionalities in reading. Prosaic *locality*, then, for Kittay and Godzich is an essentially *provisional* effect: "What is said in prose, whether attributed or not, is to be taken as grounded locally, as if in quotes, not finally" (Kittay and Godzich 1987, 133). Prose *per se* is just a management system, then, a "great container"; and if localized effects are provisional, the "providing" is actually done by a kind of peripatetic "prose-literate" reader. Rather than assuming an outside totalizing perspective or responding confrontationally to a situ-ated utterance, this reader "is to unmoor himself or herself from single or singular perspectives and travel the roads of positionality" (124).

This "provisionality" of position has become, I think, another of the modern commonplaces of the situatedness of the prosaic, including even that more politically self-conscious situatedness of the cultural critic in prose. In fact, although a self-situator like Leah Marcus on the one hand advocates an open acknowledgement and self-fixation of one's position, she too considers "local reading" to entail some sort of provisionality:

> "local" reading can be—and should be—a suspension of our ruling methodologies, insofar as that is possible, in favor of a more open and provisional stance toward what we read and the modes by which we interpret; it should be a process of continual negotiation between our own *place*, to the extent that we are able to identify it, and the local *places* of the texts we read. (Marcus 1988, 36)

But if the extent to which we *can* identify our own place is put into a ticklish situation by the probings of an early Bakhtin, the extent to which we can fix the "places" of the texts we read and take up a position with regard to their places *in prose* ourselves would seem to be put on shaky ground by Godzich and Kittay's conception of the proclivities of prose and the conventional expectations met in prose literacy. If one version of the prosaic leaves us as authors always outside other positions in a position we cannot ourselves really determine, the other suggests that *the reader* cannot finally determine *our* positions as constituted in the prosaic, but only circulate around positionalities within a pre-disposed prosaic literacy whereby we as both writers and readers must at least temporarily disappear into the wordwork. The prosaic in these two senses would not seem to lend itself to the textual confrontation of grounded positionalities. On the contrary, real situatedness would be what tends to disappear in the prosaic.

But where does it supposedly go? On the one hand, such situatedness, it seems to me, is "ideally" now *assumed* by readers, by which I mean that in unselfconscious, privatized real reading by the "prose literate," I think readers tend to *assume* the "neutrality" of the prose and their own subject positions tend to "dissolve" into reading.[1] But if this

---

[1] Of course—rather artlessly to anticipate my conclusion—this so-called "prose-literacy" probably only really reflects the comfy reading practices of a privileged white male blah blah reader reading something that has been specifically if perhaps unconsciously provided for *his* prose-literacy. I used to have a copy of an Elizabethan prose anthology (which I now can't seem to find upon my shelves) that had been previously owned by a woman who had obviously been obliged

"provisionality" of "prose literacy" can thus become an overly convenient political alibi for the privileged aestheticist writer or the more irresponsibly pomo kind of reader, it may nonetheless *really* and not just alibiquitously constitute a soporific global textual containment of once grounded persons, positions, interests, and utterances which even now continue to *demand*—against all canonically prosaic hushing-up, including the late capitalist reaccomodation to the schizanalytical inevitability of the videoprosaic—continue, you textually lobotomized *fuck*, to cry out to be *read* as militating against such prosaic indifference at however pathetic and "purely aesthetic" a *local level*.

The "totality" of the prosaic text—as opposed to a bit of it—could

to read *The Unfortunate Traveller* for a course. The margins of Nashe's text were crammed with the most lively outcries against all the misogynistic remarks in the book.

Let us not jump to overhasty conclusions, however. It may not even be such easily locatable positionalities as those of *genuine* privilege that smooth the way for the prosaic. How many women readers (for example) have grown accustomed to assuming whatever the authoritative text provided them with so as to fulfill these very abstract qualifications of prose literacy?

Perhaps I also here need to remind you that in speaking of overeasy assumptions I am of course as always thinking of *reading*, not readings. That is, I mean something like what Random Cloud calls "The Missionary Position of Reading":

> *Sit in chair back very straight hands above board feet on floor. Both hands above board. Light falls onto page over left shoulder* (just as it does when I am in the other proper posiBut *I never ever am to write in my book.*) *Open front cover eye begins tracking rightwords from upper left along horizontal of the—* . . .
> . . . At the end of each line, the eye is to dart without hesitation without *any* thoughts of my own creeping in to the beginning of the next line down and so to bottom of page, whereupon my eye *leaps* without the *least stray* thought that the object of my abstracted graze has a physical body with its own structure opening and disclosing herself to me. Both hands arI mean I mean disclosing *itself* to me. To me? Who am I? Who are *we*? No one, having given ourself over completely to the Author's Thoughts, word by word as He offers them, without peeking ahead or glimpsing the recto page just finishing, as it wells up mirror image through the verso of its leaf which you are now turning to gaze upon. (Cloud 1990, 61-62)

Obviously, though, once you stop reading and start reading for the reading you stop assuming and start making assumptions instead.

never create any effect of situatedness. One reason is because it is an abstraction, too far removed from the temporal and thus temporary *real-ities* of reading; "reading" *as an activity* is always local, never total. Thus, no piece of prose of any considerable length can be thought of as con-stituting some "unified message." Even more grotesque, then, for Michael Holquist once to have attempted to paraphrase the entire œuvre of Bakhtin (of all people!) as "a single utterance" (Holquist 1983, 68). Totalizing "readings" are in fact merely local responses, usually based on networking localized microtextual cruces. The *unreal* element in such readings is the claim to the disclosure of a *global* position (the message); unreal, except for the fact that these localized readings only ever *are* reconstituted in writing as global containments once again—unreal ones. I would go so far as to say that effects of the real in reading are always local, never global; always read, never written. And in prose, this lack of global positionality is right there in black and white. As a print culture phenomenon in the Elizabethan age, the prosaic may well have had its little topicalities—Fleet Street, St. Paul's, etc.—but it is to be found, or rather lost, *un peu partout*, and its utterances, like all prosaic utterances, seem to emerge from out of nowhere.

In the prose of the 1590s, and preeminently in the writings of Nashe, many local effects might now be optimistically read as scattered insur-rections forming the protohistory of an eventual global revolution against textual totalitarianism: the premodern that foreshadows a now rampant postmodern as (mere) "ultra-leftism of the spirit" (Barker 1984, 68). But they could just as easily be seen (in a more tragico-modernist Jamesonian kind of view) as the last vestiges of popular reaction against a final and decisive containment of all discursive opposition or genuine difference by an emergent print state of the prosaic itself. Prose might then in the Elizabethan age not yet quite have been the global state of things that Kittay and Godzich suggest has always already been its transparent "situ-ation." Prose *is* certainly always *assumed* to be the least "present," the worst situated, of the textualities into which Renaissance literary practice is traditionally distributed, and it may be significant that it is once again simply left out of the delegation of textual topicality in Steven Mullaney's distinction: "But the drama, unlike poetry, is a territorial art. It is an art of space as well as words, and it requires a place of its own, in or around a community, in which to mount its telling fictions and its eloquent spectacles" (Mullaney 1988, 7). Drama is actually there; poetry attempts to presentify the absent; prose just sits around, unobtrusive-like.

Prose may have no room of its own, but it *can* nonetheless pretend to be an art of space, and we will see Nashe's prose doing this again and again. As a *whole*, however, an apparatus, it will tend to draw readers into that space and leave them thus incapable of taking up a stand *against* its space by the continual circulation it effects through the spac*ing* of the written. No *Gegenstand* can perhaps be maintained or withstood in prosaic *reading*. And for prose even to pretend to be an art of space rather than of *spacing*, it has first of all to make us aware of its own (lack of) situation, its potential "neutrality." Only then can it obtain at a local level the feeling of what it is not globally: position, grounded utterance. This is as close as prose gets to spatial "realism," effects that are only true locally and cannot be described globally without a loss of the effect. Any effect of grounded presence is thus, I admit, an *aesthetic effect*, though not I think in any namby-pamby sense; rather in the sense that one at least temporarily *feels* here or there about something, confronted by something. But such effects can only occur in *localities* of reading, at the places where a bit of the text is being assumed by a particular reader at a particular moment. And like all such effects in the painfully prosaic highbrow aesthetic of modernity which shapes all of "our" reading and writing (James son of Jameson) they will be evanescent, and make their "presence" felt differentially by a more profound sense of textual absence elsewhere.

Such moments do not then have an aesthetic effect in any classical sense: the realistic situation will not be found to turn on any Aristotelian *unities*, but rather precisely on illusions of disjunction or movement. The profusion of the heterogenous in Nashe's prose, the sense a modern reader will have that "[n]arrative is being distended for the sake of bizarre, local effects" (Rhodes 1980, 31)—in these one may momentarily come to rest in, or bump up against, what seems a position. But the prosaic, *ça va sans dire au revoir*, never stops—it provides only the slipperiest of ground; and as "prose literate" readers we will find it impossible to assume for more than a moment any positionality in such prosaic circumstances. The glamor of the prosaic for many of us has come to rest precisely in this *Glatteis* transparency that it has, the *impossibility* of occupying a *Standpunkt* thereon, or even of establishing a *Sitzfleisch-punkt* of sufficient tenacity or mere sedentarity for a sit-in. (One slides on one's bottom as easily as on skates, as we know from Bruegel's "Numbering at Bethlehem.") The prosaic is a package deal, a whirlwind tour. Agency here cannot be placed: there is only a travel agency, booking space and projecting itineraries. And Nashe's texts from the end of the century are thus free to rejoin a postmodern situational aesthetics at roughly the place where it had planned to meet some nice natives while "knocking around," as my friend David Thomson puts it, a Third World in which one's currency still goes a long way: on a train somewhere, one can momentarily feel certain that some text of Nashe's falls into the difference-delighted proto-Barthesian category of Nietzsche's *Morgenröthe*: "A book like this one is not meant to be read through or read out, but to be opened up, especially when on a ramble or a journey; it should be possible to be constantly ducking in and out of it and never find anything familiar around one" (Nietzsche 1881, 278)—this last actually written on the spur of the moment, a spur on which we are at a standstill, Baltimore at dusk, waiting for the power to be restored (on the way back to Montréal from the MLA convention in Washington, D.C.; it's New Year's Eve, 1989).

But the local always gives way in the prosaic to a further "estrangement effect." One doesn't get off at the station, but ducks back into the text, assured that "topicality" is only the "temporarily commonplace" (Alan Liu, quoted in Marcus 1988, xii). There is no danger of presence for those who know how to "travel the roads of positionality," those who can afford to travel within the prosaic: the prose literate. We have been privileged to claim the instability of subject positions, the lack of *terminus a quo* or *ad quem* for our trains of thought. That, as poststructuralists, is part of *our* "identity politics": no fixed abode, just another train to hop. For if realism and modernism could previously still be viewed as stations on the right track to some textual destination—as in Virginia Woolf's famous essay in which that "old lady in the corner opposite" who is just along for the ride has become, through her status as pre-textual baggage, the critical double of Woolf herself (at least in Rachel Bowlby's reading [1988, 14])—postmodernism is now more used to thinking of itself as the very *vehicle*, one Foucault has characterized as "an extraordinary bunch of relationships, the train, since it's something along which you go, something too by which you can go from one place to another, and also something which goes past" (cited and translated by Bowlby, 171 n. 4).

If the postmodern trains, however, are more and more frequently getting derailed these days, in large part, of course, by the women now *really* in the corner opposite (who before had been nastily laid athwart the tracks . . . or, ho hum; is it just that, like Amtrak, the pomo train of thought doesn't go everywhere we might want it to, is already an antique, is still too Victorian a conveyance?), the result of these trainwrecks of thought has for most of us only been a few minor abrasions, followed by a little cosmetic surgery for which it has in fact been increasingly necessary that we be, like the guy in Günther Grass's novel, *örtlich betäubt*, locally anaesthetized. Further such *anaesthesia*, anti-aesthetics, is not the way to avoid the painful side of the postmodern: it will just leave us punchy, incapacitated; like one of those sidekicks of Gabriel Harvey "that houers between two crutches of a Scholler and a Traueller, when neither will helpe him to goe vpright in the worlds opinion" (Nashe 1596,

O2/3:89). To put the postmodern back on the right track, it is certainly time to stop the train, get off, open up the cattle-cars and see who we've been travelling with as stowaways, what folks have been getting carted along with us toward horrific destinations back there while we were busy picking one another up in the lounge car. But now that we've gotten off for a moment anyway, it won't hurt us to stretch our legs a bit, look around, and try to shake out our cramps. For it might only be the numbness of perpetual travel that made us so insensitive. We should not underestimate the spiritual virtues of a little dawdling in the fresh air—a bit of perambulation on our own two feet. One can see things afoot that slip right by the habitual railer, who comes no longer to give a damn about what is actually being ridden over. Detraining might be good for us, detraining from our postmodern timetables; *Unlernen*. A stroll around the premodern, when you still couldn't travel such great distances without feeling a lot of things under your feet, working your way through a lot of things, meeting a lot of the locals, might allow us a renewed footing in the theoretical itself, a useful post-stage in the postmodern or the postpostmodern before we set out again theoretically to "post on to practis," as Harvey puts it in his commonplace book (Harvey MS.b, 16/89). The post of the postmodern, as we all know and love, is never going to be delivered, never going to arrive, anyway, so why do we even post on so? I for one am saddlesore, and would be happy to be able to go about like Nashe's unfortunate traveller on my "bare tentoes" for awhile (Nashe 1594d, D3/2:241).

Much as I have suggested to be the case where the rift separating textuality from reality is concerned, I am convinced that the premodern is connected to the post- only by a narrow footbridge, and a rickety one at that. There is no *camino real* or "real road" that will lend itself to fast and easy fullscale industrial shipping to and fro between pre- and post-. The real that can be gotten across is always going to be *pedestrian*. But there's no grass growing under the pedestrian, and though you cannot even *make* it stand still (as you can the train *en panne* of the theoretical), yet you can make it run. What more, then, is there touching my position that you would be resolved of? Say quickly, as Nashe says, "for now is my pen on foote againe" (D2^v/2:241).[2]

---

[2]In the second edition of *The Vnfortunate Traueller*. In the first edition, the phrasing oddly suggests the resumption of a stance: "for now is my pen got vpon his feet again."

Your Place or Mine?

PROBLEMS FOR A PROSAICS OF PRESENSE

Texte remarquable à ce que (ici exemplairement) jamais le lecteur ne pourra y choisir sa place, ni le spectateur. La place en tout cas est pour lui intenable en face du texte, hors du texte, en un lieu où il pourrait se passer d'avoir à écrire ce qui à lire lui paraîtrait *donné, passé,* où il serait devant un écrit déjà. Ayant à mettre en scène, il est mis en scène, il se met en scène. Le récit dès lors s'adresse au corps du lecteur qui est mis par les choses en scène, elle-même. «Donc» s'écrivant, le spectateur peut moins que jamais choisir sa place. Cette impossibilité—cette puissance aussi du lecteur s'écrivant—depuis toujours travaillait le texte en général. Ouvrant ici, limitant et situant toute lecture (la vôtre, la mienne), la voici, *cette fois enfin,* montrée: comme telle.

Jacques Derrida, *La dissémination*

When we do this here with one another—when you do this to me or I do this to you—virtually every word is, referentially speaking, a "shifter." And you as well, and I, are we not too then inevitably *only* shifters? Perhaps in some sense yes, but it will not be out of place, all the same, to insert here a caveat for common cursory readers. For, as Whetstone reminds us in his disclosure of the dangers of the dicing-houses in Elizabethan London, "a plaine minded man . . . is an assured praye for al sortes of shifters" (Whetstone 1584, H2ᵛ). In fact, they did a lot of this sort of thing at the end of the century; they would appeal to you as though you were there instead of here, or not neither here nor there.

In other words, they would still try to make ostentative use of deixis here in writing, although even back then it was clearly considered somewhat impolite to try to point so. Deixis is strictly speaking that aspect of discourse which points to what is *outside* of it, and thus it can be said to presuppose its own groundedness in a real spatiotemporal circumstance. Even in its broadest usage it covers those elements of discourse that *only* mean situationally, supposing there might be some that could mean otherwise. In *The Emergence of Prose*, Jeffrey Kittay and Wlad Godzich have argued that it is the nature of prosaic discourse to be what we might call *endodeictic* (or perhaps even "autodeictic" [cf. Marin 1986, 199]), i.e. to refer locally to the intratextual circumstances which, in a much more literal sense than that in which all "circumstances" are constructed through language, *it constructs*. In other words, prosaic deixis is only finally answerable to a "context" in the most *literal* sense. A certain political situation is thus implied in prosaic positionality—theoretically, it is a positionality of impartiality, since the prose itself can assume no position, or rather "assumes" any number of positions, contains them. It is not a positionality itself, but administers other positionalities. As Kittay and Godzich see it, in the prose state, the verbal component of a signifying practice "takes advantage of certain of its material properties (as writing it can be transmitted *hors situation* and yet as language it can *construct situation* among its discourses, deictically and otherwise)" (Kittay and Godzich 1986, 6), and in this *taking* of advantage, prose itself absquatulates from any definitive deictic grounding. "Among all the discourses it contains, it takes the position that it is just holding them together, it is just what there is. The prose of the world," intone the authors, somewhat sardonically perhaps—later adding: "That is prose's subterfuge: not to be recognized for what it is but for the way things are" (116; 175).

Kittay and Godzich's attempt to define *prose* as the name for this tendency to the construction of deixis or situation among discourses is a concerted if ultimately problematic effort to understand in at least a slightly more historical and pragmatic way textual states of things that have now long been more influentially conceived of in metaphysical terms according to which *writing* is self-deferential or founded on absence, or else in generic terms whereby *the novel* is conceived as a meta-genre, containing other positional discourses, but not taking up any position itself. The latter situation became Bakhtin's great problem: how to account for the positionality *behind* the novelistic containment of other positionalities. The former is of course more the state in which deconstruction wanted to leave us; without the authority of real presence, position becomes hopelessly shifty, invisible, absent.

But what Derrida saw as the inevitable illocal "written-ness" of every situation, others may still stubbornly protest to be the specific "textuality" of a literary prosaicity which emerged to contain both poetry and speech sometime shortly before the dawn of the modern period. Speech may on the one hand be a classical phonocentric shibboleth that supports the old-style imperial regime of the *logos*, but it remains also the genuinely embodied appeal *against* the "impartiality" supposedly involved in the poetic justice of the prosaic. And thus it was precisely with *speech*, as Kittay and Godzich argue, that there were attempts to counter the neutralizing deixis of prose as it gained historical ground: "Historians such as Jean Marot (sixteenth century) provide an example of this resistance when they systematically exploit voice and speech to pinpoint the origins of their ideology."

Prose effaces the traces of places of utterance, and Kittay and Godzich here cryptically remark that "the agnosticism of modern prose with respect to its origins is but an ideological stance designed to occult the interests that would be revealed were prose's sender identified." That occultation is not, however, dropped in their own prosaic analysis, and the "sender" (one can't even identify two "senders") apparently remains uncannily transparent throughout *The Emergence of Prose*. Prose's sender cannot be pinned down, and speech will thus find it impossible to subsume prose under its practice, make *itself* the ground of prose, or prove that *it* really underlies prose, because *it*—speech—is actually *stuck in reality*, anchored in the body, grounded, *incapable of articulating the whole of its deictic circumstance*, while "prose can pretend to be both language and what is under it. That is what a body cannot do: a body relies on deixis, uses it, but does not constitute it. Prose can *hold* speech. Speech cannot hold prose." But prose does its best not to call attention to this holding, the hold it can have on us as discourse: it "under-stands" and "under-writes" speech and verse, but it does not emerge from "the background that is its ground" (Kittay and Godzich 1986, 198).

If we accept this account of prosaic deixis—provisionally, needless to "say"—it will be easier to see how sensations of presence or groundedness (speech deixis) are best created in prose precisely by disrupting or by drawing attention to the smooth circulation and "transparency" of deixis as it goes about its business of prosaically administering positionalities. Prose is a kind of invisible or recessive apparatus for the government of the circulation of reference, and Kittay and Godzich more than once associate it with the "faceless authority" of the state (e.g., 74; 102). Any resistance to that government and that facelessness begins—and probably ends—in *local* agitation. There was in fact in Nashe's day a certain tendency to the staging of such scattered insurrections.

Enclosures of the grounds of utterance of real people and of the discursive practices of collectivities could be experienced as untraceable reallocations at the hands of an emerging authoritarian state of the prosaic—itself to all appearances a groundless, abstract apparatus. If real grounded needs and interests were increasingly to be subsumed under the quasi-theatrical management of a placeless market (Agnew 1986), real grounded revendications of those needs and interests were perhaps slated to be administered henceforth by the prosaic agencies of a houseless state.

But the state of the prosaic was still at the time largely administered by institutions at a local level. Manifest hierarchies and a center which had not yet disappeared into the woodwork suggest that the state of the prosaic as it would come to be known—or rather, *not* recognized—was not yet fully in place, and maybe it was easier to make seditious elements that would later be effortlessly absorbed into prosaic "neutrality" stand their ground, to make them confront one another in a momentary pseudopresence belying the actual containedness of their deictic circumstance. Of course, even then this could only be stage presence, this was already an effect of media packaging; and such local effects could only be achieved double-negatively, by pretending *not* to be prose, by pretending *not* to *not have* a grounded position: through assuming in the prosaic state, and thus encouraging the reader to assume, a *pose*.

In an especially nicens little typo, A.F. Allison once characterized Robert Greene's *Mourning Garment* (1590) as "Pose interspersed with poems" (Allison 1975, 32). The *prosateurs* of the 1590s—and Greene in particular—were decidedly, and in a very modern sense, *"poseurs"*—posing the trenchant questions of the day of course I mean. But not perhaps able to pose them in a sufficiently direct manner to those to whom they actually needed to be posed, posing them, rather, to themselves more than anything else, posing them only in prose.

≈≈≈≈≈≈≈≈≈≈

Presence and immediacy are experiences which when and if arrived at in prose will only make readers uncomfortable. One often actually enters prose, frankly, to escape from "presence," which demands action, complicity or resistance. *Real* discursive presence constitutes allocution, address, accosting. Every utterance, including prosaic ones, may *in a certain sense* demand—and get—a response, as Bakhtin liked to think, but "prose literacy" allows for less implicational positions than those entailed in signifying practices grounded in physical or political presence. Prose does not really *confront* one with discourse. As it moves toward the extreme of transparency, on the contrary, prose seems to approach those "unspeakable sentences" (Banfield 1982) which condemn the reader to a mere *assumption* of the discourse: the reader's seems here to be the only "consciousness that is constantly available" (Kittay and Godzich 1986, 122), and is thus liable to *constitute* the neutrality of prose itself as it reads, and ground it in the only sense in which it can be grounded. Although Gérard Genette insists that he has never encountered a narrative without a narrator such as Banfield construes, and that he only opens a book so that "the author may *speak to me*" (1983, 69), the actual "dialogic" potential of prose literacy is pretty open to question; not simply because readers can close a book more easily than they can terminate an interview, but also, and more importantly, because the transparency of prose, its lack of presence, invites or even coerces the reader's *assumption* of prose's own holding pattern. Thus, to the extent that pseudopresence is created through pseudoaddress, it is unlikely that the reader will assume any confrontational position *vis-à-vis* that pseudopresence. That inexcusable reader-baiting such as Nabokov indulges in, for example, can only be effective because the positionality of the baiter can be contained, or even more probably *assimilated*, by the prose-literate reader as assumer of the prosaic discourse.

Although effects of pseudopresence in prose would seem always to be set up deictically (let me just reach over your shoulder and make that "endodeictically"), I would like to distinguish a practice that I'm going to call "pseudodeixis" (even though I know that that "pseudo" will immediately cause all blowhards to sputter). In *pseudo*deixis elements of space, time, or exogenous discourse within the deixis prosaically constructed are referred to according to conventions of, or are otherwise made to simulate, an actual present, grounded, nontypographical circumstance of utterance. In Kittay and Godzich's sense, of course—as in the views of most literary and linguistic philosophers writing "today," I think—there is no *pseudo*deixis, because deixis is simply the fact of pointing to something else, or in other words: relational reference pure and simple. But this definition *contains* within it a useful real distinction. I want to bring deixis back to its more vulgar meaning of language aspects which situate the utterance by reference to its *grounded* nonlinguistic circumstances, and vice-versa, and which rely on those grounded circumstances for meaning, and to use *pseudodeixis* in contradistinction for those elements of deixis which pretend that the prosaic print utterance *is* simply grounded in time and space, specifically a time and space other than those in which it will actually at some point be grounded, the only time and space "constantly available," that of a given reading experience. Presence, however "written," underwrites *real* deixis in a way that I hope makes clear how *pseudo*deixis is *really* grounded only

Unread Herrings

in language, which *by itself* "is inherently incapable of presence: it offers only effects of presence or at best simulacra of presence" (Kittay and Godzich 1986, 157). Such presence effects may momentarily startle readers, as if they had been floating above their beds in obdormition and had suddenly felt themselves whammed back onto their mattresses by a resumption of percipience; but they do not perhaps really remove us from the drowsy assumption of the official discourse, our imperceptible assimiliation to the neutrality of that now unquestionable prosaic state.

Making Prose Pose

THE MARPRELATE TRACTS

> The most part of men could not be gotten to read any thing /
> written in the defence of the on[e] and against the other. I
> bethought mee therefore / of a way whereby men might be
> drawne to do both / perceiuing the humors of men in these
> times (especialy of those that are in any place) to be giuen to
> mirth. I tooke that course. I might lawfully do it. I / for iesting
> is lawful by circumstances / euen in the greatest matters. The
> circumstances of time / place and persons vrged me thereunto.
> "Martin Marprelate," *Hay Any Worke for Cooper*

Presence enters the prose of Nashe's immediate precursors (or should
that be pre-*cursers*?) in the form of a brief, localized spitting in the facelessness of the prosaic state: the Marprelate tracts. A real sense of pseudopresence, here as elsewhere is created only by effects of movement,
bobbing and weaving, not by stable situatedness. Presence, like the
correspondent breeze, can only be sensed in movement against the differential backdrop of a stable state, and it is not perhaps surprising to find
that effects of positionality and presence were created by texts which had
to be composed on the run and thus emerged from no situated center of
discontent. It would be easier for prose to contain, and neutralize, such
a center. Instead, it had to follow Marprelate's own sudden outbursts
around in the form of versatile strategic *responses* (some of which have
long been supposed to have been penned by Nashe himself) much as the
Marprelate presses had to be chased bodily all over England by the
authorities. (For in-depth historical information about the Marprelate
controversy see Pierce 1908 and Carlson 1981.)

The Marprelate tracts were a series of Puritan attacks on the episcopacy which broke down the conventional hedges of prose etiquette (it is not polite to point) so as to simulate a confrontation of voices ("in writing," Kittay and Godzich put in, "all that is left of presence is 'voice'" [203]). "Martin Marprelate" got personal and named names in ways that previous satirical critics usually hadn't, but his chief means for disrupting complacent prosaic neutrality was the sporadic abandonment of various prosaic stylistic conventions for the management of the words of others in favour of a rallying prole-saic rhetoric involving the pseudo-inscription of speech with its rhythms, and the local taking up of conversationality. In the middle of an exposure of episcopal abuse, Martin will suddenly shift into the second person, thus giving a sense that he (or we in assuming his discourse) has turned upon someone present ("you" would seem to have to be either us, in which case we should feel confronted, or else "them," which again leads to a brief assumption on our part of confrontationality). In part, this is an inscription of devices from an oratorical and specifically a pulpit rhetoric, arising out of authentically grounded signfying practices, which, as in the case of the sermon, were given to the production of effects of pseudopresence (a usage that could actually lead, as I will argue, to effects of pseudo-*absence*). Such effects are obvious in the sermon, where God would be addressed, or absent miscreants (especially those in power) would be posed rhetorical questions. Change of person creates assumptions of *advertence*, the sense of a turning speaker, whose shifting pose may suddenly confront one with a *tu quoque*.

But in the Marprelate tracts such oratorical forms are undercut by a more familiar and conversational tone than even a Latimer would have made use of; and, just as importantly, boosted by a much swifter *inter*-cutting of interlocutory point-of-view than was possible in the sermon. The so-called "dissolves" of Lacanian subjectivity which, as Barthes seemed to think, might ease point-of-view shifts in traditional texts, and which would thus in our hypothetical prosaic state help readers to maintain that recessive mindless neutrality of the readerly (cf. Barthes 1970, 48-49), are here replaced by a rapid-fire montage of displacement cuts, so that each moment we seem to be posed a different pseudoconfrontation. Sometimes another voice will appear to break in with an answer to a seemingly "rhetorical" question, as when Martin and a bishop exchange utterances in *Hay Any Worke for Cooper*:

> And take heede of it brother Westchester: it is an vnlawfull game if you will beleeue me. Foe / in winter it is no matter to take a little sport / for an od cast braces of 20. nobles when the wether is foule / that men cannot go abroad to boules / or to

shoote! What would you haue men take no recreatiõ? Ye but it is an old said saw / inough is as good as a feast. ("Marprelate" 1589, [A]3ᵛ)[1]

The first and last sentences seem to be Martin's, the middle two, the response of the bishop. Citing this and other examples of rapid intercutting of discourse, Travis L. Summersgill, in his discussion of the influence of Marprelate on Nashe's style, speaks of "posturing": "that is, the author pictures himself in a variety of roles, ranging from that of a boisterous country bumpkin to that of fatherly counselor. This permits him to engage in dialog with himself, and with the bishops; it also allows for the humorous use of epithets and dialect" (Summersgill 1951, 149). It *also* might allow for momentary disruption of readerly discursive assumption. Readers here must pause and consider where the discourse is coming from and where they are in relation to it. Dialogue might further help create illusions of groundedness precisely by releasing the reader from either confronting *or* assuming the apositional discourse: for under normal circumstances a reader cannot confront prosaic discourse as such, and in assuming it must assume its groundlessness. Dialogue puts the reader in the middle, however: takes the reader out of an assumptive position. And Martin's discourse tends toward a dialogism with the gloves off; it certainly attempts (or pretends) to be *unassuming* prose. It sounds like it wants you to listen up and talk back.

The Marprelate tracts unequivocally present themselves as make-shift for an impossible presence: that of true confrontation with the bishops. The purpose of the tracts was ostensibly to incite the bishops to an open debate, and as Raymond A. Anselment argues, Martin's "defiant demand for an ultimate confrontation assumes throughout the satires that a corrupt hierarchy cannot withstand the scrutiny of the reformers' truth" (Anselment 1979, 53). This assumption, however, is pathetic consolation for the non-existence of that encounter in real space and time. In the genuine presence of a grounded, open confrontation it would no longer be possible for the ecclesiatical powers-that-be to contain differing positionalities within the endless prosaic agencies of a 1400-page tome like the *Defence of the Government Established* of John Bridges, the chief prelate whom Martin seems to hope to goad into such an actual con-

---

[1] In the modernized edition by William Pierce cited by critics, "Foe" is considered a printer's error and emended to "For" ("Marprelate" 1911, 218). But this doesn't help the sense, and it seems more likely that a switch in speaking is being introduced by an interjection (an exasperated "faugh!" if not even a demonizing "foe!").

frontation by simulating his presence in the text. This pseudopresence is thus at once provocation and fantasy gratification. For example, in the first part of *O Read ouer D. Iohn Bridges* (the "epistle"), Dean Bridges is made to respond to Martin's objections on the spot by way of quotation:

> For will my brother Bridges saye that the Pope may haue a lawfull superior authoritie ouer his Grace of canterbury? Ile neuer beleeue him though he saye so. Neyther will I saye that his Grace is an Infidell / (nor yet sweare that he is much better) and therefore M. Deane meaneth not that the Pope should bee this highe Priest. No brother Martin (quoth M. Deane) you saye true / I meane not that the Pope is this priest of Sir Peter. ("Marprelate" 1588a, C1)

Citing this passage, Anselment claims that the "omission of the standard transition and the substitution of a direct reply simulate a confrontation in which Bridges seems for the moment to be actually present" (Anselment 1979, 44).

But such "presence" does not really seem to *confront* anyone, after all; for *"the reader"* is the only person *really* "present" here, and the reader is not, except in one case (at best), John Bridges. And Bridges, for that matter, if and when he were the reader, would find himself confronted with his "own" retort, an alienation effect which could hardly lead to a *confrontational* positionality in reading.

In fact, in attempting to break down prosaic neutrality to arrive at confrontation, Martin finds his attention unfortunately focussed time and again—and we with him—on the only "presence" actually available to *him*, his own. This leads to a *self-consciousness* about his effects of presence, which in its turn may produce its own effects of pseudo-presence; but that self-consciousness only further reduces any feeling of actual confrontation. Indeed, Martin is even aware of his self-conscious-ness and attempts to distance *it* into a confrontational other by recon-verting it into others' interruptions of his own discourse and cavils which actually harangue at him from the pseudo-exterior of the margin. Thus, earlier, as Martin's own harangue had begun to escalate, an encouraging voice had broken in parenthetically to egg him on, while from the margin came a scandalized reprimand:

> The B[ishop]. of Lincolne / of Worcester / of Peterborow / and to be briefe / all the Bb. [Bishops] in England / wales / and Ireland / are pettie popes / & pettie Antichristes. Therefore no Lord B[ishop]. (nowe I pray thee good Martin speake out / if

euer thou diddest speake out / that hir Maiestie and the coun-
sell may heare thee) is to be tolerated in any christian common
welth . . . .

[Margin:] What malapert knaues are these that cannot be content
to stand by and here / but they must teach a gentleman how to
speake. ("Marprelate" 1588a, [A]3^v)

This certainly creates a "dialogic" effect, but it is one in which the
difficulty of locating positions leads to pseudo-presence without confrontationality. It is difficult to figure out if the mainbody discourse is
interrupted by a committed abettor or by what is meant to be an ironic
encouragement from his enemies, convinced that he is only going to get
himself into more hot water ([pseudo-]positionality is preeminently
obscured by irony); so it is hard to decide if the marginal objection to the
interruption comes from Martin's enemies, his friends, or himself!

On the next page, as Martin continues his attack, a more studied
criticism again comes from the margin: "M. Marprelate you put more
then the question in the conclusion of your syllogisme." Here Martin
responds from the mainbody text: "This is a pretie matter / y^t standers
by / must be so busie in other mens games: why sawceboxes must you
be prating?" ([A]4). The textual dramatization of an intradiegetical
entourage does lend atmosphere to a pseudopresence which has generally
been prepared by the rapid shift through positionalities obstructing the
easy assumption of the apositional discourse by the reader, but the
concentration on Martin's own situation and presence and the prosaics
with which it is constructed tends to defuse any elements of confronta-
tionality in such pseudopresence. As Bakhtin's attempts at a situational
aesthetics have suggested, trying to present discursively *one's own*
position, the surroundings in which one is lodged, flies in the face of the
conditions of *real* perception—my surroundings, my circumstances, the
context from which my discourse is emerging are precisely what only
someone else can see and define, from a position of privileged and
objective outsideness, and thus self-consciousness about one's own place
of utterance leads to the same *décalage* which troubles all those who try
to author themselves: positional coherence breaks down, and prosaic
dubiquity is the result.

Though self-consciousness may initially help fragment the discourse
without losing the effect of a lodging of the complaint in real circumstances, it can easily move away from pseudodeixis toward a plain deixis
that becomes absently textbound. As the "posturing" in the Marprelate
tracts becomes more self-conscious, more aware of its own *prosaic* circum-

stances, it actually becomes less confrontational, at least for the prose literate, and there is even less pseudopresence, more instead of that comfortable sense of intratextual self-reference which is untroubledly assumed in reading in the modern prose-literate world. Thus, when in the second part (the "Epitome") of *O Read ouer D. Iohn Bridges*, Martin self-consciously proposes a prosopopeic retort of the doctor which dangerously hits home by seeming to implicate him (Martin) in sedition against *the crown*, Martin temporizes from the margin in a way that calls attention to the very artificiality of the posturing: "Heere is an indecorum personæ in this speech I know / for the D[octor]. should not giue me this warning / but you knowe my purpose is to play the dunse after his example" ("Marprelate" 1588b, [D]3). Any effect of real presence is here supplied by the reader taking up a reflective exteriority (i.e., in criticism, not in naive reading) from which the anxiety-producing desperation of Martin's actual historical "situation" can be reconstructed.

Martin's pseudodeictic discourse can also lapse into a would-be literal *self*-reference, so that his deictic markers would refer to the act of utterance without *any* situation, without having grounded it in a supposed circumstance (this is where we are headed in the following pages). On an earlier page of the text just cited, for instance, having quoted a longwinded passage from Bridges, he had remarked: "I was neuer so affraid in my life / that I shoulde not come to an end / till I had bene windlesse. Do you not see how I pant?" ([C]3ᵛ-[C]4). One can hardly "see" such a thing, unless the punctuating slashes are meant to be typographical gasps. Of course, these texts were probably meant to be read aloud, and perhaps Martin anticipated the auto-production of the panting, or supposed he could rely on a performance of them in line with the pointing. A kind of "presence" may be created here even in reading by bringing the unconscious readerly assumption up short in a consideration of the question whether the panting can be seen or not, followed by a disgruntled rejoinder: "No damn cat, and no damn cradle," as someone once snorted. Any "presence" with which one is confronted here, however, is that of the actual *writing*; one steps back from the page, at least mentally, and there is a break in the ready readerly assumption of the discourse. But the "speaker" calls attention to his own very *lack* of presence (you *can't* see him panting there). When the confrontational element is played down in favor of self-conscious auto-referentiality, pseudopresence falters and something else "takes its place." What that something else is might best be described as "pseudo-absence." And to this, as the *deixis ex machina* still absurdly allows us to get away with writing, we will be returning—along with Nashe, and some of his readers.

Making Prose a Polis

GREENE'S CONY-CATCHING PAMPHLETS

In questo senso nulla è vero di quanto si dice d'Aglaura eppure
se ne trae un'immagine solida e compatta di città, mentre minor
consistenza raggiungono gli sparsi giudizi che ne possono trarre
a viverci. Il risultano è questo: la città che dicono ha molto di
quelche ci vuole per esistere, mentre la città che esiste al suo
posto, esiste meno.

Italo Calvino, *Le città invisibili*

In the early 1590s London becomes a central locus of the prosaic. The
exoticized settings of Italian novella, historical romance or Greek novel
where prose had largely taken place in the 1580s were suddenly left
behind as the printed text plunked itself down into the *Lebenswelt* in
which "the prose of the world" was most usually imprinted, the world
of *Long Megge of Westminster* (ca. 1590), Thomas Lodge's *William Long
Beard* ("borne in the citty of London," 1593) or the book by Robert
Greene's ghost: *Faire Valeria of London* (Dickenson 1598). But nowhere was
this appropriation of London by the prosaic more apparent than in the
realistic post-Marprelate satirical and exposé pamphlets associated with
Greene and Nashe. In 1591-93, Greene's cony-catching pamphlets and
Nashe's castigations of abuses reigning edged the social and topological
manifold of the sinful city into the foursquare blocks of print its prosaic
print culture so impressively could produce: from the subject of performative sermons and ballads, not only did the city now become the site
of scriptive romance and history, or jest-biographies like those of Long

Meg, Old Hobson and George Peele, but most memorably of a reassumed criminality and liminality which previously had been more often projected onto a demonized foreign sphere such as Rome. In an experimental series of self-inquisitions, these outlandish capitols of corruption were recognized and reappropriated by London as it articulated itself according to a prosaics of perver-city. Long largely exiled from its urban source, the prosaic returned like the prodigal son of its own previous generation; but it returned with a vengeance to announce that, like Prince Hal, it had all along had a morally-underwritten ulterior motive for its errancy, and that all along it had only in fact been holding up *A Looking Glasse for London and England,* as Greene and Lodge called their pseudo-biblical drama, published in 1594. But if the prosaic seems thus to re-appropriate and even re-assume its own actual circumstances of production, that looking-glass figure suggests that it could be just as accurate to put it the other way round: in terms of the timely re-investment of "mimetic capitol" (fdic). A complex of political interests called itself "London" and textualized itself either in an effort to solidify its hegemonic centripetality (North American tragicist New Historical version) or in a partially successful attempt to undermine or rezone official allocations of power and pleasure, right and wrong ways, through an appropriation of the prosaic's propensities for topological concinnation (sunnier transgressivist stance of a more early-Eagletonian stamp). In any case, of course, London appropriates the prosaic as the prosaic appropriates London.

The ubiquity of such chiasmus in the titles of criticism of late no doubt marks a salubrious attempt to get beyond hierarchical systems of binaries or the transcendence of realities by textualities or of textualities by realities, and instead to recognize politically complex dialogical interaction and mutual dependencies: the groundedness of texts and the textuality of groundedness. Yet we also know that if the curious loop into which the Hegelian master-slave dialectic can be made to engage (the master is a slave and the slave is a master) can indeed incite the odd bit of riot down in the semiotic square, it has also had a tendency to take the place of the absolving *cross* up on the hill, and sanction a philosophy of continued institutional re-accomodation. Such chiasmus are perhaps more likely to give the lie in "the West" to the whilom East German Robert Weimann's own funhouse-mirror formula according to which there continues to be *revolutionary* upheaval in the structure of articulations whereby "the literature of the Renaissance appropriates the world of the past and the world of the present appropriates the Renaissance literature of the past" (Weimann 1977, 12). In *his* discussions of narrative realism, Weimann has tried to relocate the prosaic practices of the Renaissance within the precincts of a generalized topos of sociocultural *appropriation* [*Aneignung*], but in his elaborations of this Marxian category he displays a marked predilection for such equiliberal chiasmus himself, so that the interaction [*Wechselwirkung*] of which he is fond of speaking has more recently, in his work published in North American journals, become specifically a "mode of making things one's own by which the world in the book and the book in the world are appropriated through an intellectual acquisition on the level of both writing and reading" (Weimann 1983, 465-66). With the free traffic between poststructuralism and postmarxism that such an intersection facilitates, one feels reassured that the wall has truly been opened up, at least in the unreal cities London Paris Baltimore. The socially-grounded is now free to make weekend trips into the pantextual with no complications, maybe even a little complimentary spending money, and gradually appropriate all the trappings of a sorely unrealized and all-appropriating West (the "secret referent" here, as Frederic Jameson has carelessly let slip, is "*American* capitalism" [Jameson 1983, 64]).

But what the chiasmus in our own titles and analyses in that "West" should emblematize for us[1] is not just some sort of recidivist (or even recusant) double*cross* whereby for all our good political intentions we would be the judases of a badly bourgeois aesthetic, but the likelihood that in supposing we can be something else in continuing to do our unifying "readings" we have arrived at that "Dawes crosse" (assumed by McKerrow [1908, 307] to be an "imaginary rendezvous of fools") at which the three Cambridge scholars (who may actually be Nashe's 1590s nemeses, the Harvey brothers) agree to meet in Abraham Fraunce's *Third Part of the Countesse of Pembrookes Yuychurch* (1592), by way of preparation for their exploration of the upper air. Indeed, an excursion into the "appropriation" of any supposed social and topographical realities of Elizabethan London by the prosaic and of the prosaic by London in the early 1590s would appear to be foredoomed with the Harveys "*to commence at* Dawes crosse" (Nashe 1596, B3^v/3:12).

---

[1]Lest it seem I do not recognize myself as implicated here, perhaps this is as good a place as any to advertise my own once ultra cutting-edge, now woefully démodé (but still a good read) unpublished 1985 McGill University Master's Thesis, entitled "Authors as others and others as authors: Mikhail Bakhtin's early theories of the relationship between the author and the hero." As must be sufficiently obvious by now, I personally am as bourgeois as the day is long, and don't even suppose I would *want* to be a fisherman in the afternoon, not a real one, when I could be a critical critic the whole day through, in my favorite café, with my black jeans and my Nicaraguan neckerchief.

My proposal here is much more prosaic though: to trace ever so briefly how the allocation of blame in a real city, which certainly had to circulate according to political articulations, was contained by "*literary*" prose in a textual space, and how that might conceivably lead to the assumption of the pseudopresence in complicity by readers. But here too, of course, it would be chary to at least begin our perambulation at Daws' Cross. To be "Doctors at Daws' Cross" may have been proverbial (Tilley 1950, D428, p. 162), but that Daws' Cross was even supposed to be a London topos is the kind of fact that is so far lost in the distant thuds of truly grounded utterances. We have only the endodeictic fix of the documentary to help us place such a name, a desperately prosaic discursive field just south of New Historicism (that eminently American onomastic convenience "New" always moves me with its fatuous t(r)opological alienation effect). In *Tyros Roring Megge* (1598), the eponymous young scholar, who looks "freshely come to towne," is said to enfold "*Dawes crosse* in his armes" ("Tyro" 1598, A4), but the town is not necessarily London, and indeed *Tyros Roring Megge* is likely the work of a recent university man, and as with the references in Nashe's *Haue with You to Saffron-Walden* (1596) and Fraunce's *Yuychurch*, the placement is thus strongly associated with academic situations. To be doctors at Daws's Cross may well have carried a prestige similar to that of being "vicar of S. Fooles" (Nashe 1589a, A1^v/1:10; cf. Tilley 1950, V41, p. 697), and considering St. Fools and Daws' Cross together, one is led to the possibility that both mock-tenuries were in fact take-offs on that most prosaic of Elizabethan London landmarks: St. Paul's. "*Paul's* cross" was, of course (or so one reads), the site in the churchyard of the stone pulpit from which sermons were preached.

But then, modern readers, especially North American ones, might even be far from certain that Daws' Cross was a merely fanciful location (and indeed we can't be sure); it sounds, after all, enough like what could be another (ornithologically-designated?—one hesitates) crux, the landmark on the way to which we encounter Greene's ghost in B.R.'s posthumous *Greenes Newes Both from Heauen and Hell* (1593): Pie Corner. For most of us in North America at the end of the century, Pie Corner probably rings about as true as Daws' Cross, but the former might at least be familiar to *readers* as the place the Great Fire stopped; it can be textually located on certain old maps, and is mentioned in such prosaic sources as Stow's *Survay of London* (1598), where it is said that "ouer against the said Pie corner lyeth Cocke lane" (Stow 1603, 2:22),[2] though

---

[2] I tried to go there during my honeymoon in 1991: no damn pie and no damn corner. Now there's just a wall, some dusty back streets, a couple of lorries.

"Cocke lane" (which can *still* be found on maps, and even in the dusty concrete) may itself have no more (or less) resonance of the real for most of us than "Daws' Cross." (You can see why we still need travel grants.) While there is no reason, then, to suppose that Daws' Cross is any more geographically recoverable than the reference point of a tale in *The Defence of Conny-catching* (1592) that supposedly unfolded "within a mile of a knaues head" ("Cony-catcher" 1592, B1^v/11:54/16), our very uncertainty here should put into relief the shaky ground we are on in trying to recover the chiasmal appropriation of some long-gutted Elizabethan "London" by the prosaic and of some recently gentrified "prosaic" by London. Both of them, London and the prosaic, are for us the abstract "textual constructs" of a print culture to such an extent that any attempt I might make to "map" one onto the other so as to retrieve "real places" and the textual allocations of social energies that took place in them would, in my mind, be set at the start as taking place not far from Daws' Cross, an imaginary rendezvous of fools.[3]

---

[3]This if for no other reason than the liability of one on such a formal or structuralist errand to get *taken in* along the way. To clarify the political subtext, it may be worthwhile to recall here Lacan's characterization of *l'intellectuel de gauche* and *l'intellectuel de droite* according to the Elizabethan categories of *fool* and *knave*, during his seminar for 23 March 1960 (about the time I was going through the mirror stage), entitled *"L'amour du prochain."* The digression is worth quoting at length, never mind where and when and why it was preached:

> The *fool* is an innocent, retarded, but from his mouth come truths, which are not merely tolerated but put to use, inasmuch as this *fool* is sometimes decked out in the badges of the jester. This happy umbrage, this fundamental *foolery*, is what strikes me as being the value of the intellectual of the left.
>
> . . .
>
> The *knave* can be translated on one level of usage by "jack," but it goes far beyond this. He is not a cynic, with the heroic connotations that that position entails. Strictly speaking, he is what Stendhal calls a *coquin fieffé*, or in other words, when all's said and done, John Q. Public, but a John Q. Public with more determination.
>
> Now, as we know, a certain manner of presenting oneself that is part and parcel of the ideology of the intellectual of the right consists precisely in posing as what one actually is, a *knave*, which is to say, not backing away from the consequences of what is called realism, or in other words, when necessary, admitting that one is a scum.
>
> This is of no interest unless we consider the upshot. After all, a scum is as useful as a sot, at least in terms of entertainment value, if it weren't that the scums getting together inevitably lead to collective

Cuthbert Cony-catcher's "within a mile of a knaues head" (the incident is subsequently given more natural situation as having occurred "not farre off from *Cockermouth*," which is a real place in Cumberland) is actually a parody of one of the orientational devices with which Greene had been experimenting in the two cony-catching pamphlets Cuthbert was answering, and it is from the discursive situation of London in these pamphlets from 1591-92 that my discussion of the assumptions of "appropriation" will in fact now finally begin.[4] All I am hoping to hurry through here is the shifting positionality of London and its environs in some texts of Greene and Nashe, and a few of the ways in which these *movements* problematized assumptions and now lend a kind of "presence" to the textual topoi in question. I want to trace the way in the texts of Greene and Nashe the prosaic first brings London within its discursive confines, then equates its own prosaic pseudopresence with the feel of a city, and finally arrives at a new maneuverability within that now Londonized textuality or textualized London, extending its liberties, so that London is neither deictically coextensive with the text itself nor its extra-textual ground, but a place of purely prosaic assumptions, an invisible

> foolishness. This is what makes the ideology of the right so dis-
> heartening politically.
>   But let us also point out what isn't often enough noticed—by a
> curious chiasmus effect, the *foolery* that gives the intellectual of the left
> his individual style, quite clearly leads to a group *knavery*, a collective
> scumminess. (Lacan 1986, 215)

I'm only suggesting here that this well-worn but perhaps falsely binaristic pairing needs to be supplemented by a third Elizabethan category: the *daw*; neither *fool* nor *knave*, the daw is the mark of the cony-catcher: the intellectual in the middle of the road. Those taken in by cony-catchers in Greene's pamphlets are often brought to ruin by their own slightly knavish tendencies, of course, but they are basically too clownish on their own to do anyone but themselves much harm. Still, if we imagine them standing there in the middle of the road at Daws' Cross, waiting to be had, it would seem to be at the approach of a knave and not of a fool that they need to be a little more careful of themselves these days. Of course, our sympathies are necessarily more divided when we are confronted with the collusive, charismatic old figure of a Jack Derrydaw, singing "With heigh the Doxy ouer the dale."

[4]Cuthbert may have picked up the idea of such a mock situation from the parodic and evasive publication information in the Marprelate tracts, devices immediately seized upon by other anonymous satirists and thus widespread in the 1590s. The first part of *O Read ouer D. Iohn Bridges*, for instance, is said on the title page to have been "Printed ouersea / in Europe / Within two furlongs of a Bounsing Priest."

prosaicity in which the confrontation of blame is always just around the corner of a chiasmically unassuming pseudopresence. Or somesuch.

Greene's cony-catching pamphlets certainly do not owe their realism to artistic unity. The focalization and authorization supplied through Greene's pretense of overall first-hand knowledge is increasingly disrupted by extrinsic illustrative episodes introduced through situational frameworks like those parodied by Cuthbert Cony-catcher, devices adapted from the jestbook tradition. In the collections of jests, individual anecdotes were frequently opened by naturalistic settings which contributed to their pleasure-enhancing presentation as actual occurrences. This was especially the case in collections built up around an historical or pseudo-historical figure, such as Skoggin, Skelton, or Eulenspiegel (who might move through a territory as they moved through the text), while a collection like *Merie Tales of the Mad Men of Gotam* (?1565) could even take a geographical location as its unifying and authenticating framework. Frequently situations were non-commitally approximative, of course: "not far from," "on the road to," somewhere "in Yorkshire," and so on.

There may, however, in general have been a tendency for the jestbooks to develop more and more centralizing topoi and to become increasingly underwritten by a dramatic unity of place along with the concentration on a consistent personality. This development is not really manifest in Greene's own pamphlets, which seem rather to be constantly under construction, but their experiments at redeveloping textual areas for *locally* unifying effects may have played a part all the same in an increasing *territorialization* of the prosaic.

From the beginning, Greene makes use of jestbook anecdotes as supplemental illustrations for his personally underwritten outlines of the *modus operandi* of the various confidence-trickster "crafts" he is "discovering." If supplemental illustrations of this sort become increasingly common, one assumes it is because he has run out of personal experience, but not out of consumer demand, and must extend the limits of his experience to include hearsay, merry tales set in Suffolk, or even stories from the reign of Henry VIII. This paradoxically *reinforces* (by contrast) the realism of his own personally underwritten discourse (if he were making it up, why not simply go on assuming firsthand experience?), but breaks down the continuity of the text "as a whole." As long as Greene's persona focalizes discursive assumption, the effect of unified position can attach to his discourse in accordance with any constructed entourage he allocutes. "The oral tradition," as John Dale Smith notes, in one of the few extended discussions of Greene's techniques, is "suggested by Greene's assumption of an audience to which he addresses himself directly" (Smith 1968, 68-70). This intradiegetic audience assumes the place of the implied readership and in turn might allow us as readers to assume its "presence" vis-à-vis Greene's discourse. But with the incursion of extraneous, disjunctive jestbook material, the text loses solid ground, the discursive assumption of an isotopy breaks back up into the default free-floating neutrality of the prosaic. Yet as Greene gives up his own real firsthand situatedness as guarantor of authenticity, there is some tendancy on the part of the personally "extraneous" to become more and more centralized *in London*, and the jestbook *situations* at the beginnings of discrete anecdotes become increasingly detailed. The "inclusion of himself" which was, however, one "step toward realism," as Smith says (64), is supplanted as more decisively "the illustration moves toward realism, chiefly through the use of proper names and places and through dialogue" (67). Or alternatively, the progressive use of alternative speakers and dialogue in the later pamphlets serves to position Greene himself as a character and so "allow for the presence of the author in a concrete way" letting him "remain a presence within the text," but a represented as opposed to representing one, so that a reader intermittently "must *confront* questions about his or her expectations" rather than assuming those of Greene (Relihan 1990, 13; emphasis added).

Initially, there is an effort to incorporate these extraneous details into the Greene-bounded body of the text in an unbroken assumption via his own experiential discourse. Thus, in the first cony-catching pamphlet, *A Notable Discouery of Coosenage*, he caps a lengthy abstract overview of the "cross-biting law" with "an English demonstration": "ile tel you a pretie tale of late performd in bishopsgate street" (Greene 1591a, D3^v/10:46/47). Although a quasi-jestbook introduction, incorporated into Greene's discourse and coupled with a spatiotemporally nondistancing situation and a naturalized cast of characters ("Mal. B."), or—even more effective—a scrupulous witholding of names, or changing of names to protect the innocent, such a situation can lend a sense of lived local vera-city to the main body of Greene's pamphlet. But even in this first pamphlet Greene's *vécu* narration has to be expanded by a tacked-on "Discouery of the coosenage of colliars" in which the effect of grounded situation is vitiated as the discourse becomes dissociated from Greene, and the jestbook episodes become more pronounced and are separated out from a continuity of utterance by conventional jestbook headings. Thus, "for proofe" of his remarks about untrustworthy colliers, Greene insists he "will recite you a matter of truth, lately performed by a Cookes wife vpon a coosning Collier," but then the text breaks and there is a heading in preparation of an inset narrative: "*How a Cookes wife in London did lately serue a Collier for his cosenage*" (E3/10:57/57). At the end of the story, instead of a resumption of the previous diegetical instance (Greene's "gounded" experiential discourse), there is another break, another heading: "*How a flax wife and her neighbors vsed a coosening Colliier* [siic]," beginning with the conventionally diversionary: "*NOw Gentlemen by your leaue, and heare a mery iest: There was in the Suburbs of London a Flax-wife, that wanted coles . . .*" (E3ᵛ/10:58/58). This collapse of the "authorized" narratorial quasi-confessional unity into a folk-traditional and purely recreational discursivity disrupts *narratorial* presence more and more in Greene's subsequent pamphlets. But they do not as a rule simply break down into disconnected merry tales; rather, as Greene's personal experience becomes less continuous, the unifying function is attempted more and more by the narrative assumption of other authorizing London personalities, and by more frequent and specific recursion to the cityscape of London itself as a coordinating device. For, after an overall collapse of the second pamphlet into prosaic neutrality, there is a general, though not absolute, retraction of reference into the purview of London and its environs. In *A Notable Discouery*, anecdotes had generally taken place in London, but one also heard about Suffolk, Middlesex, Surrey, and a number of other places. With *The Second and Last Part of Conny-catching*, Greene's personal experience was apparently already keenly in need of supplementation at the second hand. There are more textbreaks and subheadings, and stories come from all over: Essex, Cornwall, Uxbridge. As Greene searched for new illicit activities to "discover" or "decipher" he was initially driven away from London in the second pamphlet, and was only able to resume some local unity when he hit on the practices of cutpurses and pickpockets and could again claim personal experience of stories "realistically delineated against the background of specifically named streets and disreputable taverns" (Schlauch 1963, 116), using the familiarizing and intimating device of placename-dropping: "Paules, Westminster, the Exchange," etc. (Greene 1591b, C4/10:103/30). One "merie tale" is even set in a specific tavern: "the three tuns in Newgate market" (D3/10:110/37). A friend of his reports a "*kinde conceipt of a Foist performed in Paules*" (D4ᵛ/10:114/40) and then we are offered "a quaint conceit" that is not situated. Next follow some more generalized remarks, intermingled with more merry tales to "recreate your wits" (E4/10:123/49), all of them but the last taking place in London. In general, the effect has been one of miscellany, prosaic flitting.

It would appear that the next attempt after *The Second Part* to answer the public demand for more cony-catching pamphlets was in fact *The Defence of Conny-catching*. The narrator, Cuthbert Cony-catcher, introduces himself as a "professor" in the "liberall Artes" that Greene has been exposing. (Greene himself had used this title for "nips" and "foists" in

The Second Part). Cuthbert has recently made a circuit of the realm—a no doubt unintentional parody of Greene's having been obliged to (discursively) leave London in search of more material: "As *Plato* (my good friendes) trauelled from Athens to Aegypt, and from thence through sundry clymes to increase his knowledge: so I . . . lefte my studie in *Whittington College* [i.e. Newgate prison], & traced the country to grow famous in my facultie . . ." ("Cony-Catcher" 1592, A2/11:43/5). "Cuthbert's" pamphlet, like *The Second Part*, features a number of jestbook-type anecdotes taking place at various spots around England; but in *The Thirde and Last Part of Conny-catching* that followed it, and which also opens with an allusion to "*Whittington Colledge in* London" (apparently, the real college this time; Greene 1592g, A3ᵛ/10:140/5), all of the episodes are situated in the city. *The Thirde and Last Part* is properly a *London* jestbook, an anthology of twice-told anecdotes which Greene appropriately refers to as "our booke" (B1ᵛ/10:145/11). But while it consists of almost nothing but short disconnected narratives superscribed with jestbook headings, the topological settings no longer tend to come at the openings of tales but crop up naturalistically like urban landmarks as we peep in on scenes around town. The cinematic ease with which "impositional" prosaic discourse can cut or dissolve from one scene to another gives the collection of vignettes a feel of the documentary.

As the title leads one to expect, the fourth of Greene's cony-catching pamphlets, *A Disputation betweene a Hee Conny-catcher and a Shee Connycatcher*, consists largely of a dialogue, between a thief named Laurence and a courtesan named Nan. Their intradiegetical discourse is firmly (pseudo)grounded as taking place "here in London" (Greene 1592b, B2ᵛ/10:213/18), indeed at one point they are apparently even specifically "here in Westminster Hall" (B3ᵛ/10:217/22), so that while Nan tells a story that took place at Spilsby, one does not feel one has left a Londonian circumstance of *utterance*. Onto their dialogue is tacked a first-person narrative in the romance-confessional mode Greene had been experimenting with since his quasi-confessional 1590-91 "farewell to folly" publications, presenting the story of the "conversion of an English Courtizan" which in the epistle Greene insists is "not a fiction, but a truth of one that yet liues" (A3ᵛ/10:201/7). The account is far from having an effect of the real, however; it would seem to derive from medieval accounts of the conversion of Thais via Erasmus's colloquies (see Macdonald 1984); its first person narration comes out of nowhere, there is no name-naming, and the story is hardly underway before the conventional avuncular advisor from the Euphuean prodigal son romances of the 1580s is offering to the (transexual) protagonist the conventional avuncular advice which we know will conventionally be ignored, complete with

Latin tags and literary allusions. A dinner is interrupted by an inset tale of several pages (essentially lifted from Gascoigne), and the style, though not exactly Euphuean, is pretty similar to that of Greene's late romances, whatever satiric dialogism Macdonald thinks she can locate in it.[5]

In these pamphlets so often cited for their "realism," effects of the real, Londonian or otherwise, are only "local." None of Greene's cony-catching works after the first shows much unity of narrator or persona, and reality effects rarely have much to do with Greene's assertions that what he is telling us is "not a fiction, but a truth." On the contrary, the real seems to peep through the cracks in Greene's disintegrating under-writing of prosaic positionalities, and Greene himself seems to do some of the peeping (cf. Relihan 1990). As the series progresses, "the narrator's role as external judge disappears" (Smith 1968, 72)—we could perhaps even agree with Relihan that "narrative control and artistic authority become Greene's foregrounded concerns" (13)—and we increasingly are expected to contain our assumptions of the discourse, positionalities of many kinds, with no predetermined evaluative position by which to coor-dinate our own. Greene seems unable to provide us with the unifying authorial response that Bakhtin originally supposed would obviate our own assumption of total responsibility for outsided unification. But this does not finally make these into "writerly" texts for which we ourselves somehow become answerable. Greene continues to insist upon a personal complicity which finally will bring the freer circulation of inculpation of the later cony-catching texts back upon *him* with a vengeance, though perhaps Relihan goes too far in insisting that all of the later pamphlets serve to "focus" our attention on Greene at the expense of other, appar-ently foregrounded characters. It may simply be that he is not at all well, and prosaic neutrality suffers along with him. Maybe this is the source of local presences in the pamphlets: an authorial position or stance or *comprehension* has been assumed only to falter. Greene must have written at least half a dozen pamphlets in the year before his death, probably more, seemingly in a genuine state of moral distraction, artistic confusion, and, near the end, physical illness. His last two cony-catching pamphlets feature "confessions" which recall the "farewell to folly" prefaces and anticipate his multiple deathbed and posthumous self-accountings, and the *Disputation* is capped by a far from "merry Tale" (F4/10:276/80)

---

[5]It might, however, be of considerable interest to a feminist critic attempting to re-assess the misogyny or anti-misogyny of Greene's romantic response to and "feminization" of the Euphuean tradition (cf. Helgerson 1976, 82; Kinney 1986, 184). Thanks to David Theodore for reminding me of the Gascoigne connection and Karen Valihora for the insight she provided into the mind of "faire Nan."

about a sick man forced to lie ill in the home of an abusive cheat. Knowing the reports of Greene's death that were soon to be so greatly extenuated, it is hard not to suppose this to be quasi-autobiographical; and certainly by the beginning of the next and last pamphlet, *The Blacke Bookes Messenger*, the sick man at the beginning is Greene himself. *The Blacke Bookes Messenger* is more like the deathbed *Repentance of Robert Greene* than like *A Notable Discouery of Coosenage*. Ned Browne, a man "well knowne about London," tells his own story, though it is still broken up into jestbook episodes and there is a curious lack of unity for all the autobiographical framework. *The Blacke Bookes Messenger*, even though most of it takes place in London, seems to be on the way back to emerging from the nowhere of prose, while much of the hodgepodge in the previous two texts had seemed to draw the reader at least momentarily into a localized cityscape.

One obvious but, as I want to argue, crucial reason for this effect was the adoption in *The Thirde and Last Part* of pseudodeictics such as "here in London." In the earliest two pamphlets, among other places the prose was written *about* London—all geographical references were introduced in the same manner, as the positings of a personally unified discursivity which was itself now prosaically neutral. But in the *Defence of Conny-catching*, Cuthbert had here and there created the effect that London was not being talked about so much as *walked about* through the innovation of a simple, pseudo-self-referential, pseudodeictic formula in his attack on his fellow penmen: "Is there not *heere* resident *about London*, a crewe of terryble Hacksters in the habite of Gentlemen . . . ?" ("Cony-catcher" 1592, C3ᵛ/11:76/38; emphasis added). Cuthbert also made use of equivocal "nosism," creating a potential for writerly-readerly compli-city with the use of the first person plural: "this I talke of our London and courtly Taylors" (D4ᵛ/11:96/57). Deictic equivocation of this type (where is "here" in a printed text; whose is "our"?) immediately turns up in the early pages of *The Thirde and Last Part*: "*this famous citie* [no immediate antecedent] *is pestered with the like, or rather worse kinde of people*" or "*So if God should in iustice be angrie with vs* [where "*vs*" must mean "Londoners"]" (Greene 1592g, A3ᵛ/10:140; 141/6), but then the discursive situatedness underwritten by Greene's supposed circumstance of utterance breaks up into the merry tales, which though they all take place in London do not create the effect that their narration is *emerging from* London while one is reading them. In the dialogue of the *Disputation*, whose containment by neutral prose is more easily overlooked, this pseudodeixis is more effective. The phrases "here in London" or "here in Westminster Hall" in the dramatized dialogue of the he- and she-cony-catcher help us feel situated in the presence of two grounded speakers.

Even in the later pages of the highly artificial "conversion of the courtesan" when she reaches the point in her narrative where she arrived in town, she describes herself as "brought to London, and left *here* at randon" (F2/10:268/72; emphasis added), allowing an assumption of Londonian circumstances of utterance.

The lack of unity in these texts, then, itself coupled with by-the-way nominal situations, may at times lend a kind of metropolitan squalor to their prosaicity. John Dale Smith (1968, 71) analyzed how Greene in the cony-catching pamphlets manifests two distinct voices, one moralizing, the other merry, and later Virginia L. Macdonald, though recognizing a more dramatic playing off of "several points of view so that the reader is forced to decide among them" and in one article even cataloguing the "33 Narrative Voices" in the *Disputation* (1983, 135-36), still tends to concentrate on a "first narrator" who "avows that the tales are moral 'exempla'" and a "second narrator" who "equates them with the jest-book tradition" (1981, 128; 129). But surely she was right in her final article on the "English courtesan" section of the *Disputation* to insist on the "narrative complexity"—even if she may be wrong to assume Greene's "conscious use" of it—in "all these works," and on the "dramatic techniques" here being brought over into the prosaic (Macdonald 1984, 212; 211), a phenomenon Brian Gibbons attributes directly to Greene's experience in the theater (Gibbons 1980, 13). For there really are many more voices than Greene's duo (the moral Greene and the merry one), and increasingly, as Greene's subjective complicity decays, local unity is assumed by a *community* of London voices. Indeed, the assumption by Greene's text of the London in which it is increasingly allocating blame becomes so pronounced in the *Disputation* that as the romance narration of the courtesan peters out near the end we have a sense of Greene himself struggling through an urban textual space that has been constructing itself around "him":

> But amongst all these blythe and merry Iestes, a little by
> your leaue, if it be no farther then Fetter lane, oh take heed,
> thats too nye the Temple, what then, I will draw as neare the
> signe of the white Hart as I can, and breathing my selfe by the
> bottle Ale-house, Ile tell you a merry Iest, how a Conny-catcher
> was vsed. (Greene 1592b, F4/10:276/80)

It is here that neutral prose recounts the story that sounds so much like the circumstances in which Greene finds himself near the end (as narrated elsewhere): the sick man lying at the mercy of others in the house not his own of this text.

Making Print Repent and Point

PIERCE PENILESSE AND CHRISTS TEARES

The avowed purpose of the cony-catching pamphlets had been to "prosecute at large" the caterpillars of the community by "searching out those base villanies" they perform (Greene 1591b, *4^v/10:74/9). But the "discovery" had at first been illocal and impersonal; only as his own subjectivity broke down did Greene finally begin to name names and locate malefactors. In Greene's initial articulation, blame had been textually ubiquitous: "*I haue seen the world and rounded it, though not with trauell,* yet *with experience, and I cry out with* Salomon. Omnia sub sole vanitas" (Greene 1591a, A2^v/10:6/8). While his sense of complicity occasionally forced him to recognize a position of personal guilt, the neutral authority of the prosaic, which can so easily affiliate itself with an impersonal transcendent state, was—*assumed* to be *appropriate* for the public-good discovery and containment of these practices. Yet the malefactors who worm their way into and often fasttalk their way out of Greene's texts could be seen as enemies not only of the social but also of the prosaic state. Though prose can be used to put into custody and perhaps even panoptically to surveille criminal and liminal elements (prose and cons) it cannot obviously within itself actually prose-cute the blameworthy. They often even find it possible to get themselves re-leased—however briefly—from the prisonhouse of language through the convenient prosaic mechanism of, wait for it, *parole*. But of course it isn't long before they wind up back in the pen—or rather, neatly tucked away in a cell-block of type, having first been printed and um booked, no doubt. Prose is a faceless institution which can't be resisted but to whose judiciary apparatus access for the average inmate is also always already denied (one might confront Greene's own attempts to attach his texts to the commonwealth in his motto for these pamphlets, *Nascitur pro patria,* with Kittay and Godzich's cynical aside: "Prose is tailormade for the pros" [74]). But the attempt by the prosaic to contain iniquity without assuming it starts to break down when a malefactor, but also an author, Cuthbert Cony-catcher—whose pamphlet was almost certainly at least in part by or at least written in collusion with Greene himself (see Margolies 1985, 109-10 for the latest evidence)—began to *assume* the impartial, impersonal pervasiveness of blame, labelling Greene a cony-catcher as well ("Cony-catcher" 1592, C3-C3^v/11:75-76/37) and creating the sense of an encompassing textual dupli-city with his own pseudodeictic pseudo-presence "here in London." This in turn seems to have contaminated Greene's later pamphlets with a greater assumption of the iniquity by London and of London by the discursivity of discovery, even as Greene avoided the pandemic attribution of blame in Cuthbert's pamphlet by retracting into more personalized figures and eventually a series of projected reappropriations whereby he himself became the focal center of sin.

A further source of the dissemination of London into the prosaic and of prosaic blame into London in the later cony-catching pamphlets had been hinted at by an allusion to Pierce Penniless in Laurence's opening speech in the *Disputation.* Sometime between *The Second Part* and the *Disputation,* Nashe's pamphlet had apparently appeared. This, of course, was far and away Nashe's most popular pamphlet in his day, and his most influential work, precisely with regard to the prosaic appropriation of London. As Neil Rhodes puts it, it was by seizing on the "lively sense of topography and the teeming images of vice and squalor" therein that the next generation of pamphleteers was to continue the trend in appropriation that, again in Rhodes's terms, allowed "the city itself to move into the centre of the canvas" (Rhodes 1980, 54).

Pierce Penilesse initially displays the same pseudodeictic formulas that Cuthbert Cony-catcher had made use of, and this is one more argument in favor of the theory that Nashe had been Greene's collaborator in *The Defence of Conny-catching.*[1] *Pierce Penilesse* in turn also betrays some of the disorientation of Greene's later works, and in fact begins with a feigned world-weariness and a gesture toward repentance that echoes the

---

[1]The theory that Nashe is the "yong Iuuenall" of Greene's *Groatsworth of Witte* (1592) and, largely based on stylistic similarities, that the "Comedie" in which they collaborated (Greene 1592c, F1/12:143/44) was *The Defence of Conny-catching* was proposed as a "new suggestion" by both Nicholl (1984, 125ff) and earlier Miller (1954), and I actually seem to remember coming across this hypothesis in even earlier studies.

opening of *Greenes Vision* (probably written in 1590, but not as yet, apparently, published; see 1592d). But this *Weltschmerz* is rejected for a less extremist circulation of guilt allocation than Greene had been capable of (for him it was either *mea culpa* or *omne sub sole vanitas*). If Nashe usually roams anonymous as a kind of *flâneur* in the big compli-city, he nevertheless will often unexpectedly lash out baglady-like at one in an attempt at disturbing prosaic assumptions.

Nashe is fascinated with textually articulated figures of city-dwelling (cf. his gentleman friend's reference to "the vaward or subburbes of my narration" in *Lenten Stuffe* [1599, D3ᵛ/3:174]), and he is especially fond of constituting analogies between a heavenly or unheavenly city and his own, real or textual. The topicality of such cities is most usually concretized (and concom(m)itantly ass-faulted) in terms of the intermurally defining spaces of city proper and suburbs, whose mutual demonization makes for part of the difficulty in allocating blame in the bustling prosaicity. Pierce complains to the devil of avaricious gluttons: "if they might be induced to distribute all their goods amongst the poore, it were to be hoped Saint *Peter* would let them dwell in the suburbes of heauen, whereas otherwise, they must keepe aloofe at *Pancredge*, and not come neere the liberties by fiue leagues and aboue"; but for now it is rather left to "poore Scholers and Souldiers" to "wander in backe lanes, and the out-shiftes of the Citie" (Nashe 1592b, G2ᵛ/1:204). Virtue and vice can be seen here to occupy positionalities as center and circumference in an urbanized topography. But sometimes it seems as though the *banlieux* of blame are only the outskirts of home truth. Thus, when Nashe has described some of the minor vices and atheism of his countrymen, he claims that "[t]hese are but the suburbes of the sinne we haue in hand: I must describe you a large cittie, wholy inhabited with this damnable enormitie" (C4ᵛ/1:172). As in the previous passage, where the suburbs were subterraneously connected with heaven and the inner city was a dwelling for those bound for hell, this concentration on a conurbation of vice itself refers back to a metaphor whereby hell grew into a thriving metropolis through the capitalist entrepreneurial development schemes of the devil, "so famous a Politician in purchasing, that Hel, which at the beginning was but an obscure Village, is now become a huge Citie, whereunto all Countreys are Tributarie" (B3/1:161).

An infernal city, rotten to the core, the "supplication to the devil" which is the central hub of Nashe's pamphlet, with its parade of deadly sins that have become naturalized citizens, refuses any exorcism of blame out of its discursive position of complicity until the very end, when a margin is again formed out of the liberties, and the source of the prosaic discourse seems prepared to assume a situation within a purged center, pushing iniquity back out into the suburbs that were its official habitation. Lechery, we are told,

> hath more starting-holes, than a siue hath holes, more Clyents
> than *Westminster-hall*, more diseases than *Newgate*. Call a Leete
> at *Byshopsgate*, & examine how euery second house in *Shorditch*
> is maintayned: make a priuie search in *Southwarke*, and tel me
> how many Shee-Inmates you finde: nay, goe where you will in
> the Suburbes, and bring me two Virgines that haue vowd Chas-
> tity, and Ile build a Nunnery. (H3^v/1:216)

And here Pierce assumes an alterifying second person from the center of town: "*Westminster, Westminster*, much maydenhead hast thou to answere for" (Ibid.).

The supplication to the devil is more consistent in setting than the cony-catching pamphlets had been and it establishes a London context which the rest of the pamphlet can assume as well, so that *Pierce Penilesse* "as a whole" finally presents a kind of Londonized center surrounded by a (nondisruptive) suburbs of prosaically neutral liberties. It reinforces the sense that the text we are reading emerges from that center through a more frequent use of pseudodeictics. Nevertheless, the heterogeneity of the "suburbs" threatens to overcome unified centralized location, and Nashe recognizes that the unzoned quality of his text may annoy readers, answering a reproof which is actually self-addressed in a passage which creates its own prosopopeic pseudopresence à la Marprelate:

> Whilst I am thus talking, me thinkes I heare one say, What a fop
> is this he entitles his Booke *A Supplication to the Diuell*, & doth
> nothing but raile on ideots, and tells a storie of the nature of
> spirits. Haue patience good sir, and weele come to you by and
> by. Is it my Title you finde fault with? Why, haue you not seene
> a Towne surnamed by the principall house in the Towne, or a
> Noble man deriue his Baronrie from a little village where he
> hath least land? (L2^v/1:240)

The uncertainty as to whether his whole pamphlet is a town which assumes its name from the manor of the supplication proper or the supplication is a village from which the symbolic pseudoproperty of a unified demesne is derived is typical of Nashe's hopping between topoi of conurbation. In fact, Nashe's text is no commonality attached to an authorizing manner, but a bustling prosaicity in which it is easy to get oneself lost. Crewe begins to describe that prosaicity when he insists that

Nashe's prosaic "city emerges not as a positive material or social entity to be written 'about,' but always paradoxically as a place of deficiency and negation: deficiency of the divine poetic-creative will; deficiency of the word; deficiency of the natural order" (1982, 55). Really though, Nashe's text is more of an *arriviste* neighborhood in which the grass is always Greener on the other side of the fence. "Deficiency" is a matter of not being, or having, some *autre part*. And this implicates the prosaic deficiency in *real* estate. For all of its pervasiveness, the prosaic state can own no *real* properties, and with its increasing imperialism thus comes an increasing deficit. The position of a henceforth always Unreal City with regard to the whole of the text is usually, thus, one that must trickily *alternate* for a reader between seeming to be contained by and containing (is the deed on the property or is the property in the deed?). In the "utterance" of the supplication taken as circumscribed by the "subburbes" of the narration, however, the citified space of the letter and the literal space of the city can at times be *imagined* as isotopically coterminous with regard to central "location" (the supplication to the devil is the *down*town of an always expanding compli-city). The first sentence of the supplication places the circumstance of inditement or utterance as "heere in London" (Nashe 1592b, C1/1:165), this pseudo-deictic is repeated here and there, and at the end Westminster seems to be addressed from within the prosaically erected walls.

To go back over the same ground once again, then, London was introduced into the neutral discourse of the prosaic in Greene's cony-catching pamphlets, as one objective topos in which the blameworthy was likely to be discovered. There were local moments at which effects of presence were produced, at first through Greene's firsthand reportage and detailed coordinates, later through intradiegetical pseudopresences introduced by pseudodeictic markers in the discourse of various speakers, only occasionally including Greene. In Pierce's supplication the effects introduced by Cuthbert Cony-catcher were expanded and the voice of the supplication was made to emerge from the confines of a settled, citified *circulation* of utterance. In the cony-catching pamphlets sin and the city were still basically something written *about*, prosaically contained, circumscribed by a hovering extraterritorial prosaic. A threat of prosaic compli-city was countered by more detail and particularity: localization, pointing fingers. The author would obligingly circulate—much as the police ask the homeless to do—and eventually he turned the blame back onto himself in the confessional self-accountings that followed his cony-catching pamphlets. In *Pierce Penilesse* prosaic blame was eventually *written out* of town on a "rail," so to speak, near the end, as Nashe purged the civic center from which his own discourse was now assumed to be emerging.

But in the following year's *Christs Teares ouer Ierusalem*, either Nashe
or London seemed at first to have gone through a decisive crisis of
conscience, and to be making a concerted effort to assume complicity in
the free-floating blame. (Unless we are only witnessing a symptom of an
epidemic outbreak of pseudodeixis that was sweeping through the
prosaic as the plague raged through London.) If Greene had done much
to make prose a polis, Nashe seems to become increasingly keen on
somehow making that prose apologize—making his own native complicity face prose-cution. We in our local reading seem strangely drawn into
a textually articulated state—or rather a complicity of blame—as Nashe
adversively pivots between a self-assuming locative and an implicational
vocative inflection. The prosaic here tries to assume the discourse of the
sermon, and with it its characteristic grounding deictic usages, making it
seemingly more difficult for reader or prose to absent themselves from
a "London" overrun by blame.

There are other assumptions which hold more locally, however. The
first fifty pages of *Christs Teares* consist of the assumption by the prose
of the discursive pseudo-(well, we can't call it groundedness)-*dupli*city of
Christ, the discursive assumption which has led so many critics along
with Hibbard to mark this text on their cognitive maps as a "monument
of bad taste" (Hibbard 1962, 123). The choice of "persona" is, nonetheless,
an interesting one from the point of view of textual positionality in that,
unlike the God-like omniscient narration that is the bread-and-er-butter
of the prosaic, a Christ-like agency is one that can be assumed to be both
transcendent to the world of diegesis and retaining some immanent trace
of positionality in that world (one thinks of Bakhtin's Dostoevsky): the
implied (and implicated) author is more like Christ than God. But this is
precisely the most outrageous chicane of prosaic (a)positionality: to
pretend to have an incarnate position while at the same time tran-
scending and "embracing" (or is it incar*n*cerating?) all others.

At the end of Christ's lamentation over the depravity of Jerusalem,
narration is resumed by Nashe's persona in order to recount how Jerusalem ignored Christ's imprecations and was scourged for its unregen-
erate sinfulness. Nashe sometimes takes over the second-person address
of Jerusalem that Christ had used, and also assimilates his "weeping"
(Nashe 1593, G2^v/2:60). This covers another 25 pages, at the end of which
there is another break and adversive reorientation:

> Now to *London* must I turne me, *London* that turneth from none
> of thy left-hand impieties. As great a *desolation* as *Ierusalem*, hath
> *London* deserved. VVhatsoeuer of *Ierusalem* I haue written, was
> but to lend her a Looking-glasse. Now enter I into my true

Teares, my Teares for *London*, wherein I craue pardon, though I deale more searchingly then common Soule-Surgeons accustome: for in this Booke, wholy haue I bequeathed my penne and my spyrite, to the prosternation and enfurrowing the frontiers of sinne. (K2-K2ᵛ/2:80).

Prosternation is "laying out before," and the prosternation on the anatomy table of "frontiers of sinne" suggests that Nashe is once again going to lay blame out in strumpet-like suburban sprawl from his civic center of censure. Indeed, nearing the end it seems that Nashe will write sin out of town again as he did at the end of Pierce Penniless's supplication: "*London*, what are thy Suburbes but licensed stewes?" (V1/ 2:148). But the more characteristic dodge here is that of sermonic advertence, and London in the text interestingly now reappears in each person: I, thou, it, we, you and they. Nashe consistently declines (if I may mildly pun) to "recognize who and what in the midst of hell is not hell, and to make it last and give it space" (Calvino 1972, 170). He gives space rather only to the infernal, pays out only enough deictic rope for us to hang ourselves with. His advertence seems to lead to a kind of inescapable wheeling or circulation of blame. Each time London or we feel we have assumed a safe position with regard to blame I find myself getting confronted with it again. You think of Freud's story in "*Das Unheimliche*" about wandering the streets of an unfamiliar town and finding himself again and again back in the red light district (cf. Garber 1987, xiii). All roads here lead uncannily to home, and the economy of deixis makes it difficult for readers to avoid their pseudosomatic Assumption into the unheavenly compli-city of blame. "Us" and "them" are all but inexorably blended in the eco-nomically *unheimlich* sermonic slippage.

> The Delicacie both of men & women in *London* will enforce the Lorde to turne all their plenty to scarcity, their tunes of wantonesse to the alarums of warre, and to leaue their house desolate vnto them.
>
> How the Lord hath begun to leaue our house desolate vnto vs, let us enter into the consideration thereof our selues. (Nashe 1593, X2/2:156-7)

And yet the reader of Nashe's day may well have been possessed of a certain "sermon literacy" that would obviate an assumption of presence, implication and complicity in such prosaic circumstances. The advertence conventions of the sermon, as I suggested earlier, may in fact allow for an assumption of "pseudo-absence"—so that even when one is being addressed by a present speaker there is an element of prosaic impersonality which makes it possible to "travel the roads of positionality" without experiencing along the way—in some Saul-Paul's cross self-recognizng manner—any of the positions as implicational or confrontational. In practice, I think, any readerly assumption of presence, with the implications which a present utterance would entail, will be avoided through an assumption of complicity with the encompassing *prosaic* economy. The city thus, as the text, *constitutes* an articulation of blame, but does not finally *assume* the blame itself, and to the extent that readers assume that textual articulation, they are indeed in "London"—or rather instead they *are* London; but never the London implicated by the text— only the London *of* the text, an impersonal and groundless, unlived, a transparent, an invisible city.

Thus, in our attempt to allocate blame and meaning in the prosaic state we have not in the end made much progress from Daws' Cross. But then, however could we when we have actually all this while been safely locked away in our "studie at *Whittington Colledge*"?

Assumption

Les déictiques (*ce, ceci, cela*) marquent le passage du discours
dans le système de la langue: ils se définissent essentiellement
par leur emploi par le sujet de l'énonciation. S'il est vrai qu'ils
renvoient à un référent, ils indiquent aussi bien un autre signe
qu'eux-mêmes: ils sont métalinguistiques et sui-référentiels. Par
la multiplicité de plis de l'énonciation que possède cette
catégorie linguistique, le sujet qui s'en sert peut se mettre à
cheval sur divers espaces énonciatifs. On expliquera ainsi
l'impact des déictiques dans des discours où l'identité du sujet
parlant est en cause.
　　　　　Julia Kristeva, *Le vréel*

I haue rid a false gallop these three or foure pages: now I care
not if I breathe mee, and walke soberly and demurely halfe a
dozen turnes, like a graue Citizen going about to take the ayre.
　　　　　Thomas Nashe, *The Terrors of the Night*

I am not sure that the extent to which Nashe assumed the "posturing" of the Marprelate tracts has ever been sufficiently recognized,
despite the contribution of Summersgill (1951), a chapter by Nicholl
(1984), practically equipaginal accounts of his contribution to the controversy by Hibbard (1962, 36-48) and Hilliard (1986, 34-48), and so forth. If
the Marprelate tracts tried to cultivate effects of pseudo-presence as a
kind of *supplément* of the confrontation they could not really provoke, it
might be said that in his own efforts as it seems to supplement that
supplement, Nashe, as Hutson puts it, "deliberately pursues such an
effect of intimacy, creating a sense of shared space by allusively invoking

a contemporary locale, drawing on and intensifying current colloquial-isms and discovering syntactical patterns which heighten the sense of a sentence without sacrificing the illusion of conversational spontaneity" (Hutson 1989, 2). The impact in terms of a situational aesthetics is perhaps in part recognized by Jonathan Crewe, when he discusses the anti-Marprelate work most widely postulated as actually of Nashe's authorship, the 1589 *An Almond for a Parrat* (see, e.g., McGinn 1944). According to Crewe, in this pamphlet, "Nashe cannot finally come to rest" and consequently "[i]f radical dislocation and irresolution remain characteristic of Nashe's work (or of his personae), the cause is at least partly suggested by *Almond*: no single decorum, voice, or position can legitimately prevail" (Crewe 1982, 33). Although not yet the Jack-Wilton-of-all-sides that Crewe and others will discern in the narrator of *The Vnfortunate Traueller*, Cuthbert Curry-knave, the narrative persona of the *Almond*, already at least "appears on both sides of the issue, that of the hierarchical order and restrictive authority as well as that of carnival-esque folly and indecorum" (33-34). This duality should not surprise us, for what Nashe inherits above all from Martin is his divisive textual *self-consciousness*, self-presence, the element which can dissolve confronta-tionality in an easy (because non-implicational) assumption of the cloven pseudopresence of an author *to himself*. Nashe becomes so given to situ-ating "himself," shifting situations, and calling attention to the textual articulation of these pseudopresences that any effects of actual presence are undone by the eventual pseudo-absence to which "I" alluded "above"—which is to say, *the circumstances of utterance*, not the utterances themselves, tend to become textually "regrounded" and leave the reader confronted only with—this page. Thus, when Nashe attempts to respond to the prosopopeic critic of the thematic disunity of *Pierce Penilesse* quoted in the previous chapter, he calls attention to the fact that his temporizing has created a kind of preface, there at the end of the pamphlet, and he asks himself: "*Deus bone*, what a vaine am I fallen into?" He answers the self-posed question with more prosopopeia, usurping therein the posi-tionality of his critic (originally self-constructed):

> what, an Epistle to the Readers in the end of thy booke? Out vpon thee for an arrant blocke, where learndst thou that wit? O sir, hold your peace: a fellon neuer comes to his answere before the offence be committed. Wherefore if I in the beginning of my Book should haue come off with a long Apologie to excuse my selfe, it were all one, as if a theefe going to steale a horse should deuise by the way as he went, what to speake when he came at the gallowes. Here is a crosse way, and I thinke it good heere to

part. Farwell farewell, good Parenthesis, and commend me to
Ladie Vanitie thy mistres. (Nashe 1592b, L3/1:240-41).

Seemingly aware of its situation in the book, and able to create an effect
of taking cognizance of that situatedness (while *assuming* guilt for those
circumstances and the need of an "Apologie" in the assumption of that
situation *as* writing—see the discussion of Crewe and Hutson "below"),
Nashe's discourse deictically presents a strictly textual space, one that
depends upon but does not have to answer to political or social articulations of space outside the prosaic. His "Here is a crosse way" refers
to nothing but its own discursive enactment (the block regularity ["an
arrant blocke"] of print is nowise disrupted, no grounded circumstance
is referred to), while the Epistle to the Readers has been reallocated
according to a more effective logic of the alibi or, perhaps here, "extenuating circumstance," and could even now be tardily followed by the
subversive *coup* of a dedicatory epistle: "Now *Pierce Peniles* if for a
parting blow thou hast ere a tricke in thy budget more than ordinarie bee
not daintie of it, for a good Patron will pay for all. I where is he?
Promissis quilibet diues esse potest. But cap and thanks is all our Courtiers
payment" (L3/1:241).

The pseudopresence of book or paginal space is not a *pseudo*presence
at all, for the page is really there situated at the belated place in the book
to which the deixis refers (it's right under your nose at the moment, too,
assuming of course that you are assuming Cloud's "Missionary Position
of Reading"; otherwise, I suppose, your nose may well be right under *it*);
but, as I have been trying to suggest, this form of deixis creates at the
same time (or rather, of course, in a different moment) a sense of pseudo-
absence, as the actual sender of the utterance refers to textual circumstances that are purely virtual at the time of inditing (the articulated
space of the book), and thus creates the illusional effect of a purely
textual situation whose actual circumstances of "utterance," to snatch
Derrida's untranslatable amphibology: "[n]e se livrent jamais, au présent,
à rien qu'on puisse rigoureusement nommer une perception" (Derrida 1972a,
71). In inscribing his utterances, the "sender" gives up ground, and the
utterance is left to simulate this ungroundedness: it is as though writing
were speaking about its literal spacing: but this is the *pseudo*, for actually
the utterance can only exist as an utterance because it was once grounded
(during writing) and is again (during reading).

Jonathan Crewe has thus understandably come to consider *The Vnfortunate Traueller* as a "phenomenology of the page" (see further), and it is
true that in that text Nashe's pseudodeixis becomes even more dependent
upon bookspace. In the early pages of the pamphlet, Nashe attempts to

establish the pseudopresence of his narrator, Jack Wilton, and Jack's discourse as grounded utterance through use of quasi-isochronies and apostrophe. An example of a quasi-isochrony (in these cases, not *narrative time = narrated time*, but *narrative time = reading time*) would be: "There did I (soft, let me drinke before I go anie further) raigne sole king of the cans and blacke iacks, prince of pigmeis, countie palatine of cleane straw and prouant, and, to conclude, Lord high regent of rashers of the coles and red herring cobs" (Nashe 1594a, A2/1:209). A typical use of apostrophe is: "Gentle Readers (looke you be gentle now since I haue cald you so) as freely as my knauerie was mine owne, it shall be yours to vse in the way of honestie" (B2/2:217). The immediate effect would seem in both cases to be the creation of a conversational pseudopresence, but from the very start the pseudo-spoken passages call attention to their actual writtenness. As David Margolies has enigmatically put it: "The character of the writing is conversational and at the same time clearly literary. . . . Nashe substitutes literary time for conversation time . . ." (1985, 100).

A "spacing," as we know, intensifies the temporal absence of the written. Cynthia Sulfridge has discussed the apparently presentifying temp-orality of Nashe's reality effects, and her subtle analysis does, in my experience, represent the situation into which the reader *temporarily* is "placed" by such effects. Following E. D. Mackerness (1947), Sulfridge suggests that the

> oral characteristics are part of an effort in the text to bring the reader into a close interaction with Jack Wilton, to blur the distinctions between the reader's world and the narrator's. They nudge the reader into a casual, unguarded relationship with the narrator. They lead him to accept gradually the terms of the narrator's world as a feasible reality. They prepare him for the effects of Jack's subtle blending of the reader's reality markers with those of the narrative. Jack speaks of historic events and personalities the reader will recognize as "real." He sets the events of his narrative geographically within the reader's known world. And, finally, in his coup de maitre, he manipulates the reader's unconscious tendancy to blend the concepts of verb tense and time.
>
> Jack begins by speaking as if his delivery is taking place at the very moment in which the reader is reading it. Whatever would halt the flow of an oral delivery halts Jack's tale as well. He stops to drink (209) or to tell his reader to fill in portions of the story (227), and the discourse is interrupted. . . . All of these

are temporal interruptions to a temporal flow of narrative. They suggest that this text, unlike most written texts, is subject not to the laws of the written word but to the laws of oral discourse. Ordinarily it is in the reader's power to control the flow of the written word, to pick up the book or put it down, but here the power of interruption seems to lie elsewhere as it would if the reader were involved in a conversation. The text suggests that here there is no difference between "textual time" and "reader time." (Sulfridge 1980, 5)

Sulfridge may be correct about the intended effect, but I am not certain that discursive power resides in oral presence of the kind Nashe's text supposedly feigns, nor that on closer reading these effects do not in fact call attention to the text's writtenness even as they work all of the manipulative effects which Sulfridge puts down to their pseudo-temporality and orality. Consider the first example I quoted above, which Nashe suddenly introduces after he has begun situating the narrated time as during Henry VIII's French campaign and seems to have situated himself firmly in the English camp at Térouanne: "There did I (soft let me drinke before I go anie further) raigne sole king of the cans and blacke iackes. . . ." This seems to jerk us back abruptly from settling into an assumption of Jack's narration by apparently confronting us once again with a present speaker; the parenthesis neatly brackets the speech for the timespan of a good pull on the bottle. But the intervening text actually emphasizes the disjunction between discursive and real (present) temp*orality* by going further logically during what from a logical point of view would be "dead time" in the grounded utterance it supposedly refers to. At this point in the situation to which it pretends to refer, Jack's discourse would break off, and we would be *confronted* by his glugging mug, while here we continue to *assume* his discourse. Under cognitive scrutiny the parenthesis proves to be heterodeictic (cf. "heterodiegetic" in Genette), since the parenthesis refers to a different diegetical universe (that in which Jack is speaking to an implied audience) from that referred to in the periparenthetical utterance (the time when Jack was in the English camp at Térouanne). A device which would seem to propose a pseudopresence thus actually effects a pseudo-absence, as the textual situation is momentarily displaced and the utterance loses unified positionality. Time is not the problem, as Julia Kristeva remarks in analyzing a not wholly dissimilar utterance— "This is my body" (Matthew 26:26)—in which the Cartesian Port-Royal logicians saw a "double space of utterance," according to which the demonstrative would refer to both "the confused idea of the thing present" and other ideas that are "inspired by circumstance." Committed to the myth of a unified *cogito*, they could not explain the "identity of a subject who can assume such different 'circumstantial inspirations,'" and so they recurred to time: "*now* this is bread, and *then* it is my body" (Kristeva 1979, 27; cf. 1977, 490). If we accept this tenuous temporalization of transubstantiation (which a grammatology might also expect) we will recognize that the subsequent "blood" of "this is my blood" is already the red letters we are reading, and so the dearly departed authorial agency ("The letter killeth, but we learn this from the letter itself," as Lacan sagely points out [1966, 848]) can now be toasted: "By this blessed cuppe of sacke which I now holde in my hand and drinke to the health of all Christen soules in, thou art a puissant Epitapher" (Nashe 1592c, F1/1:188). Much more blatantly, the apostrophe "Gentle Reader (looke you be gentle now since I haue cald you so)" deconstructs any conversational presence it might have created simply by referring to a reader instead of a listener.

Later isochronies, pseudodeixes and apostrophes call attention to their print culture textuality in much the same way, even as they may appear to produce effects of grounded utterance. After Jack has told of one of the savage practical jokes he played in the English camp, we are confronted with "Here let me triumph a while, and ruminate a line or two on the excellence of my wit: but I will not breath neither till I haue disfraughted all my knaueric" (Nashe 1594a, B4ᵛ/2:285). In this there is no claim to be taking the breather that grounded speech might really demand—the pause is of "a *line* or two" (in fact it is three in the *Ur*-editions). Again, when Jack seems to apostrophize his audience at the end of an account of an Anabaptist uprising at Munster: "What is there more as touching this tragedie that you would be resolued of? say quickly, for now is *my pen* on foot againe" (C4ᵛ/2:241; emphasis added). Nashe's self-consciousness about the writtenness of his discourse, and the print textuality of its assumption by his audience seems to lead him to create effects of pseudopresence which on closer examination produce a recognition of absence (there *is* no grounded situation and thus no utterer).

This apparently demystifying performance has been hailed by a few critics, among whom Jonathan Crewe is perhaps foremost, as producing epistemological bonuses of the deconstructive variety. Wilton's status as a "page" is constantly emphasized, so that the situation of discourse is deictically grounded in writing as such. Through the creation of pseudo-absences, Nashe calls attention to the real *paginal* presence of the prosaic utterance, and thus, I guess, like Derrida, is attempting to make us conscious of the "spacing" of reality ("the articulation of space and time, the spatialization of time and the temporalization of space") which however, as Derrida himself says, will be "always the non-perceived, the non-present, and the non-conscious" (Derrida 1967a, 99).

But the realities of the *prosaic* cannot merely be collapsed into the scriptive self-difference of philosophical pro-seity. As opposed to a revelation of the "arche-writing" of time and space themselves, I think (with Crewe) that Nashe is concerned in these passages specifically with creating an effect of the *presence* of the *page*—and thus of the literal materiality (the limited ink) on which the prosaic must rely for the transparency of its own "absence." The most "impressive" example of this sort of effect (one not reproduced by, but at least remarked on in the commentary of McKerrow's edition, and one strangely undiscussed by Crewe) occurs when (in both *Ur*-editions) the top of a page begins: "In a leafe or two before I was lockt vp: here in this page the foresayd good wife Countesse comes to me . . ." (Nashe 1594d, L2^v/2:314). At this point, presence of tense helps along deictics that suggest the discourse can refer to its own print presence; and several other such moments punctuate the later pages of Jack's narrative (". . . spare we him a line or two" [K3/ 2:306]). A reading which, writely or not, might call itself deconstructionist could thus praise the demystifying performance of the text here. But this occasional presence of the page too really only bolsters the effects of pseudo-absence which are obscuring the situation of "prose's sender."

The ungroundedness of that sender's discourse has much to do with why writing is transparent, "non-perceived, non-present, and non-conscious," and thus perhaps with why it is difficult for the reader not to *assume* it. In their brilliant and subtle analysis of the narrative strategies in *The Vnfortunate Traueller*, Susan Marie Harrington and Michal Nahor Bond, inspired by Adrienne Rich, ask us to consider these "assumptions at the heart of fiction" (Harrington and Bond 1987, 243). To become conscious of such still largely transparent assumptions—I in turn would argue (inspired by them)—might lead us, better than any gramma- tology could do, to make *different* ones.

Jack's apparent presence to his audience, especially as a pseudo- grounded speaker, progressively diminishes in the later part of the narrative. As Harrington and Bond argue, this is because there are times when the narrator "finds it more advantageous to shift his audience's attention away from himself" (247). They provide us as an example the scene in which Jack narrates the rape of a woman by a brigand which he witnessed while himself in a situation where his actantial intervention would probably have been to no purpose and might have gotten him into trouble. The greater passivity of Jack's character in the later episodes of the pamphlet and the concomitant shift toward prosaic omniscience and transparency of narration had been remarked by other commentators, but

only Harrington and Bond reveal how these narrative strategies recapit-
ulate with a vengeance the cruel pranks Jack himself enacts at the
beginning by occluding his actual complicity and control and forcing *us*
to assume responsibility for experiencing and evaluating scenes of
murder or rape. As Harrington and Bond see it, this "transition from
bullying narrator to fellow member of the audience draws us into the
text, hindering our ability to recognize the narratorial manipulation"
(250). Robert Weimann (1970) was thus right to concentrate on the
relationship between *Ich-erzähler* and jestbook in *The Vnfortunate Traueller*,
but he failed to see that the movement between them is in fact the same
as that in the cony-catching pamphlets: an original evaluative narrative
position is gradually allowed to recede until the "sender" becomes transparent and the reader is forced to look *through* that now translucent positionality. Far from constituting a demystifying performance, then, the
narration of *The Vnfortunate Traueller* in general would be one more
"work of disguise and mystification" rendering us complicitous through
our reading with Jack's own "pattern of pleasure in domination, unable
to ask if it is true for us as well" (Harrington and Bond 1987, 250). Any
odd bit of pseudo-absence only makes away with the situation of prose's
sender, and leaves *us* ("us"!) to assume the discursive responsibility.

Perhaps the prosaic state which we assume upon entering writing is
finally a rhetorical manipulation, a containment, a strategy which takes
advantage of the non-groundedness of writing to take us in. But to call
this a strategy or a manipulation suggests that the assumption has been
the ulterior motive of a grounded sender, rather than—as we now more
often tend to assume—the state in which "we" find ourselves because of
writing as such. Perhaps, then, as we have begun to consider, the
mystification *would* be better fought not by discovering prose's sender but
by knowing where we stand as its "receiver," in a sense which is still
best thought of in terms of underworld connections. Yet both sender and
receiver really are continually being spirited away by the pseudo-absence
of the prosaic. It is in its nature—is it not?—to fade into the background
as the steady state of things, and take us with it; and any prosaic phenomenology would seem in the end to bump up against (or rather waltz
right through) its transparency, and to face (or rather find itself unable
to face) the problems which according to Derrida make a phenomenology
of writing impossible:

> for right here is where we exceed the bounds of pheno-
> menology. Arche-writing as spacing cannot give itself *as such*, in
> the phenomenological experience of a *presence*. It marks the *dead
> time* in the presence of the present being. Dead time works. It is

because of this, once more, despite all of the discursive sources it has to borrow from it, that thinking about the trace will never be confused with a phenomenology of writing. Like a pheno-menology of the sign in general, a phenomenology of writing is impossible. No intuition can be achieved where *"les 'blancs' en effet assument importance."* (Derrida 1967a, 99)

Impossible, indeed, it sometimes seems, *there,* or for some of us—those not known for our intuition especially perhaps. The prosaic transparency of writing may in general have constituted a "work of disguise and mystification," and perception of its positionality may indeed be practically impossible at present for those by whom the prosaic state has been constituted and who continue to re-sign ourselves to that constitution—those for whom "prose literacy" does not even seem to be a question: the blanks who make possible the "spacing" on which the faceless prosaic state depends to maintain blankness of expression. That snippet from Mallarmé with which Derrida ends will have seemed for us to translate transparently enough a prosaic platitude about the poetic: "the 'blank spaces' in fact assume importance"—a platitude, however, now beginning to yellow for us like the spermy correction fluid that has always really been used to obliterate figures that would have prevented the spacing, so that actually all along it has only been *les blancs* that were doing the important assuming. To press "those discursive emptinesses [*blancs*] that recall the sites of her exclusion, the spaces that insure by their *taciturn plasticity* the cohesion, articulation, and cohesive expansion of the established forms" (Irigaray 1974, 176)—that is now the task that has assumed importance for us. "For us" again—*"nous, mais qui, nous?"* (Derrida 1979, 47)—who's "us"? you might well ask, if there were of course any "you." In the facelessness of this state we can never confront "prose's sender."

That, at least, has been the assumption. But do we really need Benny Hill here to remind us what it is we do when we assume?

NO TIME TO UNPACK

J'en conseille la lecture aux gens déjà un peu avancées. Que ceux qui n'ont pas beaucoup de temps en lisent au moins la première partie.

Jacques Lacan, speaking of Kierkegaard's *Repetition* in his seminar for 19 January 1955

Making Print Sprint

"One must go further; one must go further." This compulsion to go further is an old story in the world. Heraclitus the obscure, who deposited his thoughts in his writings and his writings in the Temple of Diana (for his thoughts had been his armor in life and so he hung it up in the temple of the goddess), Heraclitus the obscure said: one cannot step into the same river twice. Heraclitus the obscure had a disciple who didn't stop at that but went further and added: one cannot even do it once. Poor Heraclitus to have such a disciple! With this amendment the Heraclitean thesis was amended into an Eleatic thesis that denied motion—and yet that disciple only wanted to be a disciple of Heraclitus who went further, not back to what Heraclitus had abandoned.

> Søren Kierkegaard, *Fear and Trembling*

The critical attempts to "re-route" *The Vnfortunate Traueller,* as Louise Simons expressly puts it in the title of an article that is swiftly receding into the theoretical past from us, have themselves been responsible for any plottable course it may have taken in modern accounts of Renaissance fiction. For the shifting readings of critical movements, like all "historical" transactions, are rapidly taking their place among other instances of intellectual "conveyance," in that nimble Elizabethan sense ("Oh good: conuey: Conueyers are you all," rails Shakespeare's Richard of Bordeaux in the scene removed from the early quartos) according to which Nashe can promise the reader only "some reasonable conueyance of historie, & varietie of mirth" (1594a, A2/2:201). By this is not implied any realignment of the constellation which led slightly earlier adventurers to seek the Northwest Passage of epistemology (M. Serres) in the tropics

(Hayden White *et al.*), but only that any shady figures we now find slaving away there were originally *transported* there (Parker's pun [1987, 39] somewhat improperly conferred to Derrida 1978, 7). This is perhaps especially true in "figuring out" historical accounts, whose narrativity carries a literary theoretical onus by which it would seem that "one would have to conceive of a rhetoric of history prior to attempting a history of rhetoric or of literature or of literary criticism" (de Man 1979b, 28) if one would take upon oneself what Hayden White (1966) once famously called "The Burden of History," a charge whose incumbency on a couple of salient figures now makes it seem not at all improper to speak of it as an outdated kind of White and de Man's burden. Such a burden has come to foist upon one the exigency of an intellectual extra-territoriality that allows one to cross disciplinary boundaries with a mere flash of documents, as well as a missionary sense of duty to pay one's respects in all quarters. Yet those recent readings which now seem most pointedly to have been "all over the map" have in fact almost invariably proven to be neatly chartable somewhere within that triangle of semiotic trade—with its seasoned "interpreters" and "representatives"—that is ultimately concerned with the *conveyance* of things, and whose "immaterial" profits (the wages of *Sinn*) also manage to accrue to those for whom the representatives do their representing. This is not, of course, meant to occult the existence of that contiguous Bermuda triangle (symbol : reference : referent) in which, to use the Baconian semaphore, "many other barques of knowledge haue beene cast away."[1] But the loss of however many transatlantic argosies (as the celebrated Ogden-Richards expedition earlier in the century) does not make up for the too often piratical practises of those still following a similar course even today, and who have generally been able, with a little craft, not only to stay afloat, but to outpace the more lumbersome tonnage, freighted as it is with treasured cargoes of sense, and keep those who would give chase safely at sea and, so, at bay.[2] Expedition and mobility are of the essence in

---

[1]"The reason of this omission I suppose to be that hidden Rocke wherevppon both this and many other barques of knowledge haue beene cast away, which is, that men haue dispised to be conuersant in ordinary and common matter, the iudicious direction whereof neuerthelesse is the wisest doctrine: (for life consisteth not in nouelties nor subtilities) but contrariwise they haue compounded Sciences chiefly of a certaine resplendent or lustrous masse of matter chosen to giue glory either to the subtillity of disputacions or to the eloquence of discourses" (Bacon 1605, 70-71).

[2]If, as E. R. Curtius points out, it is a commonplace that "the epic poet travels in a large ship on the open sea and the lyric poet in a small bark on the river"

bringing such negotiations to a profitable conclusion, and the famed speed and maneuverability of the text is of course ideal for the conveyance of a moving finger that is quicker than the I and the specious sociocultural *rapprochement* that comes with telecommunication. But the "Pathos of Approximation" that is thus the outcome of the global contraction of a heightened intertextuality and ever encroachinger close reading may, sprawled open but unread across the lap, just cover the swelling act with an empirical theme of the most complacent of armchair travellers, one index quivering over the surface of the remote control and one, from time to time perhaps, over the index . . . .

Now then—where wasn't I?

The course of the critical reception of *The Vnfortunate Traueller* itself can be picked up as easily as anywhere else about the time that Mikhail Bakhtin, the exilic not to say ex-iliac poetician, was lighting up the last page of the chapter on the adventure novel from his history of the *Erziehungsroman*,[3] i.e., to triangulate historically, somewhere between Fredson Bowers's 1941 essay on the genre of Nashe's book and two postbellum ergo propter bellum (cf. Mackerness 1947) stylistic analyses (Croston 1948 and Latham 1948).

Bowers wished to argue, against the current of past criticism, that *The Vnfortunate Traueller* was indeed a picaresque novel. He consequently highlights its "picaresque" aspects, which I would like to summarize under three rubrics: *topicality, an antiromantic protagonist* (often a servant), and *realism* (cf. Bowers 1941, 13):

> How then does *The Vnfortunate Traueller* measure up as a picaresque novel? First it has a roguish anti-hero, who makes his way in the world by his wits. . . . In the service of a master he sees the world, and when sufficiently affluent he travels independently. . . . The rogue tricks and lampoons his master. Manners are surveyed and satirized. . . . The tone is strictly

(Curtius 1953, 138), it will be clear that critical corsairs make use of ultraswift clippers in their endeavor, as it might drily be put, to help the pilots light their weary vessels of their loads (cf. *Faerie Queene* 1.12.42).

[3]Bakhtin, as it will be recalled, writing on the Rabelaisian body with his leg off, and short on smoking papers in the heart of World War Two in Stalinist Russia, put his own copy of a manuscript already sent off to the publisher to a most Nashean use, resurrected the leaves of his foolscap to "honor them in theyr death so much, as to drie & kindle Tobacco with them" (Nashe 1594a, A2/2:207). Meanwhile, a German tank was blowing up the publisher, making a much quicker smoke of the only other copy.

realistic and life is painted without sentimentality; indeed, the point of view is distinctly cynical and there is a wealth of corroborative detail. In general, the construction of the novel is episodic. (25)

It will be seen that what I will be calling "topicality" can indeed cover a lot of ground, including the episodic form of the picaro's peripatetic servitude and the satirical commentary on the various situations (geographical, economical, and cultural) through which the itinerant hero passes. This topicality of the picaresque has been seen at times as a function of the *servitude* of the protagonist (cf. Bowers, 13). In fact, for Bowers the entire generic question comes down to the status of the hero: "The crux of the matter is really the character of Jack Wilton" (14). It had been objected that Wilton is too often masterless to be a picaro and that the motivations for his tricks are too often not material enough for him to be classified with a Lazarillo de Tormes (Ibid.).[4] Bowers suggests that Wilton's relative independence is an anticipation of later developments in the genre whereby the motive thrust of the hero's divagation—"in order that a shifting background may be provided" (13)—would no longer depend upon the devices of penury and servitude (19). In such "topical" works, movement is the main thing, and one may recall that Bakhtin was to deal with the picaresque under the general head of "the novel of travel" and to describe its hero as simply "a point moving in space" (Bakhtin 1979, 188). Thus, the element of servitude in recognized picaresque narratives could in fact be trivial, a facilitation of the crucial element of *movement*. In any case, as Bowers himself points out, Wilton's social identity is not the entirely disenfranchised one of the *picaro* but in fact the civil servile one of the *page*. As such, however, one would expect his own movements to conform to the essentially "horizontal" processions of the *court*. The *picaresque* servant, on the other hand, jumps "vertically" as well (cf. Babcock 1978, 98), attaching himself to a wide

[4]Whether Nashe had even read Rowland's translation of the Spanish novel (earliest extant edition, 1586)—the only recognized picaresque novel in existence at the time—is a matter of some controversy. Nashe scholars (e.g., McKerrow 1910, 5:23; Latham 1948, 86) tend to assume that he had not, but some historians of generic influence (e.g. Lovatelli 1984, 112) are inclined to differ, or at least defer. Werner von Koppenfels (1976, 361 n. 1) points out that in the third of his *Foure Letters* Harvey considers *Pierce Penilesse* an attempt "to reuiue the pittifull historie of Don Lazarello de Thoemes" (sic; G. Harvey 1592, E4/1:206/56), but not even the quivering-antennaed von Koppenfels can detect any allusions to the work in Nashe's own texts.

range of masters, so as to move along with them through radically discontinuous environments. Jack has only a single determinate master in the narrative, the courtly poet Surrey, but this does not stop his own movements from being more vertically "picaresque" than either his paginal or his liveried servitude would lead one to expect. So if our page somehow *is* a picaro, then in any case that page, as Ortega y Gasset says of Baroja's picaresque vagabond, "is not a loose leaf [*una hoja inerte*: cf. Crewe's "lying page"] carried hither and yon," but rather his wandering is a matter of "disposition [*genialidad*]" (Ortega y Gasset 1910, 125).[5] In Jack Wilton's case, however, this *Flugblatt* dis-position, which Ortega y Gasset seems to see as essentially auto-motive, may actually (as Bowers claims, though not in so many weirds [*OED, sb.*[5b]]) be the uncertain maneuvering of a supercharged vehicle by an imported and unstable tenor not always able to decipher all the signs along the way. And by this

---

[5]Cf. Nashe's dedicatory epistle to Southampton: "This handfull of leaues I offer to your view, to the leaues on trees I compare, which as they cannot grow of themselues except they haue some branches or boughes to cleaue too, & with whose iuice and sap they be euermore recreated & nourisht; so except these vnpolisht leaues of mine haue some braunch of Nobilitie whereon to depend and cleaue, and with the vigorous nutriment of whose authorized commendation they may be continually fosterd and refresht, neuer wil they grow to the worlds good liking, but forthwith fade and die on the first houre of their birth" (Nashe 1594a, A2ᵛ/2:202). The "leaves" which depend upon the aristocratic sap for succour will be briskly replaced by an unanchored page skimmed along from point to point.

Marcelino C. Peñuelas made the point differently but interestingly in 1954 when he attempted to distinguish Nashe's page from Lázaro's picaro by dealing with their relative degrees of *volition*: Lázaro "is a victim of his circumstances [*del medio*] with no direction of his own; [Jack] knows where he is going, and why" (445). The distinctions between a realistic, upwardly mobile but personally immutable Lázaro's trying to survive and a labile, *habile* Jack-of-all-sides apparently going his own way are well catalogued by Stefania Albertini. Yet she makes the crucial point that Jack is actually what *Nashe* makes of him:

> When his creator is trying in every way to outdo the jestbook writers, Jack is a brash clown; when he means to compete with the chronicle-writers, Jack becomes the ablest of chroniclers; when he wishes to attack Petrarchianism, Jack turns into an estimable literary critic, an admirable parodist, and so forth, until Nashe has exhausted the multifarious semblances assumed by him in the guise of his hero. (Albertini 1985, 45)

As we can already see from these few readings, then, while Jack may thus not be a mere victim of circumstance, as Lázaro seems to be, he can still perhaps in many senses be considered a *víctima del* medio.

we are brought to the outskirts of Metaphoricity, which, as Peter Lubin reminds us in his dress-up-like-Dad article on Nabokov (Lubin 1970, 188), is just past the turnoff to Synecdoche on the Allegory bypass.

The opening move of the 1948 article by A.K. Croston, from halfway across town, is to aver that "the chief characteristic of Nashe's prose is its alertness to the possibilities of metaphor" (1948, 90). For Croston, what sets the metaphorical imagery in *The Vnfortunate Traueller* apart is the disorienting celerity of its juxtaposition: "Generalizing, we may say that Nashe's images are not elaborated: the mind is passed on from one to the next with an almost bewildering rapidity" (96). This sense of speed is partly conveyed by "far-fetched" yet telegraphic imagery, but it also has something to do with the fact that Nashe's prose, rather than con- centrating on the delivery of the narrative freight via express metaphor, "is far more concerned with the interplay between 'tenor' and 'vehicle' placing the stress, where over-balancing takes place, on the 'vehicle'" (91). This is evidently a performance vehicle, and it handles very prettily under such pressure: "the performance aims at giving the reader the sense of immediate physical action" (90-91).

The freewheeling drive of Nashe's metaphorical transitions is boosted by what Croston considers to be the "simple device" of repetition (93). He quotes: "Sathan could neuer haue *supplanted* vs so as hee did. I may saie to you, he *planted* in vs the first Italionate wit that we had" (Nashe 1594d, F2/2:260, emphasis added). Croston claims that this rapid iteration of cognates and homonyms "develops into a punning which in Nashe is generally a method for bringing into prominence the physical reference" (Croston 1948, 93). In such a movement, however, the *effect* is perhaps as often of the abstract term leaving behind the physical landmark. Indeed, these "repetitions" most often suggest the shifting of semiotic gears in Nashe's souped-up version of what Puttenham called "*Antanaclasis*, or the Rebounde" and defined, in tennis court terms that can just be squeezed into an updated image of polysemic carpooling, as the commuting in "one word written all alike but carrying diuers sences" (Puttenham 1589, 207).

Some typical instances can be gone over if we drop back a couple of pages from Croston's example to where Jack and his master, the Earl of Surrey have been impersonating one another and have just foiled the conspiracy of Tabitha the Temptress to do away with Jack-as-Surrey. To keep them from reporting her plot to the authorities, the devious Tabitha pays them off, but with counterfeit coins: "Amongst the grosse summe of my briberie, I silly milkesop mistrusting no deceit, vnder an angell of light tooke what shee gaue me, nere turnd it ouer, for which (O falsehood in faire shewe) my master & I had lyke to haue bin turnd ouer" (Nashe

1594d, F1ᵛ/2:258). Jack's counterfeiting of the noble has no sooner been transferred to a numismatic vehicle than it rubs off onto the proposed next recipient, the prostitute on whose services Jack plans to spend his ill-gotten pelf: "There was a delicate wench named *Flauia Aemilia* lodging in saint Markes street at a goldsmiths, which I would faine haue had to the grand test, to trie whether she were cunning in Alcumie or no. Aie me, she was but a counterfet slip, for she not onely gaue me the slip, but had welnigh made me a slipstring" (F1ᵛ/2:258). The counterfeit slug will thus be seen in passing to act as a kind of subway token connecting the misrepresentations of Jack counterfeiting Surrey, Surrey counterfeiting Jack (or rather "Brunquell" as he calls himself), Tabitha counterfeiting the contrite would-be "angel" (like a "noble," this too of course was a coin), and finally the prostitute who as cunning alchemist is supposed to transform cold cash into hot erotic chemistry, counterfeiting passion, but who turns out not to be a "genuine hypocrite."[6] The metaphoric "rebounds" here seem at first to represent double-clutching downshifts as Jack's momentum is momentarily stalled by death-dealing double-entendres.[7] But ultimately the "turning over" (one hears the engine rev;

---

[6]Although a paronomastic transaction involving "change" can be imagined, the use of the coin as a metaphor for metaphor does not perhaps have the prevalence sometimes claimed for it, and I do not know what stock quotations Derrida is speculating upon when he speaks (*Verzeihung!*) of the "noteworthy currency" with which such "paradigms have been doled out in all quarters" (Derrida 1971, 6, translation mollified). In the most widely circulated, and indeed worn out and usured quotation, Nietzsche does not refer to metaphors as coins, but rather to *truths* as "metaphors that are used up and bereft of sensual force [*sinnlich kraftlos*], coins that have lost their stamp [*Bild*] and now matter only as metal, no longer as coins" (Nietzsche 1873, 374-75). There *is* a long tradition of *money* being used as a metaphor for *words*, including Bacon's claim that "wordes, are the tokens currant and accepted for conceits, as Moneys are for values and that it is fit men be not ignorant, that Moneys may bee of another kind, than gold and siluer" (Bacon 1605, Pp4) and the remark of Hobbes (possibly recalling the passage from Bacon and recalled by Nietzsche) that "words are wise mens counters, they do but reckon with them: but they are the mony of fooles, that value them by the authority of an *Aristotle*, a *Cicero*, or a *Thomas*, or any other Doctor whatsoeuer, if but a man" (Hobbes 1651, 106).

[7]Indeed, though it could in a sense be seen as rhetoric's way of telling you to slow down, in serving the purposes of postponement or wheelspinning, the figure seems ultimately to draw out the discourse or even trundle it along, deferring the moment of meaning's mortality by simply keeping it moving. It is interesting to recall in this connection the example through which Quintilian (9.3.68) initially introduces the antanaclasis: "Cum Proculeius quereretur de filio, quod is mortem suam *exspectaret*, et ille dixisset, *se vero non exspectare: Immo*, inquit, *rogo expectes.*

or was that just the page once more rustling?) which "welnigh" awaited
Jack and Surrey is overturned; and McKerrow reminds us that, if a "slipstring" in the headlong hurl here appears to connote the noose, it "seems
actually to have meant a truant—one that gets away from control"
(McKerrow 1908, 4:277).[8] Indeed, that tip of the nib making a trip of
three slips illustrates well that the ugly head of dead metaphor at the rear
of those consecutive sentences may always have been a dummy left in
place of the fargone fugitive, putting the backfiring rebounds "under
erasure" (burning rubber, i.e.). The semic drive is in the end unbraked by
the antanaclatic détours: "the words," as the Rev. Grosart unexpectedly
punned, "run on wheels, and the wheels burn in their course" (qtd in
Kinney 1986, 355).

While the rebounds do ring changes on metaphors (or catachreses)
it should be clear that the interchanges themselves do not move one
along to the end of the metaphoric line (literal meaning or narrative
closure) any faster. What they provide rather is a *feeling* of movement and
even of acceleration, a sense of whipping across context lines before they
can be apprehended. And even when this sense of speed is diminished
there is always in the trusty old Nashe rambler the comforting awareness
of jostling over the concrete, passing sign after sign without ever turning
off. The freeways that make this kind of drive possible, like the antanaclatic cloverleaves in which Croston briefly loses himself, do not follow
the old roads of metaphoric elaboration, but are built up at the level of
the signifier. The narrative rides over what Puttenham called "auricular"
figures—"*Omoioteleton,* or the Like loose" (consonance), "*Parimion,* or the
Figure of the like Letter" (alliteration)—which facilitate the stretch of
discourse ahead even as they keep it rolling along through the run-on
sentences.[9]

[When Proculeius accused his son of *waiting* for his death, and the son said that
he was not waiting for it: well then, the father replied, *please do wait for it.*]"

[8]McKerrow cites Chettle's *Kind-hartes Dreame* and Lyly's *Mother Bombie,* but the
most elegant of illustrative examples would surely have been Gascoigne's
Supposes, a play whose plot may in part have suggested the master-servant
switcheroo, where in act 3, scene 1 a character complains of a lackey: "if he spie
a slipstring by the waye such another as himself, a Page, a Lackie or a dwarfe, the
devill of hell cannot holde him in chaynes, but he will be doing with him"
(Gascoigne 1575, 210). Here the slipstring is exemplified by the page and the
lackey (Jack's two servile roles) and the dwarf. "Bruquell," a dwarf and
paranymph in the 1595 *Celestina* and the 1589 *Palmendos,* is apparently the
inspiration for Surrey's "Brunquell."

[9]In choosing the motorcar as my own vehicle for Nashean troping I am of
course endeavoring to drive home that auto-motive or internal-combustion aspect

which allows it to serve as the very engine of narrative motivity. Movement might be less a by-product of far-fetched resemblances than of a concatenated series of thumbed "lifts," so that the situation would be similar to that in Proust where Genette argues that "metaphor is what recaptures lost time, but metonymy is what reanimates it and gets it moving along again" (Genette 1972, 63). It may be, as I am trying to suggest, by speeding over the *concrete* that Nashe re-topicalizes a figurativeness which has always seemed to be in danger of slipping its anchor and drifting out over the sail-veiled sea of semiosis (*"mare velivolum"* [*Aeneid* 1.224]; cf. Migliorini on "reciprocal metaphors" [1957, 23]). Umberto Eco, for example, remarks that "the chronicle of metaphor is a chronicle of a series of variations on a few tautologies" some of which, "however, constitute an 'epistemic break,' allowing the concepts to drift toward new territories" (1984, 88). One of the veiled (*voiles*: sails and veils) metaphorico-synecdochic *exempla* by which Aristotle (*Poetics*, 1457b) introduces the topic of metaphor is the Homeric "my ship stands over there [νηῦς δέ μοι ἥδ᾽ ἕστηκεν]" (*Odyssey* 1.185; 24.308), for to lie at anchor is a kind of standing. (Never mind that in neither instance of imposture does a ship actually stand or lie over there at all.) This driftiness of the ship-metaphor materializes the difficulty of mapping a metaphorics onto any topics, or for that matter, as Greimas might put it, of freezing into polar binaries the free-floating figure amid the titanic and equally unanchored "isotopies."

The substantiality of language itself, however, seems to give the ground to a necessarily *metonymic* relationship between topicality and metaphoricity, as does the textual extensivity of both generic commonplaces and literal *éspacement*. Thus, before embarking on his discussion of nautical metaphors (text as ship), E.R. Curtius, who had earlier sailed breezily enough into his discussion of topics with the potentially anxiety producing *"dubiam trepidus quo dirigo proram?* [toward what am I fearfully turning my uncertain craft?]" (Curtius 1953, 89), here must first stake out the territory now to be appropriated by but kept alien from his topics in suggesting collusively that "we place over against [*zur Seite*] our historical topics, an historical metaphorics" (138; *"zur Seite"* [which—why not?—could also mean "on the page"] manages to suggest at once putting the metaphorics "next to" the topics and keeping it "apart" from it and "by the way"): the two chapters are in fact separated by a short topical breakdown: "Goddess Natura" and sodomy.

Here I am tinkering with the idea that Nashe, like Genette in de Man's reading of *"Métonymie chez Proust,"* but in a different sense, would "stress the 'solidarity of the text' despite the perilous shuttling between metaphor and metonymy" (de Man 1979a, 72; cf. Genette 1972, 60; actually he does not have this exact phrase here, but *"solidité indestructible de l'écriture"* and a little further on *"cohésion «nécessaire» du* texte"). In other words, the possibility that the literal, or littoral, opposition between a metaphoricity settled on the solid ground of (iso)topicality as against topicality as itself an (unmappably oceanic) metaphorics would be knocked down, the pair of them, (in an unmindful vehicular manslaughter like the famous scene in *Reefer Madness*) by a joyriding Nashe, after first

But "auricular" figures for Puttenham seem to correspond to those of *"Enargia"* (vividness), though he significantly shifts the sense from visual lustre to phonic gloss (cf. Puttenham 1589, 143), while *"Metaphora, or the Figure of transporte"* (178) is quite properly classed with those that are "sententious," and thus also apparently make use of *"Energia* of *ergon,* because it wrought with a strong and vertuous operation" (143), and are concerned with sense in the sense of meaning and not only sense in the sense of the senses. Though it is the pervasive symbol of figurative transport, it is not immediately clear in what way metaphor *per se* is the overriding trope of *The Vnfortunate Traueller.* "Indeed," insists Croston, "it is no exaggeration to assert that the metaphorical possibilities of language form the essential subject matter of the prose" (1948, 90). To appreciate the full force and lustre of this assertion it is perhaps necessary to move a little closer to home. It wasn't so far back that Patricia Parker took Paul de Man's remark that discussions of mastering the "Rappaccini's garden" of figurative abstractions can begin to sound "like the plot of a Gothic novel" (de Man 1979b, 21) several steps further by suggesting a whole range of alternative (and more Elizabethan) plots "with the metaphorical 'alien' as changeling, picaro, or usurper" (Parker 1987, 38).

Parker's discussion of metaphor began appropriately enough with a rundown of the shifting but consistent critical commonplaces (from Aristotle, Cicero and Quintilian to the present) whereby metaphor is seen to involve an interchange of *property* (or *propriety)* or *position.* In the dramatic interest of "plotting" metaphorical displacements and appropriations, theorists have introduced the vying figures of proper and figurative meaning and the master/slave confrontation of tenor and vehicle. The literal/figurative pair is frequently discussed in terms more fitting to the characterization of fraternal rivalries (legitimate and bastard pretenders or true son and changeling), while the tenor/vehicle dynamic suggests a scheme in which the vehicle as *"Gastarbeiter,"* interloper, or vagabond might be identified with the shifty and unrespectable picaro-figure.[10]

The picaresque plot of metaphor is left unarticulated by Parker, and is presumably a less intriguing one than those involving rival claimants

---

having rendered both metaphoricity and topicality unfalteringly *pedestrian,* and then *run over* them for real with an auricular steamroller that would pave the way for postrealism.

[10]One regrets the absence of the quasi-oedipal *Hamlet* plot, where the metaphor, neurotic but irresistible, would be subjected to an usurpatious interloper at the literal level. We shall see as the plot thickens that it is as common for a number of proper senses to displace one another in the relationship to the metaphor as vice-versa.

(the picaro is essentially a prose personage, while the antagonistic brothers are as common in historical drama or revenge tragedy as in the romance). Parker does not even bother to spell out the role which literal meaning or tenor would play opposite the picaresque figurative meaning or vehicle, but the choice seems plain: literal meanings would be embodied in the series of masters "served" by the picaresque metaphor. The picaresque, with its jestbook glibness and prosy realism, might thus initially appear to be the least agonistic of the plots of metaphor mentioned by Parker: the picaro rarely overthrows his master or takes his specific place but at most, like Lazarillo, works his way up to a position of "property" and "propriety" through opportunistic maneuvers, or even mere lucky breaks.

The apparently anodyne variation on this plot in *The Vnfortunate Traueller* would seem then to call into question either its status as real picaresque or else the dramatic potential of the picaresque plot of metaphor. For the episode in Nashe's novel where there is a changing of places is the one already glanced at where the exchange seems quite properly enacted for the benefit of the master, Surrey, although the nature of this benefit is in fact rather equivocal: "By the waie as we went, my master and I agreed to change names. It was concluded betwixte vs, that I should be the Earle of Surrie, and he my man, onely because in his owne person, which hee woulde not haue reproched, hee meant to take more liberty of behauior: as for my cariage, he knew hee was to tuene it at a key, either high or low, as he list" (Nashe 1594d, E3^v/2:253). Presumably this means that Surrey wants to enjoy the freedom of action and speech that is denied him as a proper and propertied master, but his eventual foursquare idealism at every turn might lead one to interpret the horny logic in another direction: perhaps he wants Jack to *represent him* as livelier than he actually is. In any case, his motives would seem to be closer to those of Erostrato in Gascoigne's *Supposes* than to the uniformly highflown above e-la intentions of Lucentio in *The Taming of the Shrew*. Either Surrey really does plan to improvise an unfigured baseness as "Brunquell" or he will orchestrate from behind the scenes a more coloratura earl as performed by Jack. Either way, the exchange, as it is not in Shakespeare, is reciprocal. If the subservient "vehicle" is licensed to take on the "cariage" of the pretty little Surrey with the fringe on the top, the narrow-ranged "tenor" supposedly gets to tackle the rambling part of the base figure here. And there is assuredly little of the tragic felony of the overreacher or the runaway violence of the Henriads or the futile foul play of the revenge tragedy in the displacement.

Dramatic interest *is* perhaps lent to the metaphorical plot in *The Vnfortunate Traueller* by the division of the role-changing act into three scenes which together can be read as an allegory of metaphoricity as a hermeneutic *comedy of errors:* the episode in which Jack and Surrey are entertained in Venice by Petro de Campo Frego and Tabitha the Temptress, the episode in which they are thrown into prison and meet Diamante, and the episode in which, having through Diamante's "provokement" parted from his master but still retaining his false identity, Jack is suddenly reunited with the real earl in Florence.

Scene one: come to Italy on a pilgrimage to the homeland of Surrey's Platonic paramour, Geraldine, the travellers find themselves in Venice where, "hauing scarce lookt about vs, a precious supernaturall pandor apparelled in all points like a gentleman, & hauing halfe a dosen seueral languages in his purse, entertained vs in our owne tongue very para-phrastically" (E4^v/2:255). Petro de Campo Frego, as this procurer is called, convinces them to be his guests and quickly conducts them onto his own territory: "The place whether he brought vs was a pernicious curtizãs house named *Tabitha* the Temptresses, a wench that could set as ciuill a face on it as chastities first martyr *Lucrecia*" (Ibid.). Since they are "loaded," both master and man are at first "vsed like Emperours," but soon, unaware of the previous exchange of identities, Petro and Tabitha attempt to conspire with the supposed servant "Brunquell" (Surrey) to do away with his "master" so that they can seize his whole fortune to themselves. "Brunquell" pretends to go along with the scheme, but at the last moment feigns a loss of nerve ("for he could counterfeit most daintily" [F1/2:257]) and betrays the conspiracy.

The plot might serve as something of a cautionary tale for revisionist exegetes who would enlist the less respectable aspects of what is apparently the vehicle in their attempts to dispose of what seems a tiresomely highborn tenor. Petro and Tabitha's "subornation" (Ibid.) of Surrey-as-Brunquell fails because they cannot see that Jack-as-Surrey is in fact already the former's "suborned Lorde and master" (E3^v/2:254). The proper meaning has thus protected its *propr(i)été* (O to be in Paris now that Jack and Surrey are in Venice!) from "misprision" by dis-simulating in advance its place in the tenor/vehicle dynamic.

The connivance of Petro and Tabitha fails, but in the buying-off countertransfer of fake crowns to Jack (see above) both tenor and vehicle are nonetheless brought into jeopardy. Having capitalized on the abortive plot, Jack decides to try his false profits on the touchstone of Flavia Aemilia (who happens to dwell at a goldsmith's), but she proves a most pseudo "doxy" and the confederate of Tabitha, and *she* exposes *him* as a counterfeiter. Metaphorically, money here would, in good humanist fashion, represent rhetorical resources, "words as what a character in *Great Expectations* calls 'portable property'" (Parker 1987, 36), a reading to which credence is improbably but happily lent by Lorna Hutson when she confirms that "for the pander, Petro de Campo Frego, linguistic mastery becomes portable property; he carries 'halfe a dosen seueral languages in his purse'" (Hutson 1989, 220). Petro can figure the rhetorically resourceful eisegete, Tabitha his collaborator or editor, her house the "reading" in which the metaphorical duo are temporarily lodged, and the prostitute the meretricious theory which comes to the aid of the critics in their attempt to overthrow the authority of the traditional tenor. The counterfeit coins would thus represent the *falseness* of rhetorical resourcefulness, but they would represent it as in itself a potential agency of metaphorical subversion. The contrived exposure is a fraud, indeed more of a fraud than the perpetrators realize, since the true subordination remains reversed as the pair are interned: "To prison was I sent as principal, and my master as accessarie, nor was it to a prison neither, but to the master of the mintes house" (Nashe 1594d, F1^v/2:258). But once they are in the hands of the authorities, some curious countrymen who have heard that an English earl has been "apprehended" point out the true hierarchy: "at the first glance they knew the seruant of my secrecies to be the Earle of Surrie, and I (not worthy to be named I) an outcast of his cuppe or pantofles" (F1^v/2:259). The master of the mint, scenting a conspiracy, immediately commits them to "a straighter ward" (F2/2:259). Thus the connivance of Petro and Tabitha, merely by focussing the attention of the authorities on the duo, leads to the discovery of the "truth."

Scene two: with Jack and Surrey now under lock and key, Petro de Campo Frego is ironically called upon to be their interpreter and proceeds "most clarkly" to misrepresent them: "He interpreted to vs with a pestilence, for wheras we stood obstinatly vpon it, we were wrongfully deteined, and that it was naught but a malicious practise of sinfull *Tabitha* our late hostes, he, by a fine cunny-catching corrupt translation, made vs plainly to confesse, and crie *Miserere*, ere we had need of our neckeverse" (Ibid.). It is here, more or less, that Jack accuses Petro before the reader of having "supplanted" them and "planted" in them "the first Italionate wit" that they had (F2/2:260). Responsibility for all the foregoing "counterfeiting" is thus displaced onto the hermeneutic moment of the perfidious interpreter who has usurped their discursive function with that neapolitic erudition that Sidney called "counterfeit lerning" of the Italians (Sidney 1912, 3:127).

While they "lay close and tooke phisick in this castle of contemplation," a "magnificos wife of good calling" was thrown in with them, supposed to be unfaithful through the false reports of a vengeful courtier who had been unsuccessful in his attempts to borrow from "her doting husband" (Nashe 1594d, F2/2:260). But for Jack, connubial fidelity is at first an all too forward facet of this Diamante, as she is called, a depressing syndrome he retails in a metaphorical mine of moneys and metals:

> It is almost impossible that any woman should be excellently wittie, and not make the vtmost pennie of her beautie. This age and this countrie of ours admits of some miraculous exceptions, but former times are my constant informers. Those that haue quicke motions of wit haue quicke motions in euery thing; yron onely needs many strokes, only yron wits are not wonne without a long siege of intreatie. Gold easily bends, the most ingenious minds are easiest mooued, *Ingenium nobis molle Thalia dedit*, sayth *Psapho* to *Phao*. (F2ᵛ/2:261)

According to Jack, it would seem, the Golden Age of fast women has in general given place to an irony era of inflexibility. But as it turns out, this particular "magnificos wife" simply hasn't yet been "molded and fashioned as it ought" (F2ᵛ/2:261-62). Diamante's obdurate name is finally belied, for she proves to have "mettall inough in her" for Jack to bend her to the inclinations of the "supple soul" (*ingenium molle)* that the muse of comedy has made him. His master Surrey is "too vertuous" to attempt this physical manipulation of the inmate, but he does practise a species of *méconnaissance* or warping "suppose" upon her, whereby "he would imagine her in a melancholy humor to bee his *Geraldine*," and bend and bow *himself* as would befit his ideal: "from this his intranced mistaking extasie could no man remoue him. Who loueth resolutely, wil include euery thing vnder the name of his loue" (F3/2:262).

Metaphorically speaking, the relationship between Jack, Surrey and Diamante is extraordinarily complex, although the literal action is uncomplicated enough: "My master beate the bush and kepte a coyle and a pratling, but I caught the birde, simplicitie and plainnesse shall carrie it away in another world" (F3ᵛ/2:263). In this allegorical world of metaphorical plots, however, Diamante must perhaps first be seen as pairing with Jack on a different axis from that whereon Jack is paired with Surrey. At the same time, an initial homology can be set up on the basis of heterosexual coupling between Jack and Diamante and Surrey and Geraldine. We could plot this development in a number of metaphorical ways, but I think the following foursquare diagram is appropriate enough:

	Literal Meaning	Figure	
Figure	SURREY	JACK	Signifier
Literal Meaning	GERALDINE	DIAMANTE	Signified
	Tenor	Vehicle	

The relationship that develops during interment would thus plot some of the intrigues that can occur in the interpretation of metaphorical *ménages à trois*, triangles of desire, or oedipal threesomes. Diamante figures the initially suspicious physical "property" of a third party (her husband), becoming attached in close keeping to the vehicle as part of its sememic ensemble of signifieds. Geraldine figures the established abstract signified of the sublime tenor, for which the signified of the vehicle must be mistaken. But precisely through its abstractness ("as I perswade my self he was more in loue with his own curious forming fancie than her face" [F3/2:263]), this signified, the supposed pretext for the trip, remains absent from the scene of examination. Instead, emphasis is transferred from the more stable and idealistic aspects of the present signified of the vehicle (upright fidelity) to its more fickle and sensual side (horizontal slipperiness). The vehicular page's tangible advantage over his tenorial master here leads in a way into the final scene of the tenor's "subord-ination" to the vehicle.

Scene three: through the good graces of none other than Pietro Aretino, Jack and Surrey are in the end explicated (*explicare:* to disentangle, to explain, to set free) and examination is turned upon Tabitha the Temptress, who under his scrutiny reveals her falsifications; she and Petro are summarily executed. But the "inlargement" (F3^v/2:264) of tenor and vehicle is not without a narrative dilation, including a lengthy peroration on Aretino, whose terminal image (a toad swelling with venom) seems to give the metaphorical ground to the next expanse of plot: "*Diamante Castaldos* ye magnificos wife, after my enlargement proued to be with child" (F4^v/2:266). Her husband (her former signifier) meanwhile has wasted away (either through famine or jealousy) and with Aretino's help she is left with his estate. As the signified of the vehicle, Diamante can bring to Jack the semic wealth that belonged to her former signifier/husband, and now seems to be pregnant with the new meaning that she and her present signifier have engendered together in close quarters. But this is significantly a gravidity which is adroitly forgotten (miscarriage?) in the course of the ensuing episodes, so that the noseyparker is left with the suspicion that it was a ruse designed to get them on the move (cf. Hibbard 1962, 163). Jack's habitual dissimulation of position is now abetted by the newly propertied Diamante: "Being out, and fully possest of her husbands goods, she inuested me in the state of a monarch" (Nashe 1594d, F4ᵛ/2:267). She lades Jack with the "properties" that belonged to the late husband, and at her provocation Jack departs from his master without leave and once more assumes his position: "Through all the cities past I by no other name but the yong Earle of Surry; my pomp, my apparel, traine, and expence, was nothing inferior to his, my looks were as loftie, my wordes as magnificall" (Ibid.). They make their way to Florence; but Surrey, amazed that Jack would think "to separate the shadow from the bodie" (G1/2:267), overtakes them almost immediately, and Jack must bow low for survival: "My soule which was made to soare vpward, now sought for passage downward" (Ibid.). His shortlived ascendancy comes peacefully to an end, however, as he assures an indulgent master that the stunt has been effected only so that Jack could expend the wealth with which Diamante has endowed him under the aegis of the earl: "some large summes of monie this my sweet mistres *Diamante* hath made me master of, which I knew not how better to imploy for the honor of my country, than by spending it munificently vnder your name. No English-man would I haue renowmed for bountie, magnificence, and curtesie but you, vnder your colours all my meritorious workes I was desirous to shroud" (G1/2:268). Thus Jack argues that he has been operating for the greater amplification of Surrey: "if the greatest men went not more sumptuous, how more great than greatest was he that could cõmand one going so sumptuous" (G1ᵛ/2:269). Since such stratagems may indeed have been part of the reason that Surrey employed Jack in the ruse in the first place, and since Jack has apparently in fact "inhanced his obscured reputation" (Ibid.), Surrey is content, only insisting that Jack not drag his "curtizan" (the low material baggage connotively stowed in the vehicle) along with him. Jack argues that she is his "treasurie" and his "countenance and supporter," and resigns his earldom rather "than parte with such a specyall benefactor," insisting, however: "your seruant am I, as I was at the beginning and so wil I perseuer to my liues ending" (Ibid.).

Rather than give up the more substantial "properties" which Diamante represents and possesses, Jack-as-vehicle gives up the possibility of further being mistaken for the privileged tenor, and the narrative promptly shifts focalization back to Surrey and his pilgrimage to the home of the ineffable Geraldine, leaving Jack's Diamante temporarily by the way, never to be delivered of the meaning with which she had briefly become pregnant. With her conveniently absented from the diegesis, the conventional master/servant routine returns: "Wee supt, we got to bed, rose in the morning, on my master I waited, & the first thing he did after he was vp, he went and visited the house where his *Geraldine* was borne" (G1ᵛ/2:270-71). Introducing Surrey and Jack into this context allows the tenor an opportunity to counter the base vehicle's bending of Diamante to his will with a sublime rarification of Geraldine—"the soule of heauen, sole daughter and heir to *primus motor*"; and Jack does his best to represent "[t]he alcumie of his eloquence," which "out of the incomprehensible drossie matter of cloudes and aire, distilled no more quintessence than would make his *Geraldine* compleat faire" (G2/2:270). Clouds and air, the least "comprehensible"—or tangible—of materials are still too "drossie" with base matter to convey the transcendental signified. But Surrey's sonnet, of neoplatonic necessity, moves through concretizing images that can be mistaken for bodily movements—indeed, as with "The towre where Ioue raind downe himselfe in golde" or "prostrate as holy ground Ile worship thee," even those of what Bakhtin's translator called "the material bodily lower stratum"—and can only be supplemented by the reinscription of "body-wanting mots" from Ovid, words which make every effort to *lack* corporeal substance, but which can always still be read as the expressions of *desire for* the body which they literally constitute (G2/2:271). The absent living body of Diamante, in its subjection to the attempted inscription of the transcendental signified, is doubly transfigured, first to inanimacy, then to ethereality: "Diamonds thought thẽselues *Dii mundi*, if they might but carue her name on the naked glasse" (Ibid.). The nakedness of the glass of the signified mirrors the multi-faceted diamond of another signified here functioning as a signifier in its turn in the final obstructed coupling of Diamante and Geraldine, both absent, the glass taking its apparent body from the diamond and simultaneously metamorphosing it into an extramundane *dea mundi* by reflecting its own transparency. A refulgent smaragdine Geraldine could only be figured through the solid inscription of the adamantine Diamante, but Surrey has insured that the clarity of his beloved's absence will not be impaired by the impedimental presence of Jack's "baggage" in her enshrined birth-chamber.

We could no doubt unpack these metaphors a little further here, if we had come to this room for more than a quickie.[11] What is important

___

[11]This preposterously reductive phallocratic distribution of the *actants* not into a semi-idiotic rectangle but into more of a soft-ball diamond in which the tenor can never come into home because its signified cannot get to first base (the signified of the vehicle) since she is "struck out" at the plate, would not necessarily play more smoothly with the assumption of a threesome that deconstructed a patriarchal schema so that the ladies were the signifiers more interested

in terms of the picaresque plot of metaphor, I think, is the essentially un-Shakespearean close of the comedy: master and servant resume their conventional roles, and the servant even winds up with a frisky rich widow, but Orlando, so to speak, is still in the woods, with neither "bagge and baggage" nor "scrip and scrippage" he can call "his own." The servant or vehicle carries away the "goods," so that in the end it may seem that the master really would have more to gain by the exchange of positions. Thus, rather than overthrowing the privileged tenor through violence or insubordination, the vehicle does so symbolically, by acting as a foil, setting off the immaterialness of the tenor it quite "faithfully" serves. In other words, the plot of metaphor in *The Vnfortunate Traueller* would operate through an assumed *parity* of tenor and vehicle which is a *parody* inasmuch as the class difference actually leaves the *tenor* at a

in connecting up with one another than in the staying on top of fatuously phallogocentric signifieds. One can imagine the fantastically convoluted and evaginated plot of metaphor that could be traced in the New *Arcadia* for instance, and there could even be some politically more correct content wrung out of the so-called feminist inversion of *Euphues* to be detected by some in Greene's *Mamilia* (cf. Jordan 1915, 15-16, quoted and discussed in Kinney 1986, 184). Something at least potentially more satirical of phallogocentric "agenders" could have been rigged up by Nashe if he had been less inclined to the dramatic. If he had "sung *George Gascoignes* Counter-tenor" (i.e., been incarcerated; cf. Nashe 1592c, I1/1:310), with the falsetto for his little *huis clos* having been chosen not from the *Supposes* but from *The Adventures of Master F. I.*, the triple play might have caught out the noble tenor as a wimpy and valetudinarian insignificato. But of course, this plot too, like that of *Master F. I.* itself, would be easily recuperable to a misogynistic reading in which the duplicity and slipperiness of the tenorial signifier (Elinor) rendered it unworthy of the singleminded if now and then upright signified (F.I.). Indeed, Harvey, annotating the already post-moralized reworking of *Master F. I.* that appeared in Gascoigne's *Posies* (1575), drew precisely the lesson from it that women have no use for men "who cannot bestead them" and suggested well that their roles in the bedroom scenes need not be so different from that in the birthchamber scene in Nashe, referring to them, indeed (inspired by *The Steele Glas*) precisely as complementary *specula*: "the one, a glas of brittle Bewtie; the other a Mirrour of during Honour," and only possibly suggesting a tenor-vehicle reversal in referring to the former, presumably (Elinor-Leonore, who would be the tenor in the plot not plotted here), as "a false Diamant" (Moore Smith, ed. 1913, 167). Given the sexist, and indeed heterosexist, assumptions of all the gory allegories of metaphor so far explored (Geraldine and Diamante may have been made to engage in a little bit of titillating twin fun, but we have not paused to wonder what the early risers Jack and Surrey did when they climbed back into their old routine), it would hardly be politic to pretend that all of this is meant tongue in cheek.

"material" disadvantage, textually. Put the other way round, in the looking-glass confrontation of literal and figural properties, "parody," to pun outrageously on the theorem which makes Martin Gardner's *Ambidextrous Universe* possible, "is *not* conserved."

But the insuperable difference of rank might seem *here* to have been exaggerated for picaresque effect. The picaro is typically of the lowest order, often an orphan. But Jack Wilton reminds us more than once that he is "a Gentleman at least" (A3/2:209), which, despite the jocular tone, is not, I think, meant to be sarcastic. The term "gentleman" denoted definite class affiliations of not inconsiderable status, and when Nashe signed himself "*Th. Nashe*, Gentleman" (or, as he seems to claim, was thus signed by his publisher; cf. Nashe 1592c, I2-I2ᵛ/1:311-12) he was mocked for the presumption both by Harvey and by Richard Lichfield, the demon-barber author of the sickly tonsorial *Trimming of Thomas Nashe, Gentleman* (1597). Jack's insistence on his gentle nature suggests that his relationship with Surrey is meant wistfully to hark back to that Golden Age of reciprocal rapport described by the author of *A Health to the Gentlemanly Profession of Seruingmen* (1598), when, just as Adam had needed an Eve, "Gentlemen and States considering their calling, thought it very meete and necessarie to haue a helpe, to further them in euery of their actions," and "this helpe or Seruaunt should be made of their owne mettall" so that "the Gentleman receaued euen a Gentleman vnto his seruice, and therefore did limit him no other labour than belonged him selfe" (I. M. 1598, C1-C1v).[12]

The "mettall" of which both metaphorical master and servant are ostensibly made is language, and one would never want to deny anyone the "intellectual pleasure in the perception of unexpected similiarities between tenor and vehicle" (Larson 1975, 20); but as metaphors are recast, this metal does become stamped with heads and tails. (Even the bicephalous coin with which the Jack/Surrey switch would beguile us is after all still marked as a noble on one side, a groat on the other.) Their substantial linguistic parity, however, allows for the flipping of that coin

---

[12]The "commensal" nature of this relationship is, incidentally, brought out in part by an allusion to a ballad, "*It is merrie in Haul, when Beardes wagges al*" in which mention is made of "Beardlesse Brian, and long toothed Tom, whose teeth be longer then his beard" (C1v). This may in fact be a glance at Nashe, whose want of beard and whose gagtooth are alluded to in several texts. I. M.'s pamphlet, which shows the influence of Nashe, especially echoing *Pierce Pennilesse*, and of Greene's somewise proto-Nashean *Quip for an Vpstart Courtier* (1592), was brought out by William White the year before he surreptitiously published the herring-infested, possibly Nashe-prescribed *Pil to Purge Melancholie* (?1599).

and the par or chiasmal crossover whereby the master is a servant and
the servant is a master. Ideally, this would constitute what Bruno
Migliorini once called a "reciprocal metaphor" (Migliorini 1957, 23ff), but
in fact it is closer to what, with its quasi-grammatical ingrained pre-
cedence/presidence, is known as antimetabole (the Master is a Servant
and the Servant is a Master), or as Puttenham spells it, "*Antimetauole* or
the Counterchange," and one hears the Latinate purloining of the coin
(why, it's in your ear!) in his allophonic penultimate. Patricia Parker is no
doubt right to call attention to the prevalence of politically charged
illustrations in Puttenham's discussion of the figure, but it should be
remembered that his closing example is the rather Harveyesque "*In trifles
earnest as any man can bee, / In earnest matters no such trifler as hee*"
(Puttenham 1589, 209; cf. Parker 1987, 92). Ultimately, the metaphorical
plot in *The Vnfortunate Traueller* may subtextualize any political content
by denying the fall from a Golden Age in which master and servant were
of the same metal: for in reality, as Surrey is a Tudor aristocrat and Jack
a mere "gentleman," if that, they *cannot* finally be recast into one another,
just as in a metaphor with an implied or virtual tenor unable to sully
itself with the dirty work of material signification only one term is of any
substance: the *vehicle*. In the fallen world, the master does not employ the
servant to do "no other labour then belonged him selfe," but precisely to
do what he no longer *can* properly do, what no longer belongs to him as
labour or is no longer his productive "property." The vehicle must be
palpable and real in the tenor's place: "*Vivre? les serviteurs feront cela pour
nous.*"[13]

Parody does not conserve parity; in its very mirror symmetry right
is made sinister, and in any event, "Imitation is Criticism," as Blake told
his incurious copy of *The Works of Joshua Reynolds*. It has become common
in recent years to accept Nabokov's distinction, "Satire is a lesson, parody

[13]Obviously, not only Hegel and Marx are cooling their heels and wagging
their beards, though Hegel, heartlessly, had none, in the hall, but more especially
Nietzsche with his eternally discursive and semantic understanding of subversion
and his awareness of how a ruling-class word may go from signifying "one who
is, who possesses reality" to a metaphysical *property* of "spiritual *noblesse*," from
being to *having* (the phallus, and so on, cf. Nietzsche 1887, 277). But something like
the implied dichotomy (concrete vs. spiritual *property* of nobility) was indeed in
circulation in the Renaissance, even if at that time the "subversive" gesture would
have been the privileging of the *spiritual* property. Nashe's parody of parity thus
becomes proto-post-Enlightenment in its refusal to subvert the established nobility
by recourse to a "more authentically noble" interiority. Instead, by projecting an
already bourgeois vacuity onto nobility *as such*, the text proves to be *fin-de-siècle*
indeed.

is a game" (Nabokov 1967b, 30), but Barbara A. Babcock rightly points out that "[t]he impulse to parody is fundamental to the satiric mode" (Babcock 1978, 100) and the page's metaphorical imitation of the noble could well therefore reflect criticism. In *The Vnfortunate Traueller*, I would suggest, a critique tends in the direction of valorization of the concrete vehicle at the expense of the abstract tenor, and in doing so parallels at least the picaresque privileging of the servant's material realism over the nobleman's inane sprezzatura, exemplified in Lazarillo's provisioning of his proud but purse-poor master. Because he has an established symbolic pedigree, the master, unlike the servant, has no need of "references," but this ultimately conditions his lack of integration in a meaningful *Lebens-welt* and leaves him at a material disadvantage which the picaresque plot can reflect.

Surrey does of course rule Jack in the sense that the page can only take his place by his leave; but ruling a page only makes it a wee bit less crooked. As long as the superior must rely upon the inferior to do for him there is always, not the danger, but the discursive inevitability, of *mis*rule. "[G]ood sir, be ruld by me," Jack collusively advises the tiresome captain whom he supposes he is sending to his death early in the book, but "good sir, be *served* by me" is eventually a far more subversive proposition. *The Vnfortunate Traueller* could, then, *in a certain sense*, be said to chronicle what Parker (1987, 39) calls the "ambiguous genitive" of *"The Rule of Metaphor,"* recalling the insubordinate rendering of Ricoeur's title (as though *La métaphore vive* had been misread as *Vive la métaphore!*). Through a parody of disparity, really, the servant convinces the master to let the vehicle undertake the concrete labor and the sensual play, the *Arbeit und Liebe*, that make for real life. The plot *would* therefore be pica-resque inasmuch as the polymorphous page of the vehicle is meant to outdo the master trope of the tenor.

But as I suggested earlier, it may be more in relation to *mobility* than *nobility* that the picaro must be defined. The whole issue of servility may be ancillary in the determination of the picaresque, and thus of any picaresque plot of metaphor, to exigencies of movement. Umberto Eco reads Aristotle through Ricoeur: "In the *Rhetoric* (1411b25ff) there is no room for doubt: the best metaphors are those that 'show things in a state of activity.' Thus metaphorical knowledge is knowledge of the dynamics of the real" (Eco 1984, 102). But *pace* Ricoeur and Eco, this need not mean that metaphor is necessarily mimetic, only pseudokinetic. Every master-trope becomes the pretext for the unrelieved mobility of the vehicle and as such the tenor in fact becomes the temporary "vehicle" or "ride" of a shiftless hitchhiking figure. To the extent that the tenor or "proper meaning" is thus instrumentalized in the plot of *The Vnfortunate Traueller* that plot of *aufhebend* (Jacking-up) "lifts" becomes not metaphorical but "metaleptic."

Metalepsis, or transumption, which involves the intervention of further figurative terms between tenor and vehicle, and thus, as Quintilian put it (8.6.37), *"ex alio tropo in alium velut viam praestat,"* provides a path as it were from one trope to another, is identified by figures as apparently remote as George Puttenham and Harold Bloom with distanciation, whereby the master is *denied*, as Tranio denies Vincentio, through a further charge of imposture. But in Nietzsche's theory of metaphor and the work of those deconstructionist rhetoricians who have followed him, metalepsis becomes the real translation of *Uebertragung*, a figure of endless figurative relay, and hence of unpointed and unchecked movement. Nietzsche's theory, as Sarah Kofman once showed, "rests on the loss of the 'proper'" (Kofman 1971, 77) so that "the concept of metaphor becomes totally 'improper' since it no longer has reference to an absolute essence [*à un propre absolu*] but always already to an interpretation" (79). Nietzsche had recognized as early as his 1874 rhetoric lectures that language is tropological through and through and that "there can be no talk of a 'literal meaning' [*von einer «eigentlichen Bedeutung»*] which would be transported only in certain cases. . . . In actuality everything that is commonly called discourse is figuration" (Nietzsche 1874, 300). Every tenor is consequently only a further vehicle, and vice-versa.

In picaresque, the chain of masters thus becomes a series of *pis-aller* whereby the "topicality" of the narrative movement can be maintained. Put another way, the rogue's progress is not movement toward a goal, or movement in the service of another, but movement for its own sake. Consequently, as Bakhtin says, "in the absence of historical time, contrasts are brought out through difference [различия] alone" (Bakhtin 1979, 189). As a metaphor of *différance*, the picaro becomes an image of the ultimately "improper" modes of transport of the unpropertied classes of signifiers whereby literal meaning or the signified is trivialized or dropped out of the endless circulation of significance, all metaphors referring only to further metaphors as every signifier can lead only to another signifier. But in the absence of a proper master or any personal property, the floating signifier of the metaphor can only be defined by context, which because contexts are in motion as well, is no real definition at all, so that in the end, as even G.R. Hibbard asserted, though perhaps unaware of the Einsteinian ramifications (*ein Stein wird geschlagen*, though Berkeley no longer stubs any toes on such lapidary confutations), "[t]here is no Jack in the proper sense of the word" (Hibbard 1962, 177).

Such endless vehicularity, by the way, seems to be what licenses the "interminable analysis" (to drive home the Freudian transference) of much of the eternal deferral of modern criticism, where even for such a Sunday driver as I.A. Richards, it became invidious to distinguish between a "whither" and a "way" in poetic meaning—as he remarked in a misty passage in *Coleridge on Imagination* where we are made to hear the forlorn dwindling foghorns of the great Anglo-American lines in that echoic "wither away" (cf. Richards 1934, 213). But at the very origin of the age of discovery, it would seem, when such an offputting trajectory would generally have been viewed as peculiarly pointless, there was already inscribed in the picaresque the romantic détour which down the road would come to usurp discursively the teleonomic itinerary of the Capitalist-Imperialist settlement. Still, discursive or otherwise, transportation was more usually, for the Elizabethan, or so we are told, designed to carry freight to a destination, eventually *home*. Unlike the postromantic, the patriotic Elizabethan capitalist-humanist would be interested in the whither, not the way. Travel was dangerous and suspect, and a book like *Turlers Traveiler* (1575) warns that "as in all humain affayres, we must consider to what ende, and for what commoditie they are taken in hande: then ought wee most especially to bee myndefull thereof in traueill" (Turler 1575, C1). Rhetorical transport must serve the *oratorical* conveyance of "resource capital" (cf., most recently, Hutson 1989, Ch. 2). But the metaphorical picaro, the unindentured vagabond of the graphic, is going nowhere fast, and his endless movement is a scandalous reminder that all further ends are finally next ends (cf. Sidney 1595, C3^v/29). He is the Juvenalian *"vacuus viator"* in Pierce Penniless's self-characterization (Nashe 1592b, B2^v/1:160-61)—later picked up and taken for a quick spin by Harvey (1592, E4^v/1:206/56)—the empty-handed wayfarer who sings for the highwayman, offering pure materiality in place of transactional dolors and sense (Juvenal 10.22). The picaresque plot of metaphor thus would eventually become a discursive alibi of extenuating circumstances; and such an unmotivated plot, as Babcock points out (1978, 111) can only end arbitrarily. The last page of *The Vnfortunate Traueller* returns us to the English camp, the "truculent tragedie of *Cutwolfe* and *Esdras*" (a parable of the hunting down and extermination of the metaphorical libertine) having left Jack Wilton "[m]ortifiedly abiected and danted" and moving him to commit himself to "such straight life" that he marries Diamante, wedding himself apparently for good to a single signa-fide (Nashe 1594d, M4/2:327).

But in the end Jack "wilt on" if it will serve anyone's turn: "All the conclusiue epilogue I wil make is this, that if herein I haue pleased anie, it shall animat mee to more paines in this kind" (M4/2:328). In true picaresque fashion semiotic closure is a matter of physically closing the book, for inasmuch as the picaro enjoys a "position of constant mobility" (Babcock 1978, 96) he can obtain no real position, but only, as Derrida put it, "a travail in which I find myself *engaged:* which is not thus any more my own property for having been seized at this point" (Derrida 1972b, 7, translation [but how could it be otherwise?] modified). The page has come to an end, but more pages may always follow and be animated to more pains; for no other signifier will take the "place" of the Melmoth the Wanderer of the metaphor, it has no real "home" to go back to, and the endlessly "resourceful" metaphorical picaro is thus an unfortunate traveller indeed.

Topical Reading and
the Metaphorical Traveller

Cantabit vacuus coram latrone viator.
Juvenal, *Satire X*

Agnes M. C. Latham's 1948 article, "Satire on Literary Themes in Nashe's 'Unfortunate Traveller,'" denies realism to the text and implicitly rejects Bowers's claims for its picaresque status, insisting that "[w]hatever Nashe may have intended when he began the book, before he had finished it it had turned into a spirited parody of popular literary themes and styles of the day" (Latham 1948, 86). But such parody grading into satire coincides with the *topicality* of picaresque; the "hit-and-run style" of the picaro (Babcock 1978, 96) is in fact equivalent in effect to Nashe's "lightning transitions" which leave readers "giddy, gasping and weak with laughter, as though they had just come off a switchback" (Latham 1948, 99). Latham's disorientation may be due to her concentration on the Bowersian category of "realism" since for her *The Vnfortunate Traueller* "is not realism, it is criticism, and the form it takes is literary satire" (90). Though she makes the connection between satiric parody and criticism, she has missed the boat that connects them with the picaresque in a passage sailed through by Babcock: "While we tend to dissociate criticism and satire, defining the former as literary critique and the latter as social critique, it is interesting to note with regard to the picaresque that Roman satire (*satura*), from which picaresque ultimately derives, was the traditional vehicle for literary criticism. The *satura* or 'plate of mixed fruit' consisted, like the picaresque, of an admixture of genres and their reciprocals" (1978, 100).

By the 1950s this kind of mixed fruit was of course available tinned, pre-cut in bitesize bits in Frye's *Anatomy*, but Nashe's peculiar brand of

131

fruit cocktail, "a medley with picaresque elements," as C.S. Lewis calls it, was suspected of having been spiked, seeing's how Nashe "does not drive on so steadily as we could wish" (Lewis 1954, 428). Lewis was disgruntledly aware, however, as was G.R. Hibbard, that anyone wishing to apprehend him for driving under the influence "has difficulty keeping up with" his "rapid changes of direction" (Hibbard 1962, 178), and that, paradoxically, it is Nashe who displays an "arresting manner" (147), hi-Jacking his would-be apprehenders and taking them tied up in the trunk along with his bootlegged moonshine across the line, so that he "does succeed in conveying a number of discrepant attitudes to morals and to literature with a peculiar force and vitality, giving them the quality of immediate sensations" (179). Parking for a few hurried gropes with Lewis in '54 one still felt comfortable with the style taking a back seat, but with Hibbard we are already barreling precariously up into the sixties.

Ignoring Sister Marina Gibbons's graphic admonitions of an impending thematic pile-up (1964, 421), David Kaula seems initially bent on turning "the primary vehicle for Nashe's 'view of life': the style" (1966, 44) into a hot rod to hell in which he exploits "the possibilities of the rogue-hero who brashly exposes himself to hazards far beyond his ability to control" (48). But finding himself eventually committed to "such local effects as metaphor, alliteration, wordplay, proverbs, Latin tags, and mock-learned allusions" (Ibid.), this rebellious spirit's characteristic recursion "to the low style" (55) brings him back to the place he was trying to get away from, where he winds up, not unexpectedly, "grounded" (57). Still, Richard A. Lanham argues that Jack is ultimately grounded *by Nashe*, and for his own good. This is tragic in a way, though, since the narrative's "profuse speed is one of its great virtues" (1967, 209), but it is nevertheless necessary if the angry young man is to subdue the "free-floating aggression" and *"angst"* (206) by which he "protect[s] himself against what today we might call the 'system'" (208), and so finally kill off that part of himself "that blocks his establishing a harmonious relationship with society" (215). According to Lanham, this is eventually accomplished by transforming his anarchic performance of violence into a discursive *representation* of violence as a form of social protest in the later stages of the novel, so that "the Jack Wilton who emerges from the admittedly unrelated episodes he passes through, the identity that accretes around his name" is that of the "satirist" (207). In his following of critical "paths" and "approachs," then, Lanham concentrates on the figure of the protagonist as the existential key to the meaning, even if the critical "conveyance" of that meaning is unwittingly complotted in a construction worthy of Crewe, whereby the vehicular

page seems to become the proposed freeway site between major menda-
cities: "The most promising approach to the novel, then, would seem to
lie through Jack Wilton" (203; emphasis added).

Not waiting for the seventies' shift back away from character analysis
to intertextuality, Katherine Duncan-Jones (1968) proposes, incontinent,
that the way to Sidney lies through Surrey. The identification had been
urged previously (e.g. Hibbard 1962, 156), but no one had explicitly
pointed out that Surrey's tournament in *The Vnfortunate Traueller* presents
"a mosaic of references to tournaments and single combats in the *Arcadia*"
(Duncan-Jones 1968, 3). Duncan-Jones's breakaway analysis will eventually be surpassed by the high-powered von Koppenfels (1971), so we
will leave the tournament aside for now and take another turn at it later.

Walter R. Davis returns to bring the sixties to a close (although
Frederic Jameson [1983 and 1984] has convincingly suggested that this
may actually only take place in 1973) and put an end to that decade's
concern with the character analysis of the developing literary delinquent:
"The development of the persona of Jack creates the narrative curve of
the book" (1969, 218). For Davis, Jack is an easy rider whose "position as
a court page places him in a socio-economic no man's land" (216) and
whose "experience of reality . . . constantly gives the lie to ennobling
formulations of the real, be they literary conventions, intellectual aspira-
tions, or codes of life" (215). Meanwhile, behind the iron curtain, Robert
Weimann was putting this realism less liberally down to the "specificity
[*Besonderheit*] of the point of view" of the first person picaresque narrator
leading "to the discovery of humano-social actualities" (Weimann 1970,
25). The anecdotal jestbook turns into the fictional novel "precisely when
a made-up figure presents himself as the originator of fictive proceedings.
Only through such a figure is narrated actuality replaced by an image (or
similitude [*Gleichnis*]) of reality that is actualized *in the process of
narrating*" (23). Perhaps this makes *The Vnfortunate Traueller* more than
anything else a kind of *Bildungsroman* of the figment.

In 1971 we return to literary satire in an article which niftily contains
the first critical statement about Nashe's treatment of women, obliquely
alluded to in an analysis of the Petrarchism of Surrey, again arrived at
via Sidney, or in any case via Dorothy Jones, who is indeed a woman
from down under (Kensington, New South Wales). The reins of the
Surrey subplot are picked up again the same year by the redoubtable
Werner von Koppenfels, who enters the lists (cf. von Koppenfels 1971, 15;
16; 18) and manages at the very least to keep up with the Joneses and the
Duncan-Joneses, although he repeats much of the course already covered
by the latter (1968). Von Koppenfels catalogues the allusions to the
Arcadia in the description of the tournament in *The Vnfortunate Traueller*

which Surrey organizes to defend Geraldine's beauty after he has visited
her birth chamber, but the discussion is really useful for the stress it lays
upon the ecphratic tradition on which both Sidney and Nashe are playing
off. In Nashe, the tournament is largely a pretext for farcically overblown
and impractical armorial costumes and impresas. Sidney's elaborate
devices, while they most artificially create "the illusion of life and movement in mimetic effort" (von Koppenfels 1971, 2)—reins are disguised as
snakes or grape-vines; tail-furnishings mimic an eagle so that "as the
horse stirred, the bird seemed to flie" (Sidney 1590, 423)—are designed
as emblematic vehicles to convey the essences of the riders. But in
Nashe's description "the piling up of heterogenous emblems within one
portrait often borders on the grotesque, and this is doubtless what he
intends. The overall meaning of his devices frequently remains obscure,
whereas Sidney's are generally intelligible even at first sight" (von
Koppenfels 1971, 23). Nashe's emblems celebrate "the concept of art
copying natural movement" (22) at the expense of definitive meaning;
they are "quicke lives" (cf. Nashe 1594c, G3/1:380), evolving, as all things
do in *The Vnfortunate Traueller* by auricular and metonymic ramification.
Thus Nashe begins by retailing Surrey's armorial devices and explaining
the significance of each, but both description and explication are
generally so elaborate as to leave one with only the sense of the running-
on. Surrey's horse is elaborately decked out as an ostrich with spurs like
the "sharpe goad or pricke wherewith" the ostrich "spurreth himselfe
forward" (Nashe 1594d, G2ᵛ/2:272). But unlike the aquiline imagery of
Argalus's armor in Sidney, Nashe's strutting enumeration of struthious
details defers fixation of both the organic image and its moral significance. The emblem comes alive and takes on a life of its own. Indeed, the
ostrich-symbology unfurled as an allegory of Surrey's relationship to
Geraldine even harks back to the vivacious Diamante, "the birde" limed
by Jack while Surrey "beate the bush" in prison (F3ᵛ/2:263). "Like a bird
she tript on the grounde," Jack recalled her arrival in the dungeon, "and
bare out her belly as maiesticall as an Estrich" (F2ᵛ/2:261). On the wings
of Surrey's ostrich armor, ostensibly figuring forth the ocular influence
of his neoplatonic paramour, are actually "embossed christall eyes . . .
wherein wheelewise were circularly ingrafted sharp pointed *diamonds,* as
rayes from those eyes deriued" (G2ᵛ/2:272; emphasis added). We have
returned to the mirrored crystals of diamond and glass of the birth-
chamber scene. The rays shot from the eyes produce "a fine dim shine"
like "a candle in a paper lanterne, or a gloworme in a bush by night"
(G2ᵛ-G3/2:272). Geraldine is thus emblematized both in the bush that
Surrey is still beating around (her eyes spurring him on are sado-
masochistically inverted into his spurs guying forward his mount), and

the Diamantine "enranked" tremulous-truculent bird no longer in the hand, now the inaccessible content of a signifying bush. In the impenetrable depths of the "bolne swelling bowres of feathers" would seem to lie the secret source "glistering through the leaues & briers" (G2ᵛ; G3/2:272) of Surrey's symbolic action. Yet lover, bush, diamond and bird telescope back in a *mise-en*-a-beam which defers meaning while "animating" both symbol and interpreter.

The emblems of the other knights similarly represent what Davis had called "breathing literary artifacts" (1969, 225), inasmuch as they purchase life at the expense of definitive meaning. The extent to which this life depends upon a deferral of interpretational closure is itself emblematized in the armor of the eighth knight, "throughout engrailed like a crabbed brierie hawthorne bush" with "a solitarie nightingale close encaged" and "Toads gasping for winde, and Summer liude grashoppers gaping after deaw, both which were choakt with excessiue drouth for want of shade" (Nashe 1594d, G4/2:275). The themes of imprisoned signifier, caged or cached bird in the bush, and the reptilian "impedimentes" (G4/2:276) to ramification expiring in the reductive brave clearness of noontide scrutiny are foiled by the emblem on the knight's shield, "the picture of death doing almes deeds to a number of poore desolate children. The word, *Nemo alius explicat*. No other man lakes pittie vpon vs." Jack comments: "What his meaning was herein I cannot imagine, . . . I cannot see howe death shoulde haue bin sayd to doe almes deedes, except hee had depriued them sodainly of their liues, to deliuer them out of some further miserie; which could not in anie wise be, because they were yet lyuing" (Ibid.). Jack leaves it at that, and, needless to say, *nemo alius explicat*: for the emblems are plainly *not* topics for explication, but explorations of "the concept of art copying natural movement" (von Koppenfels 1971, 22). And if they *are* mistakenly taken as occasions for exegetical techniques, they display, in my experience, sufficient evidence that *explicats* have at least nine lives.

Alexander Leggatt connects the life-like ostrich armor with the birds of the pleasure garden in the banketing house in Rome, into which Jack and Surrey ride on a humble pair of assonances once Surrey's won the tourney. Like the armorial devices, this mechanical reconstruction of the unfallen world, an apparatus of twittering "clockwork toys," pipes, gears and painted surfaces is, according to Leggatt, in direct contrast to the real life of vulnerable flesh and chaotic horrors in the greater part of Nashe's book: "The outside world is real but horrible; the garden is beautiful but unreal: each world mocks the other" (Leggatt 1974, 33). The vitality of both the "breathing literary artifacts" of the tournament and the "enwrapped arte" (Nashe 1594d, H2ᵛ/2:282) of the wheeling works of the garden is considered by Leggatt to be a function of their mechanism. Their artful life can persist since, being unreal, they cannot die: "The birds are indestructible, because they are mechanical" (Leggatt 1974, 33). A different, but equally bloodless, survival is posited for Jack, who, in Leggatt's view, is not a growing person or developing "character who reforms his attitudes under the pressure of experience, but a narrative voice which changes tone to fit the changed nature of the events described" (40). This "fitness" of the agency of the *Ich-Erzähler* is, as Reinhard H. Friederich agrees, "elevated . . . above any pretence to a consistent persona" (1975, 211). The narrative agency of the picaresque Jack is officially a travel agency [*instance de voyage*], and Friederich has confirmed reservations about the "static nature" of the hermeneutic and automatonic "vitality" of the tournament and pleasure garden set pieces as against "scenes in which everything is in motion" (212). He books the characters as figures that "neither live nor exist, but function on principles external to themselves" (218)—structural literary principles. But Friederich seems to agree, at least tacitly, with Leggatt's view that Jack, even if he doesn't exist as a flesh and blood person, displays, as a disembodied voice, what one theorist of natural selection has termed "*adaptativité*" ("an ability to adapt and readapt in diverse directions" [Morin 1980, 48]). This also fits well with Friederich's viable hypothesis that "imagery" in *The Vnfortunate Traueller* "depends on verbal instead of visual movement" (Friederich 1975, 213). A convenient tag for this verbal associative evolution might be arrived at by doubling back on a term swiped by Gérard Genette from film theory ("diegetical metaphor," where metaphoric vehicles are borrowed from the universe of the narrative [the classic instance is the train going into a tunnel at the end of Hitchcock's *North by Northwest*; see Genette 1972, 48 n. 1]) and calling it "metaphorical diegesis" (where the universe of narrative and indeed its developmental plot cruces are generated by random tropes or verbal signifier-level swerves [cf. clinamen]). The production of text would thus be the work of a matrix of *voices*, with Jack's displaying superior adaptivity (*pun*ctuated evolution) and hence a canalizing influence on the trends of a stochastic narrativity for whose elements "survival potential" is essentially a matter of avoiding becoming "unsympathetic in literary terms" (cf. Friederich 1975, 217).

But Charles Larson would bring us back to the reality of human nature re(a)d in tooth and claw, insisting that Nashe "reveals a sensibility toward life to at least the same extent that he demonstrates formal attitudes toward art" (1975, 19), and stressing how the life-extending devices of anti-interpretation to some extent only come down to an animation to further pains, so that the ecphratic contraptions of the narration parallel the extenuated artistic execution of "the incredibly complicated death machines in Kafka's 'In the Penal Colony'" (25-26). Ultimately only prolonging an excruciating inscription (for the reader searches in vain for a definitive "crux"), the devices draw out the painful dying which is narrative "life." Influenced by Bakhtin, Larson sees the book as "a comedy of violence," in which the necessity of death to continued vitality has been extrapolated.

But of course the violence can only be comic because it does not put an end to the *reporter*. The constant and hence the selective element in the prodigal stochastic evolution of the narrative is the narrative agency: Jack. "The work moves in a randomly incremental fashion," remarks Patrick Morrow: "Nashe piles up units of incidents, while Jack, who is frequently but not always involved in the action, functions as a continuity device" (Morrow 1975, 640). According to Madelon S. Gohlke, on the other hand, Jack's initial involvement in the action is what leaves room for him to adapt. She too stresses the basically "violent, fragmentary, and accidental" (Kaula 1966, 55) evolution of "a mere chaos of events" (Davis 1969, 236) and initially concurs with the "continuity" view of the picaresque protagonist, according to which "the context of action alters, the hero does not" (Gohlke 1976, 401). One might put in here, that it is difficult to reconcile this with what I called the "adaptativity" view of the narrative voice put forth by Friederich, although it is true that evolutionary adaptation may not entail real, definitive alteration, indeed might preclude it. But in *The Vnfortunate Traueller*, as read by Gohlke, "the hero continues to escape death" not so much through adaptiveness as through a genuine alteration in his picaresque strategy: "The key to his invulnerability lies in his switch from an active to a passive role, from participant in events to narrator of events" (407). This rejoins Latham's reading of a decade earlier, according to which Jack is reconciled with society in the latter part of the book by displacing his life-threatening tendencies into the aesthetic.

Barbara C. Millard agrees with this neo-developmental reading, although uneasy about the positive valorization of the shift in the narrator's character. For her, the plot development charts "Jack's movement from anti-hero to non-hero, from victimizer to victim" (Millard 1978, 44). Yet the passive role is what protects the continuity of his vision; encountering scenes of mass carnage and formalized torment, "Jack remains secure from danger and his tone is aloof" (44). His adaptive strategy is finally an adoption of a grotesque modality in his picaresque narrative agency, "exposing the 'reality' of a primitive undercurrent in a growing urban civilization, and reassessing the lines between the natural and the unnatural in human beings and their constructs" (40).

In his full-fledged study of the *Elizabethan Grotesque*, Neil Rhodes agrees that it is this grotesque impulse which drives Nashe's "restless experimentation with topical satire and the picaresque novel" (Rhodes 1980, 4), but refocusses attention away from Jack and back onto the "new and dazzling kind of speed" with which "grotesque images in Nashe's writing seem to flash cinematically past the eye" (21). The long running time of Jack's "swift, colloquial banter" (37) distends the narrative "for the sake of bizarre local effects" (31). As a kind of avant-garde director, "Nashe literally sets the image in motion, epitomising his imaginative procedure as a whole" (52). But Ruth M. Stevenson critically claims that this rapid montage ultimately "unfolds . . . in a series of patterns which contribute to and culminate in a thesis about the artist's relationship to chaos" (1980, 292). The overarching message is presented by intercutting "Art and Evil," juxtaposing tableaux of artistic unity like the banketting house with images of stark violence such as the massacre at Münster. As the documentary footage unreals, however, there is a degeneration which culminates in the "Art *of* Evil" (295) exemplified in the Kafkaesque "death machines" in the final scenes of painstaking artistic execution, so that "[t]he reality of *The Unfortunate Traveller* is the gradual, cumulative dissection and destruction of ideas of value, beauty, harmony, coherence" (306).

Cynthia Sulfridge attempts to render the acuteness of Jack's angle in an isosceles obliquely cornered by "Nashe" as paratextual narrator and the reader. In cony-catching terms the reader is the cony and the "role of the fictive Nashe [in the induction] is not unlike that of the 'setter'" who puts the reader-cony into "a mood of relaxed congeniality," leaving Jack as "par excellence, the cony catcher" to "unsettle" the victim in a series of conveyances leading "through a maze of narrative maneuvers which leaves readers baffled and uneasy" (Sulfridge 1980, 3; 12; 2). But Sulfridge suggests that in so "victimizing the reading audience upon whom its own success depended," the book "became itself the ultimate victim of its author's peculiar humor" (14). By promoting their own selfish interests at the expense of their lectorial hosts, Nashe and Jack thus condemned themselves to an extinction which, however, as Sulfridge somewhat ironically fails to consider, is belied by the atavistic resurgence of the work's popularity in recent years. "The lifespan of a work of art" after all, "is the same as that of its utility," as Valéry once remarked, adding: "This is why that lifespan is discontinuous. There are centuries during which Vergil is of no use to anybody" (Valéry 1960, 562). Sulfridge insists that Nashe's "text lacks . . . an 'adaptive strategy'" (8), using the term in Norman Holland's somewhat different sense; but the narrative cozening that was maladaptive in the Elizabethan era may after all contribute, along with the horror and cruelty which "assume an aesthetic function, within the show offered by the author both to his readers and to *himself*" (Cuvelier 1981, 48, emphasis added), to its renewed vitality in an age of lurid and masochistic readerly tastes.

Margaret Ferguson inaugurates the poststructuralist ergo propter structuralist reception of the text when she accounts for the shifting positions of Nashe, Jack and the reader in terms of moves in what Nashe calls the "newes of the maker" game (Nashe 1594d, A2/2:207), where "competition among various makers" involves new authorities "constantly replac[ing] old ones" (Ferguson 1981, 167). Ferguson's own gambits tend to turn the game into one of *"fort-da"* or Oedipal competition in micro-analyses where the moves are not the aleatory outcome of *coups de dés* as in the stochastic accounts, but more of the "slurred die" lurking in the "line of life" (cf. Nashe 1594d, A3; B2/2:207; 217) that is displacement or even, in some cases, countertransference. But Ferguson ultimately stresses the reader's unfair advantage in the life-and-death game she conceives of: characters killed off in authorial forfeits can be brought back into play by the reader and "[i]f the reader does reanimate the pages, the 'newes of the maker' game will begin again" (Ferguson 1981, 182). This should serve to remind us "that commentary is not an innocent activity. If it is a game, it requires its players not only to engage in the risky enterprise of replacing the old with the new, but also to ask themselves as Nashe does, 'Is this a game?'" (Ibid.).

If it is, John Wenke seems to suggest, it is immoral and deadly. Wedged between Ferguson's eclectic Yale poststructuralist commentary and Jonathan Crewe's bookletlength deconstructionist study, Wenke's ethical interpretation is actually the most radical rereading of the decade, even if it essentially replaces the "new" with the old. According to Wenke, "Nashe affirms the same general moral vision represented much earlier by Wyatt and Ascham and dramatized contemporaneously by Sidney and Spenser" (1981, 19). For him, "Nashe persistently attacks the art of fiction-making when used both to define the self and to control the world through which one moves" (17). Indeed, moving through this world at all is a form of inauthenticity as one will only thus circulate among immoral fictionalizers on the make, who "seek to make life the subject of their art and . . . try to control people as an artist manipulates characters" (22). As Wenke sees it, Nashe critiques this aestheticization of life and affirms in its place the neoplatonic aesthetic of courtly lovers who "create a closed world of sympathetic identification" (Ibid.) rather than attempting to blur distinctions between life and art. The only episodes that hold out a "chance for an ordering vision, and in the sixteenth century," according to Wenke, "the presumption must always be that that is what the artist is trying somehow to attain" (24), are the one in which Jack responds to the Anabaptist uprising with a re-affirmation of Anglican ideals and the one in which, having saved Jack from the noose in Rome, a banished English earl unsuccessfully lectures him on the evils and follies of travel and proposes "a value—home in England—which the corrupt European landscape cannot supply" (22). As Wenke sees it, Nashe's narrative serves to affirm values of private (as opposed to fictive) selfhood, reformed Christianity, and insularity: the abiding, indwelling values of the age. Forced to reside among the mobile, continentalized fiction-makers of the eighties, Wenke seems a banished English earl himself, and not surprisingly his advice has been little heeded.

Jonathan Crewe is back to insisting that "style is the substance of *The Unfortunate Traveller*" (Crewe 1982, 68), but grants that the book "is also an antiromance, first-person narrative, and even a 'critical fiction' of its period" (69). For Crewe, however, the work is pre-eminently "an informal phenomenology of the page" (Ibid.), with pun—dare I say?—intended, by which "the endless succession of pages, constituting their own spurious order, threatens an infinite deferral of true order or ultimate significance" (70). Crewe's pages would rewrite the medieval *liber mundi* topos as perpetuated in the Renaissance in configurations such as that in the first week of Du Bartas, in Sylvester's translation:

> The World's a Booke in *Folio*, printed all
> With God's great Workes in Letters Capitall:
> Each Creature, is a Page, and each effect,
> A faire Caracter, void of all defect.
> (1.1.173-76; Du Bartas 1605, 1:116)

However, as a page in the *liber mundi*, each creature is bound into a paginal position to which a reference can presumably be meaningfully made, whereas in views such as Crewe's the page would seem to be a loose leaf in a three-ring binder at most, largely full of doodles of cute professors; and narrative or historical progress can thus become a matter of dwalmy "leafing," dumped sheets hurriedly reassembled after class, and so on. In this event, any ultimate "signature" can only be a contextual index for the convenience of whoever would gather and bind the actually unmassed quires of polyphonic *discursus* (fueilled again)!

Unredeemed Rhetoric at first seems eager to reveal the verso of the page—indeed can't wait to see the backside of him. Crewe cuts formerly bunched leaves, veritably pulls out the stitching. But then he un-expectedly trims, aligns, rebounds and even provides a "guilt-edge." He suggests that the page becomes an "'unfortunate traveller,' a restless fugitive conscious of his own problematical and threatened identity" because of "guilty knowledge" (73). By this seems to be meant not just the pandemic "culpability of authorship in the 1590s" (Hutson 1989, 15), but also an emerging epistemological self-consciousness and anxiety over *décalage* between appearances and reality—or rather appearances and other appearances—which would lead to an *après-mauvaise-foi* embrace of rhetoric. But Jack/Nashe "deflects" from this destiny "to engage in more innocent forms of by-play" (75), even if finally "violence remains inescapable, at least within the closed circuit of author and reader" (87). Jack thus is still for Crewe, as the last leaf is overturned, a "lying page," and we "would remain among Jack Wilton's 'creditors' if we assumed that anything had been constructively resolved" (Ibid.). We know, of course, the resolutional alternative.

But the ease with which a *de*constructively resolved deferral of meaning can be rehabilitated to a structure of systematic irony which "tempts us with the idea of a perennial modernism" (68) is itself epistemologically and politically now called into question by Ann Rosalind Jones, who comes to ponder the patently modernist comparisons of Nashe with Joyce or Wyndham Lewis suggested by Haworth (1956) and G.R. Hibbard (1962), the latter of whom, in a kind of semiotic slippage *au pied de la lettre*, had briefly become "G.W. Hibbard" in Ferguson's text (1981, 167 and n. 6) only to turn here into first "J.K. Hibbard" (*à rebours?*) and then "G.K. Hibbard" (A.R. Jones 1983, 79 n. 2; 63). Jones uses Bakhtin as read by Julia Kristeva (J.K.) to repatriate *The Vnfortunate Traueller* in the pre-modernist picaresque tradition by shifting, like Crewe, "from a thematic and stylistic focus to a rhetorical one" (64). Countering the keen temptation, as Crewe had called it (*"pour qui se laisse séduire à ce genre de choses,"* of course, as Genette once scrupled [1979, 79]), to situate Nashe's text in a modern context where, as Wayne Booth regretted, "[t]he successive annihilation of seemingly stable locations has been widespread" (cited in A.R. Jones 1983, 67), Jones sees the work as straining, in the Bakhtinian Menippean tradition, but also as what Simons will call the "proto-postmodernist novel" (1988, 36), toward Kristeva's "unbounded text." This reading itself falls apart in exemplary fashion as Jones interrogates the potential for real subversive or contentional dialogicity in a work which plays out fantasies and anxieties of the author, or at least of "a writer in Nashe's position" (A.R. Jones 1983, 74). But though New Historicist in spirit, her attempts to situate the work historically move recurrently toward intercontextuality, just as her version of "Bakhtin's polyphonic novel" overlooks, to employ the Apollonian

pun, that theorist's own historical shifts.[1] "The view over carnival," as
in Bruegel's famed framed and overarching image of "The Battle Between
Carnival and Lent," is an overview which Jones resists but cannot wholly
relinquish (for as Bakhtin also pointed out, one's unavoidable position of
exotopy with regard to all that is not oneself necessarily entails a unifying
perspective). This meta-unification is inevitable for all modernist poeticses
of vision, subject as they are to "yearnings," as Raymond Stephanson
says, apparently without irony, which "are perhaps inescapable traits of
literary critics and human beings alike" (Stephanson 1983, 23 n. 10). Thus
Stephanson makes no, or only pedepaginal apology for trying to argue
that *The Vnfortunate Traueller* can be redeemed "as a serious and perhaps
consistent expression of some 'view of life'" (22). This meta-view, he
claims, is precisely the (itself stable) observation "that meaning seems
always to be in a state of flux" (24). Yet this mimo-kinetic, if that is what
it is, reading ignores Stephanson's own insight into Nashe's "preference
for tropes (the transference of meaning) rather than schemes (the trans-

---

[1]Using Bakhtinian theories of carnivalized or dialogical Menippea to valorize
"picaresque" episodicity (the genre had indeed been seen by Bakhtin as a stage
in the evolution of the polyphonic novel) contains within it its own historical
ironies. Not available to Jones, though they had been published in Russian in
1979, were the notes to the smoked "Goethe book" or study of the *Erziehungsroman* in the history of realism. This work had been accepted for publication
when the outbreak of World War Two cancelled its future, and, had it appeared,
we would have had a somewhat different view of Bakhtin's thought, and one
more prone perhaps to a developmental reading itself. In his theory of the novel
we would now be presented with a progression *back* in history from the
polyphonic novel of *Problems of Dostoevsky's Poetics* (first edition, 1929), through
the *Dialogic Imagination* articles (themselves misleadingly presented in reverse
chronological order of composition in the selection edited by Michael Holquist)
and the book on Goethe with its emphasis on the element of *development* (1930s)
and finally back to Rabelais and concentration on the carnivalesque (the War era).
Bakhtin's most extensive comments on the picaresque are the essentially negative
ones found in the section on the "travel novel" in the notes to the "Goethe book,"
where he apparently intended a valorization of character development as a
landmark in the history of novelistic realism, and where he consequently belittles
the picaresque in which the protagonist has a fixed (lack of) identity and does not
change or learn in the course of the adventure (see Bakhtin 1979, 188-90). Nashe's
flaunting of historical sequentiality, celebrated by Jones as a prime quality of the
"self-revealing text," is one of the evident *failures* of the "travel novel." One may
also get some idea of how Bakhtin might have viewed the quasi-picaresque of *The
Vnfortunate Traueller*, at least at this point in his development—with charity, but
with little respect—from the writings on various "adventure time" genres in
"Forms of Time and of the Chronotope in the Novel" (Bakhtin 1981, 84-258).

ference of order)" (Ibid.). The *schematic* representation of shifting contexts is provided not by Nashe, then, but by Stephanson's own reading. Nashe's style does not *represent* a picture of meaning in motion; it *is* meaning in motion. It is thus Stephanson who wishes to settle the "unsettling effects of the work" (36). But in all fairness to him, one must also gainsay his conclusion that our view of the book "is a question of how far we are willing to go" (ibid.), since it may finally be more a question of how far we *can* go. Can one ever get outside of the frame, beyond the margins that the conditions of perception prescribe?

Furthermore, the series of attempts to unify the chaos can themselves take on an aspect of random violence at a critical moment. As Mihoko Suzuki puts it, "Nashe acknowledges the problem in interpretation resulting from the absence of proper meaning. This insistence on the figurative violence of textual interpretation parallels the proliferation of literal and physical violence . . . in the Italian section of the book" (Suzuki 1984, 361). But in the midst of an "omnipresent crisis of authority that engenders chaos and violence" (371), Suzuki attempts to redeem *The Vnfortunate Traueller* as a more realistic version of what Crewe called the "phenomenology of the page." In her reading, what's more, one can glimpse the possibility that violence can be avoided by *living through* the narrative; the attempt at synoptic unification, on the other hand, does indeed leave one with an image of chaotic violence. "Although the book's subtitle, 'The Life of Jack Wilton,' implies an autobiographical narrative that is ordered according to a retrospective principle, it is as if Jack tells his story as he lives it," argues Suzuki, adding: "Jack's horrible experiences at the end do not affect his breezy humor in the opening episodes" (369). As long, then, as one's "reading" is that—the process of moving along with the turnings of the page—the history can not *add up* to a vision of violence. If the "crisis of authority" and the violence it entails do finally lead Jack and Nashe to a Beckettesque silence, at least as long as there are further pages to be read the ultimate vision of violence can be *deferred*, and the reader can go on living through any number of deauthorized and mutually destructive positions. The banished Earl, as Suzuki points out, in fact "recommends reading as a substitute for travelling. . . . The Earl's equation of travelling and the state of exile, however, implies that reading, though a safer substitute for travelling, is a double displacement from one's origin" (370). Only by failing to close the interpretive circle, or remaining an exegetical exile, can violence thus be deferred.

Robert Weimann comes back to allude as well to the violence inherent in the oppressive unification of any, to speak with the Volga, Germeneutics. But the violence of *opposition* to totalitarian aesthetic or semantic programs is also brought out in his image of the "incisive" criticism to which this "Hegelian tradition" has itself "been subjected" (Weimann 1984, 15-16). Weimann sees the textual strategy of *The Vnfortunate Traueller* as an example of the "appropriation" of "a newly self-determined manner of authority" in which the narrative could conflate *fabula* and *historia* until "[t]he classical distinction between fictional 'pictures, what should be' and true 'stories what have bin' is thoroughly inverted," with the discourse thus "moving between topos and topicality, rhetoric and experience" (17; 16; 17). In such a movement is played out a new development of being *as* writing, appropriating a sociotextual mobility which goes beyond Nashe's historical situation as well as the "feyned no where acts" (Nashe 1589a, A2/1:11) of romance, and thus tempts even Weimann, citing Harvey for support, with the idea of a perennial modernism (cf. Weimann 1984, 24; Crewe 1982, 68, cited above; Harvey 1593b, D2/2:63 [actually, here Harvey is supposedly quoting]; Z4^v/2:278); a modernism which, as we now know, approximates nothing so much as the "detachment and distancing" of "a writing that has no end apart from itself," to quote Eliane Cuvelier. Thus, "[b]y taking being as the object of his violence, exaggerating its real fragility to the point of absurdity, and dehumanizing it under the impression of an abundant grotesque so as to take its annihilation finally into artistic account, [Nashe] confers upon his narrative the ultimate status of absolute satire" (Cuvelier 1986, 66).

Antoine Demadre, in his posthumously published unfinished monograph on Nashe seems to disagree with this kind of view, seeing the Nashe of *The Vnfortunate Traueller* as an historical ultra-realist to whom it "falls to make up a few events" but who "most of the time takes off from real facts" (my translation may be a little misleading here) in line with his "tendency to documentary realism" (Demadre 1986, 405-406; 407). Demadre sees Nashe's innovativeness not in his departure from historical events, nor in any "upheaval of the chronological succession" (359) of those events, but quite simply, and as Sulfridge (1980, 6) had suggested earlier, in Nashe's acceleration/deceleration abilities—"less than two pages, for instance, correspond to four years (1513 to 1517), while the previous eighteen pages concern only three weeks, so that one winds up with a kind of 'accordion-time'" (Ibid.)—reminding one of the "road test" or actually "test bench" Genette had proposed, where the performance of *A la recherche du temps perdu* ("from a page for one minute to a page for one century" [Genette 1983, 24]) would show up not only Balzac (Genette's foil) but Nashe as well.

Stephen S. Hilliard seems to agree with Demadre, but without his optimism, that in *The Vnfortunate Traueller* "the iron world of history prevails" (Hilliard 1986, 125). For him, as for Crewe and Bowers before him, the book is "antiromantic" (123) and its presentation of idealistic positions or textual practices leaves one with the sense of "an idealism that has become grotesque in its interaction with historical contingencies" (125). Resisting this idealism, "[t]he work is not schematic; any attempt to delineate its themes or make articulate its structure contradicts the random effect of the actual narration, which is as capricious as fortune" (157). Yet Hilliard ultimately uses this Elizabethan notion of Fortune to help articulate a structure of intercalcated pride and punishment. Jack "appears to be wandering, but his travels are centripetal" (162): he moves, through a series of episodes emblematizing prideful vanity offset by scenes of violence and fickle Fortune, to Rome, "the city that sym-bolized pride and intrigue to the Elizabethans" (162). Hilliard argues that "Jack's metaphorical travels are unfortunate not because he encounters ill luck but because he travels into the uncertain realm of fortune" (153). It is the aspect of alienation which makes for the unfortunateness; finding himself in a strange land the traveller lacks the sociocultural anchors to his proper English context which might protect him from vanity and the freewheeling of Fortune. Thus, for Hilliard, "travel is not a movement from place to place but a relationship between a person and a place. . . . Jack is closer to his listeners or readers than to anyone he encounters on his travels . . ." (151).

But it is on this approximation to the audience that Susan Marie Harrington and Michal Nahor Bond would blow the whistle with a foul call of ball-bearing "travelling." They would deny the view of Jack implied in descriptions such as Hilliard's reference to him as an "empty . . . vessel" or a "*tabula rasa*" (135), for they see the narrative movements as a series of manipulations which render the reader complicitous in the narrator's enactment and enjoyment of aggression. The shifts of Jack and Nashe lull and lead the reader on, "consistently translating and reorganizing violence and victimization" in what proves "a pattern of domination and manipulation" (Harrington and Bond 1987, 243). From this scheme eventually emerges a developmental pattern that is a dark parody of those put forward by Lanham and Gohlke: as Jack becomes less powerful and is no longer in a safe position to enact violence himself, he adopts an aestheticizing, depersonalized, authorial domination where-by his "omniscient narration . . . disguises his powerlessness and his absence from the center of the action." Thus, "[b]y suggesting Jack's ubiquity when Jack is really most helpless and desperate Nashe subtly and effectively manipulates his readers, for we neglect to question the authority of Jack's omniscience" (247). At the same time, these moves toward an aesthetically distanced and disengaged attitude occult Jack's responsibility as a diegetical actor—he looks on mutely while the pathetic rape of Heraclide takes place—and solidify his subornation of the reader by shifting "responsibility for evaluating . . . from himself to his audience" (249). Harrington and Bond draw attention to the "anonymous introducer" (i.e. Nashe) in the induction who had harped upon the fact that the public could do as it liked with the book, a variation of Nashe's typical sense of *readerly* hermeneutical manipulation. But as Harrington and Bond point out, though they "underscore the audience's ability, and even responsibility, to evaluate freely a text," these disclaimers "obscure the manipulative capabilities of the storyteller" (249-50). Thus Nashe's text might well seem to be, as Philip Edwards styles it, "a classic of victimography" (1987, 295)—not, however, as he suggests at the beginning of his "Unfortunate Travellers: Fiction and Reality," because of Jack's vivid communication of *his own* sufferings, but rather, as he argues at the end, in "the revelation of the universal irresponsibility of fiction" (306). But, as I was trying to ask earlier, is this irresponsibility really so universal, and not in fact to be located somewhere between the prosaic as such and the intradiegetic agent Jack, on whose movement "from bullying narrator to fellow member of the audience" Harrington and Bond blame our being drawn "into the text" so that "we face a pattern of pleasure in domination, unable to ask if it is true for us as well" (Harrington and Bond 1987, 250)?

In "Rerouting *The Unfortunate Traveller*," however, Louise Simons seems to suggest that it *is*, like original sin, true for them as well, a "universal irresponsiblity," and that Jack's implication of the audience actually serves an edifying purpose in what is after all "a kind of *Bildungsroman*" (Simons 1988, 17): "Compromised by sin through implicit approval, the reader must perforce share in the punishment; Jack and the reader become immersed for cleansing purposes in the bloodbath of the later scenes. Jack has been an impudent upstart to whom the reader has not been immune; thereafter, the book's moralizing lesson sinks in on both protagonist and audience through gory depictions of lingering death" (34-35).

Lorna Hutson, most close to us, reasserts how Nashe displays a "Lucianic mockery" of approaches that would leave the text "moralized or 'mangled' by interested readers" (Hutson 1989, 151), but eventually capitulates to the unifying impulse herself in claiming that "[t]he lack of integrity that has so troubled critics of *The Unfortunate Traveller* is in fact a measure of its integrity." Thus she seems to embrace a Sidneian (or perhaps Nietzschean) concept of meta-mendacious fictive integrity: "for it is only by disclosing the lies and contradictions on which they depend that these pages can begin to reveal the truth about themselves" (217).

But self-subversion is surely a version of Simons's putrefacting "lingering death" and in spite of all relativizing and reanimating recurrences to parody and dialogism, "every new departure in narrative flattens into an admonition of its own punishment" (219), so that finally the text only "reveals how a literature which is obliged to conform to criteria of rhetorical effectiveness and providential 'profit' on a simultaneously political and moral level inevitably operates to curtail its own freedom, and to obliterate *itself* in order to exculpate itself from the crimes of wanton amorality or political subversion" (243-44), the inevitable fate of any text committed to the institutional imperatives of the capitalist-humanist settlement at the end of the century.

Personally, I am ready to concur with Harrington and Bond's incisive criticism that the narratorial agencies manipulate readers into collusive acts and observations of violence. But prosaic manipulation is a two-way street, and it seems straightforward to me that the traveller in most of these readings becomes unfortunate not where he cheats but where he's cheated. Unfortunately, our sense of whom is victimized and who manipulates in textual transactions is itself always etc. a manipulation (and the outcome of manipulations), but it does seem that the amoral or immoral page taken out of Nashe's text and into protective custody by the critics assumes the role of pretext and loses any picaresque "autonomy" when incarcerated within each new critical con-text. In a sense, like the picaro in *Don Quixote*, the page is, to recall Nabokov's pun (1967a, 96, pointed out by Carroll 1974, 208), a "galley slave" whose continued travels constitute thralldom (a good Spenserian kind of term) to an egregiously exploitative "press gang." The misrule of metaphor, the wheel-spinning of a levanting and gallivanting signifying chain, finally becomes the unstoppable Fortune's torture-wheel on which the body of the text is broken; in the hollow circulation that rounds the mortal templates of sense-making; for there the semantic sits, allowing the semiotic a breath, a little scene, and then comes along at last with a little pen, bores, and farewell *opera aperta*. But then there are perhaps fates worse than death; to wander with Cain in shades of endless night, e.g.

Criticism, along with hermeneutics and "meta-scientific" epistemologics, has come to take a progressively more theoretically tentative tack in many of its attempts to convey the meanings that are its work and which theory has to barter with ("Science deals with meanings; criticism produces them" [Barthes 1966a, 56; translation tendentiously paronomastic]). But the movements of theory are obviously not so unexploitatively exploratory as is occasionally supposed, both by its backers and by its competitors, and the never mark-finding Zenonian archery of the stochastic speculation that Michel Serres wants to call a *"randonée,*

forasmuch as an old hunting term, *randon*, gave birth to two close yet
divergent relatives—the French *randonée* [joyride or ramble] and the
English 'random'" (Serres 1980, 14), perhaps always comes back down
once again to a good old Peirce-snatched act of "abduction." Looked at
from this way station, the real role in meaning conveyance of the metaphorical traveller is not that of the critical picaresque "shifter," who
serves a series of masters and purloins a few measly senses from them,
but that of an infinitely subjected syllepsis, a figure Puttenham suggested
"may be likened to a man that serues many masters at once, being of
straunge Countries or kinreds" (Puttenham 1589, 165). A kind of Francis
the tapster's boy, the sylleptic unit need go nowhere; indeed can't *make*
a definitive move in any direction. Its polymorphic syntactic exploitability
insures that its position is always *subjected* to any number of simultaneous displacements. This, according to the banished earl, is the true
unfortunateness of travel, "the highest step of thraldome":

> It is but a milde kinde of subiection to be the seruant of one
> master at once, but when thou hast a thousand thousand
> masters, as the veriest botcher, tinker or cobler free-borne will
> dominere ouer a foreiner, and thinke to bee his better or master
> in companie: then shalt thou finde there is no such hell, as to
> leaue thy fathers house (thy naturall habitation) to liue in the
> land of bondage. (Nashe 1594d, I4/2:297-98)

As a traveller, each text that survives wanders not like Melmoth or like
Cain, but like Jack Wilton. And we too *are* those texts, for we can none
of us ever go back to our father's house from that land of perpetual
bondage, because we are not prodigal sons, like the heroes of Greene's
romances, but orphaned metaphorical picaros, destined to travail for, and
travel along, an endless chain of masters; for, as long as there are pages,
it would seem, they will serve the interests of those who would get on
with the sometimes all too alienated labor of making sense. Montaigne
still saw the chain of interpretation in terms of the unmasterable homogenous hitheringdithering waters of his friend La Boëtie's engagement
poem (*Essais*, 3.13: "Water in water still, one riuer still, / Yet diuers
waters still that riuer fill," in Florio's translation): "It is a movement
irregular, perpetual, patronless, and without end" (Montaigne 1588, 2:520;
"sans patron" is my translation here, which Florio more fluently renders
"patternlesse"). But that fluvial force will often appear frozen for us into
some seemingly stationary Wordsworthian blast, a sheet of holdless
rinksheer prosaicity that does indeed oblige us to recognize as "normal"
our experience of an "endless slipping of signs in erring and changes of

scene (*Verwandlungen*), linking re-presentations (*Vergegenwärtigungen*) one to another, without beginning or ending" (Derrida 1967b, 116).

Bakhtin the Peripatetic, who smoked what he wrote, for most of his writings were only loose leaves, papers, and quite properly he used them for rolling, Bakhtin the Peripatetic (unless it was Vološinov) has pointed out that one cannot ever make the same utterance twice. But Derrida, while Bakhtin was still a gleam in Kristeva's eye, did not let it go at that, but hastened to add: "One can't even do it once!" By this a dialogical doctrine of the cruciality of context is turned into a deconstructionist doctrine that seems to deny meaning. But the ultimate thralldom of a figure like Jack Wilton suggests perhaps more terribly that one can never *stop* doing it, and that Puttenham's figure would be better renamed "*Metaphora*, or the Unfortunate traveller," whose meaning is endlessly being conveyed, and whose emblem therefore might well be that of the alms of semantic death, with the motto: "*Nemo alius explicat.* No other man takes pittie vpon vs."

THE RHETORIC OF THINGS

Inutiles Cardani subtilitates negligendæ: Sola pragmatica, et
Cosmopolitica curanda: that carry meat in yᵉ mowth; & ar daily
in esse. quae alunt familiam et parasitos: quæ semper ædificant.
        Gabriel Harvey, marginalia to Οικονομια, *seu Dis-
positio Regularum vtriusque Iuris in locas communes breui interpret-
atione subiecta*

The Four First Things

Mithin, sagte ich ein wenig zerstreut, müssen wir wieder von
dem Baum der Erkenntnis essen, um in den Stand der Unschuld
zurückzufallen?
Allerdings, antwortete er: das ist das letzte Kapitel von der
Geschichte der Welt.
Heinrich Kleist, «Über das Marionettentheater»

To. ... Does not our liues consist of the foure Elements?
And. Faith so they say, but I thinke it rather consists of
eating and drinking.
To. Th'art a scholler; let vs therefore eate and drinke.
William Shakespeare, *Twelfe Night*

Wie man wird, was man ißt—this takeoff on the subtitle of Nietzsche's
Ecce Homo can serve as a delicate little entrée to a bit of logy tabletalk on
the meataphorical incorporation of *things* that takes place in writing and
reading: *you are what you eat*.[1] The connection between the legible and the
edible was, we read, obvious to "the Renaissance." Neil Rhodes, for
example, discusses how both Aretino and Nashe were given to speaking
of "verbal communication" as a "gastronomic experience" (Rhodes 1980,
32-33), and Bakhtin's unique allusion to Nashe quite properly comes in

---

[1]Cf. Kilgour 1990, *passim* the *biscotti, bitte*. Much of this must now come forth
as little more than an unwise midnight snack after the mouthwatering fare of
Kilgour's typically Rabelaisian seven-course feast, which appeared only after I
had badly spoiled my appetite on the cates in this section. I know, though, that
this fascicular collation will not be begrudged me. There will always be room for
biscotti.

a chapter on "Banquet Imagery."[2]

[2]Critics have understandably rushed to lash Nashe to the Russian, but he appears in the Bakhtinian text in name only, if that. The English translation, as always quite sloppy, puts it like this: "To a certain extent this [democratic] spirit pervaded English prandial tradition as well, in the time of Shakespeare, Thomas Nash, Robert Green, and their circle." This renders, more or less abattoirly (arbitrarily), Bakhtin's "Такова была еще в значительной мере и его английская разновидность эпохи Шекспира — застольный либертинизм кружка Неша и Роберта Грина . . . . [Of such a kind was also in some wise its English variety in the age of Shakespeare—the prandial libertinism of the circle of Nashe and Robert Greene . . . .]" (Bakhtin 1965, 322/297). The English here, choppy as it is, is still a little happier than the usually more reliable French translation, which, apparently nonplussed by the cyrillicization or *coquillage* of Nashe into "Nesh" [Неша] concocts the rather unappetizing allomorph "Newsh" (Bakhtin 1970, 295).* Of course, on precisely this sort of cacoepistic slipperiness, it used to be supposed, depended much of the fun in Elizabethan topical reference. Indeed, in their efforts to argue that Moth and Armado represented Nashe and Harvey in the old New Cambridge *Love's Labour's Lost*, Quiller-Couch and Dover Wilson pointed out that Armado's references to his page as "tender Iuuenall" in act 1, scene 2 (TLN 318ff) did not merely constitute veiled reference to the writer whose combination of youthful looks and incisive wit had arguably led both Greene and Meres to dub him a new "Juvenal," but additionally alluded to his actual name: "The epithet 'tender,' moreover, is not to be overlooked. Neshe was a recognised variant of the surname Nashe, and 'nesh' or 'nash' at that time = 'soft, delicate, pitiful, tender'" (Quiller-Couch and Wilson 1923, xxii). Similarly, "Moth," then pronounced "mote," inasmuch as it is "a little sparkling, dancing, irritating object ... does well enough as a descriptive name for Nashe," in addition to proving to be, "by Elizabethan spelling, just Nashe's Christian name reversed" (xxiii). In his reconsidered preface to the 1962 revised edition, Wilson seems to have harkened to the sensible strains of the Prologue in *Summers Last Will*: "Vayne glozers, gather what you will. Spite, spell backwards what thou canst" (1600, B1ᵛ-B2/ 3:235), and he trips somewhat more glibly over such speculation as had meanwhile been thoroughly worked through by Yates and Bradbrook and admirably articulated and augmented by Schrickx in '56. As recently as 1983, J.M. Maguin proposed in an article entitled *"Nashes Lenten Stuffe*: The Significance of the Author's Name," that said name appears as part of the title in a pun on *ashes*, the latter being "indeed *Lenten Stuffe* since they belong liturgically to Ash Wednesday which marks the beginning of Lent" and at the same time relating to the book's dedicatee, the "tobacconist" Humphrey King (Maguin 1983, 73). Gabriel Harvey in his pamphlets against Nashe had evidently thought it reasonable to confound "a Nashe" with "an ass."

Nashe, however, who actually does seem to have had a peculiar interest in Russia, suggests the most farfetched but also here the most pertinent of parono-

It will be recalled that Bakhtin connected such imagery with "prandial libertinism [застолний либертинизм]": food goes glibly in and unobstructed language comes out. Images of eating in the "popular festive tradition," he insisted, have nothing to do with that complacent *"ready-to-hand* contentment and satiety of the selfish individual" stuffing himself in bourgeois privatized consumption (Bakhtin 1965, 327/301, tr. modified). Rather, the Renaissance banquet was a scene of outspoken conviviality, a gay celebration of the eating up of all that was ripe for it, and of the triumph of man over the world through labor: "a feast for all the world [пир на весь мир]" in which the world is regenerated in a celebration of human freedom.

But as an all-consuming utopian expression of metaphorality, in the Renaissance or any other time, prandial *out*spokenness is hardly the obvious discursive concomitant of *in*gestion, hardly the sole textual scenario. As Louis Marin has well observed, it is difficult to talk with one's mouth full, and "thus one is not supposed to talk and eat at the

mastic allusions when he quotes a snatch of a Russian prayer picked up in Hakluyt (McKerrow 1908, 322) which he promises to make the Harveys intone upon their knees: *"Ponuloi nashe,* which is in the *Russian* tongue, Haue mercie vpon vs" (Nashe 1596, G1/3:40). *Ponuloi* (presumably a version of помилуй [*pomiluj*]) would be the imperative plea, and наш (nash) is in fact the first person plural possessive in Russian, often used in a pronominal fashion: наши (nashi: "us folks, our side"); so that it would seem that we have met the enemy here and he is as usual ourselves.

* The spectacular nonconformity between the 1965 Russian text of the Rabelais book, the 1968 English version, and the 1970 French translation has baffled more than one scholar. Thus, Richard M. Berrong, perturbed by a reference to the well-acknowledged Rabelaisian "charm" at the end of Bakhtin's introductory chapter in the English version, appealed to the corresponding passage in the French translation, only to find that it had "a completely different paragraph in its place" (Berrong 1986, 9; 128 n. 10). Actually, Bakhtin does indeed refer to the "exceptional charm [обаяние: enchantment] of Rabelais" (cf. Bakhtin 1965, 67/58; Bakhtin 1970, 67). The confusion results from the fact that *neither* translation is reliable, so that while the English omits the concluding paragraph of the introduction, the French leaves out the penultimate. Similarly, when David Hayman complains of the omission of a phrase in Rotsel's Englishing of *Problems of Doestoevsky's Poetics* that he has himself picked up from Kolticheff's French version (Hayman 1983, 108 n. 15), it turns out that the phrase in question has actually been rendered faithfully in Rotsel's (otherwise far from always trustworthy) translation and it is the Kolticheff version which is misleading. The English and French versions of the Rabelais book are so various in their omissions and misrepresentations that even reading both of them together does not guarantee reception of everything in the original (and does guarantee a degree of "supplemental" material). In a random sampling of two pages, however, the English version left out a considerably larger number of words and phrases than the French, even if a few words and phrases were left out by both.

same time for fear of an ever possible short-circuit and an inversion of the two functions between lips and throat, inasmuch as speaking consists of expressing breath outward while articulating it as it passes through the 'mouth,' and eating in ingesting food inward by breaking it up through grinding and mastication in the same place" (Marin 1986, 47). But it is not simply because it is difficult to talk with one's mouth full—even to talk shit—so that the two oralities, ingestion and expression, are bound to get in each other's way—that "prandial libertinism" confuses the reality of orality: it is also and more obviously because one has little call to be outspoken with a banqueted belly. *Pace* Bakhtin, it is easier to *write* while eating than to speak out, and he himself mentions the *sprezzatura* alibi of humanistic composition which Rabelais parodies in the prologue to *Gargantua*: written during stolen moments; e.g., while eating (Bakhtin 1965, 309/284). But writing, ultimately, may be as just as little compatible with eating as speaking is, though for different reasons. As Deleuze and Guattari have suggested, there is "a certain disjunction between eating and speaking—and, even more so, appearances notwithstanding, between eating and writing: of course one can write while eating more easily than speak while doing so, but writing does more to transform words into things capable of competing with food. A disjunction between content and expression. To speak, and above all to write, is to fast" (Deleuze and Guattari 1975, 36). If it is both easier and more incongruous to write than to speak while eating, it is easier still—and perhaps finally more condign—to just read: we reach almost instinctively for reading matter as we consume our solitary meals. Going hungry and speaking up (or writing down); growing replete and mutely reading. Nor, then, are writing and reading so comestibly, commensally commensurate. Reading may be a kind of consumption, but we know since Freud that writing isn't ingestion, it's excretion, and that any attempt to collapse the binaries of self and other in some form of supercommunicability that we might call "reating" (the specious laddergram whereby *writing* would become *reading*) will lead only to further attempts to perform the last writes on the souls of the read. Maggie Kilgour has thus recently demonstrated how Rabelais adopts a Reformation eucharistic logic in his discussion of reading and writing, but how their communal commutability is always in danger of breaking down once again into a nature read in tooth and claw. Reading, like interpretation, can too readily become "a darker sort of feeding, in which the complementary relationship between author and reader becomes one of unambivalent antagonism" (Kilgour 1990, 88).

The confusability of materialized language with the most obvious forms in which matter enters and leaves us—eating, drinking, shitting and pissing—certainly struck Nashe no less than his continental, or is it incontinental?, contemporaries; and his use of the imagery of eating, drinking, shitting and pissing could probably form the basis of yet another counter-sublime *escatology* (sic)—a term I would like to be deriving both from Latin *esca*, food, and Greek σκατ-, from σκορ, dung. My own "escatological" reading of Nashe, however, has lacked the banquet ritualism of theoretical interpretations like Bakhtin's. Bakhtin insists, for example, that in the grotesque Rabelaisian celebration of the "victory over the world in eating" there was "no trace of mysticism, no abstract-idealistic sublimation" (Bakhtin 1965, 310/285). But such can hardly be said for his own account of it, and I am frankly more interested, reading for *things* as I here am, in "the level of the private way of life" rejected by Bakhtin, where such imagery has—wrongly according to him—been defined as "vulgar realism" (328/302). "Vulgar realism," as you know by now, is my bread and butter; and in my view Nashe is just my kind of vulgar realist, in no wise promoting these gestive functions to discursive crowning glory, origin, destiny, or symbol of epulary democratism (nor for that matter does Rabelais always do so, as I read the writing of Berrong 1983, 34ff). So while eating, drinking, shitting and pissing are, insistently, part of the *sine qua non* of life, this little *hors d'œuvre* you are reading or eating or reating is called The Four First Things only because food, drink, shit and piss would be the first four things that emerged from my reading of the Nashean "scheme of things," *if* I were really going to do one.

But it is precisely the proposal of my little toast (and celebratory roast) that the "things" in Nashe's text not be seen as the *originary*, but as the ordinary—the square meal; that "pease porredge ordinary" (Nashe 1589b, B3ᵛ/3:324) of which one should consider oneself fortunate still to be able to partake this late in the game. Nashe's text does not present us with some "mighty aspiration to *abundance* and populism [всенарод-ность]" (Bakhtin 1965, 302/278, tr. modified), but with the actual *menu*: the small, the nourishing, without which we could not go on, or even *go*, for that fæcal matter. (For while one might not want too hastily to rush from the apéritif *clinical* discourse to the dissertive, all too digestive *critical* discourse [recalling Derrida's delectably fluffy *"parole soufflée"*] as suggested by Dr. Rondibilis's corrected version of the couplet in chapter 35 of the *Tiers livre*,

> Stercus et urina Medici sunt prandia prima,
> Nobis sunt signa, vobis sunt prandia digna,

yet it would be wrong to read any scatalogical reality Nashean textuality might have to offer as *signifying* the unfolding of some grand cosmic

ordure or the disclosure of some offal truth.) There is no gastronomics of
the word to be derived, no metaphysics with anything *eschatological* about
Nashe's morsels. If the Christly *hoc est corpus meum* is the paradigmatic
semiotic act which seems to turn a thing into a sign, and thus leave one
finally eating not things but *signs* (cf. Marin 1986), Nashe's text would
appear rather to serve up signs as things, so that one is left just *reading
things*. And indeed texts, in the cheering old sense of written documents,
have been edible things; Nashe correctly tells Harvey that he could have
been made literally to eat his words by Greene if the pamphleteer had
lived: "he would haue made thee an example of ignominy to all ages that
are to come, and driuen thee to eate thy owne booke butterd, as I sawe
him make an Apparriter once in a Tauern eate his Citation waxe and all,
very handsomly seru'd twixt two dishes" (Nashe 1592c, C3^v/1:271). In
both cases—yes, yes, of course—we are dealing with a semiotic illusion;
one neither eats *signs* nor reads *things*, no; but if food *can* be a literally
readable thing, a sign *can* also be a fritterally edible one. Hungry
parishioners double up on the masses to get the wafers into their guts;
Elizabethan scholars can only sink their teeth into signs; but the figurative
effects of eating signs and reading things are complementary. If the eucharistic utterance is anti-substantial, Nashe's escatology is anti-symbolic.
The medium is the messuage.

  This is not merely to insist once again, along with Lorna Hutson, that
Nashe appreciates that once-touted aspect of the text which will not fail
to excite a titter today: "the materiality of the signifier." He does show
such an appreciation, of course—the far more radical one of the pre-
modernist who can bequeath the read pages of *The Vnfortunate Traueller*
"to stop mustard-pottes": "To anie vse about meat & drinke put them to
and spare not, for they cannot doe theyr countrie better seruice" (Nashe
1594a, A2/2:207). It is worth pointing out, however, that even as signs *per
se* (penniless) Nashe's rhetorical exertions cater to the needs of the ordinary, in marked contrast to the overdaintiness of the euphuists, or the
verbal *embarras de richesses* in Harvey's neo-Ciceronianism. Harvey's
language is overdetermined allegorically—things get lost in it: it is overprocessed. In *Haue with You*, Nashe as Pierce Penniless Respondent offers
to cart out some samples of Harvey's fancy fare, and his prosopopeic pal
Don Carneades hungrily eggs him on:

> Carn: Then good gentle Frend (if you will) let's haue halfe
> a dozen spare-ribs of his rethorique, with tart sauce of taunts
> correspondent, a mightie chyne of his magnificentest elocution,
> and a whole surloyne of his substantiallest sentences and
> similes.

Resp: And shal; I am for you; Ile serue you of the best you may assure your selfe: with a continuat *Tropologicall* speach I will astonish you; all to bee-spiced & dredged with sentences and allegories, not hauing a crum of any cost bestowed vpon it more, than the Doctors owne cooquerie. (1596, G1ᵛ/3:41)

Nashe considers Harvey's "cooquerie" to be overly processed, too pre-packaged, full of additives. Ordinary fare, things with some real value, are lost in it, refined out of existence. Harvey's text is like cuisined food (nothing but sign-value, prodigal of comestible resources). Nashe complains of the diets of the effete Roman emperors who "would feede on nothing but the tongues of Phesants and Nightingales: other, would spend as much at one banquet, as a kings reuenues came too in a yeare. . . . It is enough for me to licke dishes heere at home, though I feed not mine eyes at anie of the *Romane* feasts" (Nashe 1592b, F4-F4ᵛ/1:199). The need to dispose of consumables in fully-articulated cuisines leads to textual wastage, as when Harvey's accomplice Master Bird is predicted to "shape you a messe of newes out of the second course of his conceit" (1592c, F1ᵛ/1:289), displaying the same ample waste which Harvey exhibits in his own writing.

Nashe's words, on the other hand bear simple fare, or serve as the savoury side-dishes of conviviality—tasty scraps that bring on a greater appetite: "onely let this suffice for a tast to the text, and a bitte to pull on a good wit with, as a rasher on the coles is to pull on a cup of Wine" (1594a, A2ᵛ/2:208). Harvey had in fact equated Nashe's writing with the wine itself: "It is for Cheeke, or Ascham, to stand leuelling of Colons, or squaring of Periods, by measure, and number: his penne is like a spigot; and the Wine-presse a dullard to his Inke-presse" (Harvey 1593b, Z4/2:278). Nashe's verbal virtuosity spurts uncontrollably out, bulging almost to the bursting point the lines of a withered Cheke and distending nearly to a rending blast the colon of an Ass-cham (cf. Jonathan Goldberg's recent *punctua*—no, I did that one already . . . ?polanalytical colonization/de-colonization of Spenserian pointing [1992, 90-91]—alternatively, though, the she-Nashe's period might just be given to an unusually heavy flow). In a way this kind of gushing could fairly be considered more characteristic of Harvey's run-on "Ciceronianism" than of Nashe's supposedly jimper, more "Senecan" vein, but then Harvey frequently accuses Nashe of his own worst (or most wished for) excesses. Indeed, in the Nashe-Harvey cross-addressing, there is a strange kind of hooking of arms in much of the banter; this is clearly "intertextuality" with the gloves off (constant cross-quotation), so that it is often hard to see who is drinking (and who is pouring) whose drink. Each, for example, at one

point or another was to accuse the other of employing speakeasy nonce-
words to spike their stylistic punches (cf. Nashe 1592c, I4^v-K1/1:316;
Harvey 1593b, Z3-Z3^v/2:275-76). And Harvey had gone so far as to
identify Nashe's newfangled language literally with evanescent bar-fare,
"diuers new-founde phrases of the Tauerne" (Harvey 1592, D4^v/1:195/
45), attempting thus to leave him under the table in that Tarltonic
Elizabethan chronotope of chronic toping (comedian Dick Tarlton's image
became a kind of logo for alehouses). To Harvey's always half-admiring
admonishments, Nashe had replied that his own neologistic quaffs were
in fact of rarer vintage, though jolly good drinking all the same:

> Heigh drawer, fil vs a fresh quart *of new-found phrases,* since
> *Gabriell* saies we borrow all our eloquence from Tauerns: but let
> it be of the mighty *Burdeaux* grape, pure *vino de monte* I coniure
> thee, by the same token that the *Deuils dauncing schoole in the
> bottome of a mans purse that is emptie* [an old chestnut quoted by
> Harvey], hath beene a gray-beard Prouerbe two hundred yeares
> before *Tarlton* was borne: Ergo *no gramercy* Dicke Tarlton. But *the
> summe of summes is this,* I drinke to you M. *Gabriell,* on that con-
> dition, that you shall not excruciate your braine to be conceited
> and haue no wit. (Nashe 1592c, H2^v-H3/1:305)

Harvey's quite possibly imaginary Gentlewoman accomplice had res-
ponded convivially to Nashe's pissproud twisting of Harvey's "new-
founde phrases" with her (his?) own boast in Harvey's *New Letter of
Notable Contents:*

> Sirrha, I will stăpe an *vnknowne grape,* that shall put the mighty
> *Burdeaux grape* to bed: & may peraduĕture broach a new *Tun of
> such nippitaty,* as with the very steame of the *nappy liquour* will
> lullaby thy fiue wittes, like the sences of the drunkenest sot,
> when his braynes are sweetliest perfumed. I fit thee with a
> Similitude for thy capacity: or belch a new Confutation against
> the long tongues of the *Stilliarde,* and some twenty *Tauernes in*
> London. I could be content, a *drunken Prose,* and a *mad Ryme,*
> were thy deadlyest sinnes. But they are sweet youthes, that
> tipple their wittes with *quaffing of knauery,* and *carowsing of
> Atheisme.* (Harvey 1593a, C2^v-C3/1:283).

The homebrew of knavery and atheism may be Nashe's downfall, but
Harvey's stamping Gentlewoman can nowise ignore the intoxicating
sparkle of his *"drunken Prose."* What Nashe's discourse is, is good old

wine fresh-mixed in rinsed goblets; he can chug out his soul in innovative language as "potable property"—to pun like the Dickens—"sprinkle
it into a sentence, & so make euerie line leap like a cup of neat wine new
powred out" (Nashe 1592c H4/1:307). There is nothing, however,
"proper" about the properties of Nashe's linguistic leaseholds, idiosyncratic though they may be, for Nashe treats words as *things*, and
things, like beer, can really only be a kind of potable property ("you
don't buy it, you rent it," goes the t-shirt). Keep in mind here that of the
three nominal categories of the real (persons, places, things), only the first
two are "proper," and thus the common italicization of them in Elizabethan texts: things cannot be emphasized as property. They are always
being "exchanged": eaten, drunk, shat and pissed. Words for Nashe are
an expendable, existential *pot de vin*, an epistemological bribe, *ein anding-
endes Dingen*. Heidegger was right to speak of "the thing" in terms of a
jug which bequeaths a "gushing present [*Geschenk des Gusses*]": "The gift
of the pouring out is a drink for mortals. It revives their thirst. It
refreshes their leisure. It enlivens their conviviality." But he was wrong
to consider the "real present [*das eigentliche Geschenk*]" to be a consec-
ratory libation: "Should the pouring out be for consecration, then it does
not ease the thirst. . . . Then the gift of the jug is neither given in an inn,
nor is it a drink for mortals. . . . In the presenting of the consecrated
libations, the gushing jug essents as the presenting present" (Heidegger
1950, 45).[3] Wrong. The gift of the Nashean thing bears the greater
presents: wine unconsecrated by the pseudopresence of the de-vine,
meaning fourfold, onefold, four last bids, and now it's time for you to
fold indeed, quit your bluffing, and drink up; a drink for mortals: down
the hatch, and out into pissing conduit. For Nashe's cards have always
been on the table; he always calls the bluff of hermeneuticism's last desperate raise; his mug is neither half-full with parasitic *parousia*, nor
half-empty with Parisian porosity, nor even overbrim with parergastical
parrhesia; it is "pease porridge ordinary" with the pouring out of pot-

---

[3]"... *west der gießende Krug als das schenkende Geschenk*." Though (rather happily,
given the the choice of thing that he found most exemplarily at hand: the jug)
Heidegger is probably popularly best known these days for being ". . . a boozin'
beggar / Who could think you under the table," those who were only following
orders of discourse are aware that he has untranslatable ways of making
morphemes talk, not least effectively by wringing the semantic ranges out of them
with the ropes of a pseudetymological laddergram whose plunging rungs lead
down into an ever tenser past (*trinken, Trank, Trunk; Schenke, Schank, Geschenk;
Schinken, schenken, Henker*, etc.). In my own translation, of course, the puns have
been changed to protect the inessent.

ations for mortals. And though its blushing Hippocrene may at times be conversationally asking itself *do I slake or weep?*, Nashe's *jug, jug* always calls ominously in re: the forlorn last bids to sweeten the epistemological pot at the folding of philosophy as eschatology. As Ralegh ominated in his prophecy "On the Cardes, and Dice":

> Full many a christians heart shall quake for fear,
> The dreadfull sound of trump when he shall hear.
> (Ralegh 1957, 48)[4]

[4]Cf. Frère Jean's interpretation of Mellin de Saint-Gelais's "prophetical enigma" in chapter 58 of *Gargantua* as "a description of the game of tennis." If these pseudapocalyptic tonalities are to be reduced to sublunary sports coverage, in what direction would the pro-mundane lines from the enigma in chapter 2 be expected to be taken?

> *Et mieulx aima le feu du ciel empire*
> *Au tronc ravir où l'on vend les soretz,*
> *Que l'aer serain, contre qui l'on conspire,*
> *Assubjectir es dictz des Massoretz,*

which we might yet feel warranted to translate in the mid-range (though cf. Marc Berlioz's lower bodily stratagems of interpretation in his too-close-for-comfort, gloves-off examination; 1985, 57ff):

> And preferred to ravish the Empyrean fire hence
> From the hollow stump where the herrings red are sold
> Than the serene air which they conspire against
> To subjugate to some Massoretic code.

Rabelais *is* arguably the most obvious precarouser of the Nashean prosaic *prosit!* to the text and the world as potable property. The well-known critical brawl over the true intent behind the prologue to *Gargantua* has pre-emptied a full appreciation of the equally debatable exemplary reification of text coming between that prologue and the earlier one to *Pantagruel*. In the latter (actually the former) prologue, the text is itself balm and restorative; in *Gargantua*, in the famous figure of the Silenus box, it comes to *contain* a curative drug. Marc Berlioz, however, has even managed to argue himself, and Rabelais, back out of that tight spot by questioning the meataphorics of the author's later image of breaking the bone to get at the marrow, and querying the sense of the phrase "*a plus hault sens interpreter*," incidentally tearing into the meat-seeking missile of the English scholar once again in the rather owlish person of M.A. Screech, whom he cunningly identifies with Rabelais's anglophobic caricature (Thomas More?), Thaumaste:

Nashe makes that apocalyptic trump from the empty jug which he has cordially dashed into our narrowing eyes; and its messuage is plain: eat, drink and be merry, for tomorrow we diet. His gift of gab consecrates the drink *as drink*. He often likens his discourse to a toast and its attendant quaff: "Before I vnbowell the leane Carcase of thy book any further, Ile drinke one cup of lambswooll, *to the Lambe of God and his enemies*" (Nashe 1592c, C3ᵛ/ 1:272). His book against Harvey is *"a cuppe of newes"* with which he carouses his reader (A2/1:255).

But if Harvey's style does amount to a form of *cuisinage* or *gourmandise* in which impotably proper things are consumed with no attention paid to what is in them or even their particular flavor, it could perhaps be objected that Nashe for his part indulges in a kind of textual temulence (he certainly always casts his pamphlets as "three sheets to the wind"). I can accept as much, but I insist that Nashe's brand of *ale-thia* is genuinely barmy rather than philosophically barmecidal. He himself was

And so we find Our English Master (for Mr. Screech does hail from London) with his mind firmly made up that we are to seek the marrow of words, which is to say, their covert meaning, it being understood that this covert meaning cannot but be deep, which is to say, well beyond and above the appearances. And his questing will is supported by the exhortation to interpret in a higher sense, a phrase which he takes theologically as an incitement to rise above the literal or prosaic to the spiritual, necessarily passing through the levels which he has indicated for us. In other words, the law of academic gravity has precluded his considering the possibility that the phrase interpret in a higher sense might be a jest most perfectly elaboured by nature. (Berlioz 1985, 4-5).

In other other words, it would seem, the high-minded, bone-breaking Brit (I keep thinking of that walking skeleton in the Ray Bradbury *October Country* story) can consider himself *bel et bien con-futé (chic)* by the *risus sardonicus* which Berlioz, in whose *modus operandi* I seem to see inklings of my own, has here produced: "he showed all his teeth, and with his two thumbs plucked down his two eyelids very low, making therewith a very ill-favoured countenance, as it seemed to the company" (*Pantagruel*, ch. 19; here, and throughout this footnote—with the exception of the four lines of verse in my own translation above—I have tried to adopt or adapt Urquhart's versions for quotations from, or where Berlioz nonchalantly slips into, Rabelais's discourse; but it seemed to me that it would have made for an unfair clinker in his *symphonie fantastique* to accept Urquhart's "in a sublimer sense" for the Rabelaisian "a plus hault sens"; and, what's more, there is some case to be made, a little Silenus box at least, for the view that in sniffing out Rabelaisian "sense" there will always be found the two hundred meanings in Gargantua's mother's smock, *"car il y a sens davant et sens derriere"* [ch. 12]).

fond of the Renaissance likening of poetic inspiration to a form of inebriation, and contrasted the poet's bibaciousness with the temperance of the
studious:

> Let frugall scholers and fine fingered nouices take their drinke
> by the ounce and their wine by the halfe penny worths, but it is
> for a Poet to examine the pottle pots, and gage the bottome of
> whole gallons; *qui bene vult* poiein, *debet ante* pinein. A pot of
> blew burning ale, with a fiery flaming toste, is as good as *Pallas*
> with the nine Muses on *Pernassus* top: without the which, in
> vaine they may crie, O thou my Muse, inspire me with some
> penne, when they want certaine liquid sacrifice to rouze her
> forth her denne. (1589b, B2ᵛ/3:321-22)

Yet according to Bacchus in *Summers Last Will*, even academic types like
Harvey only need moisten their lips: "Giue a scholler wine, going to his
booke, or being about to inuent, it sets a new poynt on his wit, it glazeth
it, scowres it, it giues him *acumen*. . . . There is no excellent knowledge
without mixture of madnesse. And what makes a man more madde in
the head then wine?" (1600, F1/3:265). The relationship between cognac
and cognition, then, apéritifs and apprehension, eggnog and knowledge,
whisky and *Wissenschaft*, sack and sagacity, drink and think, spirits and
er spirits could doubtless be ale-gorized in a microreading of that
infamous episode from the opening of *The Vnfortunate Traueller* where
Jack Wilton as "Lord high regent of rashers of the coles and red herring
cobs" (Nashe 1594d, A3/2:209) takes on a "peere of quart pots" (A3ᵛ/
2:210), the camp cider merchant, and extenuates his drinking bout by
playing on the cider merchant's "reading-for-the-plot" epistemophilia (the
plot here is actually against the cider merchant himself). Maybe the cider
merchant figures the real, which must be bam*booze*led of its reality
through linguistic technique, maybe he sits in for the critics who must be
cozened of their ci*dereal* time (sec) by an un*alego*rizable text; but the real
point here as always is: "Well, *Tendit ad sydera virtus*, thers great vertue
belongs (I can tel you) to a cup of sider" (A3ᵛ/2:210).

Rather than trying to defend Nashean inebriation on the shaky
ground of some e-pissed-emological bonus, then, I am concerned in the
end with how rhetorical intoxication might actually lead to renewed ac-
quaintance with the feel of the real. This is not so insensible as it might
at first sound. After all, when one has been drinking, one is indeed more
likely to bump into things. Thus, if Nashean lightheaded rhetoricity
clearly trips over the "clodderd garbage of confutatiõ" in Harvey's
cloying style (1592c, H4/1:307), it also might accidentally overturn the

dry new "Senecan" plainstyle of "objectivity," which, as Bacon's smelly name so well suggests, has proved to be bad for the heart. Nashe does cultivate a rhetoric of intemperance, of slips of the tongue, stumbles into things. But with that rhetoric, always poured out in Rabelaisian or Hemingwayesque draughts, he usually serves a square meal of matter as well—things you can smell and taste and that fill you up.

Critics have become too accustomed to assimilating the overly rich, often disgustingly meaty texts put out by Nashe's better-heeled compatriots. He offers us a nice little red herring "to pull on a cup of Wine," such as with any luck would flap winningly out of our hands before we could even consume it, and we proceed to prick it and pound it and pepper it and powder it and pinch it and rinse it and cinch it and sauce it and salt it and batter it and malt it and melt it and mint it and tint it and hint it and lemon it and curdle it and coddle it and model it and mould it and fold it and foil it and boil it and broil it and braise it and raise it and date it and currant it and candy it and sweet and sour it, and then brew it and stew it, distil it and pill it, dice it, slice it, grate it and chop it, cube it and flake it and sweeten it and flavor it and color it and add to it and subtract from it and nitrite it and freezedry it and shrink-wrap it and safetycap it, all too like to the cooks of the Pope's kitchen with the dear-bought little cob they take for the King of the Fishes (1599, H4ff/3:207ff), treating it as the read meat we are so accustomed to preparing for consumption: "Nay, we are such flesh-eating Saracens, that chaste fish may not content vs, but we delight in the murder of innocent mutton, in the vnpluming of pullerie, and quartering of calues and oxen. It is horrible and detestable, no godly Fishmonger that can digest it" (1592b, G1/1:201). Continue to digest it we scarcely can, but we go on overreading all the same, until it's a wonder we can even still sleep at nights, knowing, as we do, that "[i]t is as desperate a peece of seruice to sleep vpon a full stomacke, as it is to serue in face of the bullet: a man is but his breath, and that may as wel be stopt by putting too much in his mouth at once, as rūning on the mouth of the Cannon" (Ibid.). Yet we go on running on at the mouth, running into the mouth of that canon, cooking up more and more of the same overprocessed stuff. Is it any wonder if some of us now have latched onto that rhetoric of intemperance just to conk ourselves out for awhile? For intempretation (*sack!*) has really become a form of dyspepsia—an inability to read untroubledly, absorb, be restored—and wine, as we know, is, if nothing else, a notable aid to digestion, and a useful inducer of sleep. The problem with getting pissed, though—to return to the final two elements of the escatological reading, for which material is frankly somewhat lacking in Nashe's text itself—is that when you wake up you feel like shit.

The habitual overreaders will no doubt be finding all this a little hard to swallow, having doubtless, as usual, bitten off more than they can really chew. "Haue with them," says Nashe, "for a riddle or two, onely to set their wittes a nibbling, and their iobbernowles a working, and so good night to their segniories" (1599, I4ᵛ/3:216).

Things that Go Bump in the Knight

THE DISCOURSE OF APPARITIONS

The Athenians were noted for lauish amplifieng: the Cretensians
for craftie lying, the Thessalians for subtle cogging: the Cartha-
ginians for deceitfull perfidie: *Hanniball, Fabius, Agathocles, Iphi-
crates, Vlisses,* and a thousand such, for counterfeit pollicie, but
all their forgeries were seasoned with the salt of probabilitie, &
onelie vsed at occasions of aduauntage: and although the Gre-
cians generallie were ouer-lightheaded, and vaine-spoken, yet
their leuitie sauored of elegant wittinesse, and the flying birde
carried meate in the mouth.

> Gabriel Harvey, *Foure Letters and Certaine Sonnets*

Der Nüchterne spricht von Traum, als spräche er aus dem
Schlaf.

> Walter Benjamin, *Einbahnstrasse*

Rom. I dreampt a dreame to night.
Mer. And so did I.
Rom. Well what was yours?
Mer. That dreamers often lye.
Rom. In bed a sleepe while they do dreame things true.

> William Shakespeare, *Romeo and Juliet*

"Anie meate that in the day time we eat against our stomackes,"
Nashe tells us at the end of his discussion of the external causes of
nightmares in *The Terrors of the Night*, "begetteth a dismall dreame"

(1594c, C4^v/1:357). It is with reference to a similiar such "popular saying" that Freud *begins* his discussion of the stimuli and sources of dreams: "dreams come from the stomach" (Freud 1900, 2-3: 22/4:22). This is the hearsay evidence that nourishes the "somatic" account so attractive to lay opinion but which needs to be supplemented by the more metapsychologically *geistreich* theoretical explanation which Freud will provide. Nashe for his part goes on to describe how discontented blood allows "light imperfect humours" to ascend to the head (1594c, C4^v/1:357). But the straightforward demotic explanation might have provided both oneirologists with a little more food for thought.

Digestion *covers up* the transformation from the external and the physical to the internal and the mental because in the proprioception of the stomach it is no longer possible to *see* whether it is the thing that has been swallowed or some part of ourselves that is the source of the discontent. The thing may or may not have, has and has not already become a part of us; the discontent arises in the digestive absorption of what is known as a *content*, the process whereby a thing becomes part of us. We can no longer see the thing and so can no longer be sure whether *it* is still there, whether there is still a difference between it and us.

The properly external things that can cause dreams, as discussed by both Nashe and Freud, are frequently equally hard to place; not because they are inside us, but because we can't tell *where or what* they are: things that go bump in the night. An alarming number of the "things" that can serve as the external stimuli to dreams in both Freud's and Nashe's accounts are actually *noises*. Indeed, the shiftiness of the audible rightly haunts Nashe's whole "discourse of apparitions," as *The Terrors* is subtitled. "A Dreame is nothing els," he concludes at the end of a page, "but the Eccho of our conceipts in the day" (1594c, C4/1:356). But at the top of the next page he changes his mind:

> But other-while it fals out, that one Eccho borrowes of another: so our dreames (the Ecchoes of the day) borrow of anie noyse we heare in the night.
>
> As for example; if in the dead of the night there be anie rumbling, knocking or disturbaunce neere vs, wee straight dreame of warres, or of thunder. If a dogge howle, we suppose we are transported into hell, where we heare the complaint of damned ghosts. If our heads lye double or vneasie we imagine we vphold heauen with our shoulders like *Atlas*. If wee bee troubled with too manie clothes, then we suppose the nightmare rides vs. I knew one that was crampt, and hee dreamt that hee was torne in peeces with wylde horses; and another, that hauing

a blacke sant brought to his bed side at mid-night, dreamt he
was bidden to dinner at Iron-mongers Hall. (C4ᵛ/1:356-57)

Freud's account of external stimuli is frequented by the audible as well, ·
and the dream-content produced by these noises is similarly largely
violent in nature. Many of the dreams caused by outside things involve
torture, and a surprising number are centered around social insurrection:
the French Revolution, the Reign of Terror, and "the June days of 1848"
(Freud 1900, 2-3:2/4:25). Thunder becomes battle; a cockcrow, a cry of
horror; a hot poultice suggests the scalping blade of the "Red Indian";
gout, a session on the rack; scissors being sharpened, alarm bells. A
dream of Maury's, Freud tells us, has become famous: his headboard
having fallen across the back of his neck, he apparently back-dreamt an
elaborate fantasy leading up to his heroic guillotining during the Reign
of Terror. Much later Freud returns to this notorious dream to suggest
that the *nachträglich* lead-up to the dreamified external stimulus could
only have been elaborated so swiftly if this "wish-fulfilment" fantasy was
already present in Maury's unconscious, biding its time until a physio-
logical pretext should present itself: a dream just waiting to happen
(Freud 1900, 2-3:499ff/5:495ff; a presumably more obvious wish-fulfillment will be recalled from Mercutio's Queen Mab speech, where,
when the gossamer waggoner drives her cart over the neck of the soldier
it is *he* who dreams of cutting *other people's* throats, foreign throats).

Peculiarly, Nashe too speaks of executioners, but in dealing with the
egress of discontenting matter and dream-stuff from out the portals of
sense perception (the nose, the mouth, the eyes, the ears), rather than
with the *ingress* of such matter through them: "There were gates in *Rome*
out of which nothing was carried but dust and dung, and men to execution: so, manie of the gates of our senses serue for nothing but to con-
ueigh out excrementall vapors, & afrighting deadly dreames, that are
worse than executioners vnto vs" (Nashe 1594c, D1/1:357).

Frued's discussion of Maury's dream of execution centers on an
heroic wish-fulfillment. In progressively purpler prose, Freud imagines
Maury's identification with one of "those formidable figures who, by the
power alone of their thoughts and flaming eloquence, ruled the city in
which the heart of humanity beat convulsively in those days." Maury's
recollection of being led to the guillotine "surrounded by a throng of
people stretching as far as the eye could see [*unübersehbaren Menschen-
menge*]" suggests to Freud that his dream was "in fact of this ambitious
type" (Freud 1900, 2-3:501/5:497). (Freud seems to suppose that this
crowd represents popular admiration in Maury's dream, not a lynch mob
or host of bloodthirsty gawkers.) In Nashe's dream-execution, judge,

prosecutor and executioner are demonic rather than demotic, cross-examining us somewhere inside dark and isolated selves: "so when Night in her rustie dungeon hath imprisoned our ey-sight, and that we are shut seperatly in our chambers from resort, the diuell keepeth his audit in our sin-guilty consciences, no sense but surrenders to our memorie a true bill of parcels of his detestable impieties. The table of our hart is turned to an index of iniquities, and all our thoughts are nothing but texts to condemne vs" (Nashe 1594c, B1/1:345). The two executions make an unexpected juxtaposition: for it is not the fin-de-siècle Freud's, but the Elizabethan Nashe's that converts external detail into psychic interiority. The devil's whispered "audit" in Nashe *privatizes* the "fatal summons" of the *Comité* in Freud's version of Maury's dream; Nashe's "hart" that is "an index of iniquities" is *expanded* to the throbbing urban "heart of humanity" in the Freudian Paris, and the inability to see beyond the throng there is reduced to the inability to see outside *oneself* in Nashe's night. The persecutors in Freud are a socially and politically conditioned tyrannical collectivity carrying out "the will of the people"; in Nashe a demonized self or other (difficult to say), acting "as Gods executioner" (B3/1:348), an autocrat of the abandoned soul. The night is the devil's, to whom "our creator for our punishment hath alloted it . . . as his peculiar segniorie and kingdome" (B2/1:346). The difference between the devil and the poor souls he subjugates is sometimes discernible; now and then he reveals himself as the nocturnal potentate of woe he really is, but otherwhiles he travels disguised through his kingdom trying to persuade us to share his malcontent state: "Like a cunning fowler, to this end he spreadeth his nets of temptation in the darke, that men might not see to auoyd them" (B2/1:346-47). At the top of the page Nashe had been comparing day and night themselves to birds in the Bible: the dove sent out from Noah's ark "that returneth to our eyes with an Oliue branch of peace in his mouth (presenting quiet and securitie to our distracted soules and consciences)" and the "raven of the valley" (Proverbs 30.17) that "pecks out mens eyes in the valley of death" (B2/1:346). Blinded, "[i]n the quiet silence of the night" we turn to these birds, and it is we who will be trapped in the springes of his empiry of evil if once *we* grant *him* (disguised as us) "audience": "Those that catch birdes imitate their voyces, so will hee imitate the voyces of Gods vengeance, to bring vs like birds into the net of eternall damnation" (B3/1:348).

The voice that tells us here of the day-doves and night-ravens is also the voice that tells us of the devil's ability to imitate bird-calls to capture the aviform bodies of our souls, the same voice that tells us that "the least thought of faith" will cause the apparitions with which the devil would trap us to be "quite vanished and put to flight" (Ibid.). The devil, we hear, is a voice-varier, a form-shifter, and the legerdemain of his illusions will be swifter than the unheeded "faith" of the I, if we give in to his patter; for he "can cogge as quicke as thought." But how do we know in the dark to whom we are listening? The devil is polyphonic, multiple: "there is not a roome in anie mans house, but is pestred and close packed with a campe royall of diuels," and their "segniorie and kingdome" seems to be founded precisely on our inability to see: "Don *Lucifer* himselfe, their grand *Capitano*, asketh no better throne than a bleare eye to set vp his state in" (B4/1:349).

The opening of Nashe's "discourse of apparitions," then, tells how the night is the realm in which our vision, forced inward, is subject to the hypnagogic rule of the devil, made possible by our vulnerability to his discourse, our inability to shut out the audible. As birds are caught by bird-calls, our thoughts are caught by voices that imitate other thoughts, other voices; God, the devil.

But Nashe goes on to try to separate out the devil from the self by putting something between them; dreams result from an intoxication of the senses (those emissaries between inside and out, head and stomach), when the lower strata churn in melancholy and discontent, "those organicall parts which to the minde are ordained embassadours, doo not their message as they ought, but by some misdiet or misgouernment being distempered, faile in their report and deliuer vp nothing but lyes and fables" (C3/1:354). They have been drugged by this melancholy, which may have resulted from the infiltration of a foreign agent ("misdiet") allowed in through "misgouernment" of the body. The state of unrest is displeasingly dyspeptic, like the upset caused by whatever disagrees with us. Whatever we have failed to accomodate in governing our selves sticks in our craw and comes back in other forms to haunt us: "A dreame is nothing els but a bubling scum or froath of the fancie, which the day hath left vndigested" (C3ᵛ/1:355). But the result of misgovernance in the dream-state is a violent anarchy:

> No such figure of the first Chaos whereout the world was extraught, as our dreames in the night. In them all states, all sexes, all places are confounded and meete together.
>
> Our cogitations runne on heapes like men to part a fray, where euerie one strikes his next fellow. From one place to another without consultation they leap, like rebells bent on a head. (C4/1:356).

The head that rolls during the insurrection of the dream-state is the head that has allowed the discontent through misgovernance; to the guilty conscience night brings the treason of thought. Such a misruling head can swiftly become the "slaue" of superstition (D1ᵛ/1:358), but the examples Nashe now gives are of actual political leaders who had unquiet sleep and whose mental forebodings were then more or less borne out by real life upsets:

> *Darius* King of the *Medes* and *Persians*, before his fatall discomfiture, dreamt hee saw an Estrich with a winged crowne ouer-running the earth, and deuouring his Iuel-coffer, as if it had been an ordinarie peece of yron. That Iuel-coffer was by *Alexander* surprized, and afterward *Homers* Workes in it carried before him, euen as the Mace or Purse is customably carried before our Lord Chancelor.
>
> *Hannibal* dreamed a little before his death, that hee was drowned in the poysonous Lake *Asphalites*, when it was presently his hap within some few dayes distance, to seeke his fate by the same meanes in a vault vnder earth. (D1ᵛ-D2/1:359).

This "poysonous Lake," perhaps, leads Nashe into a digression on Iceland, with its "bottomlesse Lake *Vether*, ouer which no fowle flies but is frozen to death" and round which the inhabitants "are deafned wyth the hideous roring of his waters when the winter breaketh vp, & the yce in his dissoluing gives a terrible cracke like to thunder, when as out of the midst of it (as out of *Mont-Gibell*) a sulphureous stinking smoak issues, that welnigh poysons the whole Countrey" (D2ᵛ/1:360). This groaning lake (actually in Sweden) is the orifice that eerily doubles the gaping volcano of Mt. Hekla, which "a number conclude to bee hell mouth; for neere vnto it are heard such yellings and groanes, as *Ixion*, *Titius*, *Sisiphus*, and *Tantalus*, blowing all in one trumpet of distresse, could neuer conioyned bellowe foorth" (D3/1:359). Nashe says he has wandered into this insular realm because his "theame is The terrors of the Night, and *Island* [as he spells it] is one of the chiefe kingdomes of the night" (D2ᵛ/1:360). With this discovery of Iceland, Nashe has reached the infernal center of his pamphlet, which has thus far been haunted by devils, birds, discontent humors, uneasy rulers, rumors of war, voices or noises in the dark, and an overall indigestion. The second half will be somewhat glibber and given to a bit more garrulous whistling in the dark, but many of the phantoms of the first part come back like recurrent nightmares to turn the game grim when we least expect it. These uncanny revenants are somewhat prepared for by Nashe's midpoint recognition of the oneiric nature of his own discourse of apparitions:

I care not much if I dream yet a little more: & to say the troth, all this whole Tractate is but a dreame, for my wits are not halfe awaked in it: & yet no golden dreame, but a leaden dreame is it; for in a leaden standish I stand fishing all day, but haue none of Saint *Peters* lucke to bring a fish to the hooke that carries anie siluer in the mouth. And yet there be of them that carrie siluer in the mouth too, but none in the hand: that is to say, are verie bountifull and honorable in their words, but except it be to sweare indeed, no other good deedes comes from them. (D3/1: 360-61)

In the second half, Nashe takes on a more skeptical tone, distinguishing more minutely historically-verified true "visions . . . sent from heauen to foreshew the translation of Monarchies" (D4/362), from mere dreams, interpreted by those conjuring silver-mouthed opportunistic courtiers who would "prognosticate treasons and conspiracies, in which they were vnderhand inlincked themselues" so that their complicity could not be suspected if the treachery came to light (D4-D4^v/1:362-63). Such pseudo-diviners have now set themselves up around London, "not in the hart of the Cittie" but "in the skirtes and out-shifts" (E1^v/1:364), where they ingratiate themselves with noblemen and eventually are entertained "for one of their priuie counsaile" by "great Peeres" (E2^v/1:366). A conjuring courtier of this sort is a "medium" in a twofold sense; a spiritualist double agent, he traffics between factions: "All malcontents entending anie inuasiue violence against their Prince and Countrey runne headlong to his oracle. Contrarie factions enbosome vnto him their inwardest complots, whilest he like a craftie Iacke a both sides, as if he had a spirite still at his elbow, reciprocallie embowelleth to the one what the other goes about; receiuing no intelligence from anie familiar, but their own mouths" (E2^v-E3/1:367).

One may recall the alchemical arguments of M.C. Bradbrook (1936) *et al.* whereby Nashe would be here alluding to and half-mocking a mysterious "school of night" patronized by Ralegh and overseen by the archimage Thomas Harriot, a coven of crypto-catholic "scientists" and intriguers. With them, in fact, even Harvey and some of the others Frances Yates was formerly wont to team up with him (Yates 1934) could probably now be allied—thanks to the lucubrations of W. Schrickx (1956)—under a general giddy head of "inspired melancholy" (Yates 1979, 144), as against the sanguine enclave, postulated by Bradbrook, that included Shakespeare and Southampton, with Nashe as a craftie Iacke a both sides. But the passage can be related to "inspired melancholy" in a different way, for its worry over malcontents who would disrupt the crown running headlong to this sorcerer uncannily recalls, does it not?, the very vapors invading the head on account of discontent humors which in the first part of the pamphlet impeached melancholy for being "the mother of dreames, and of all terrours of the night whatsoeuer" (1594c, C4ᵛ/1:357). Melancholy, like the malcontent, does not actually invade the head itself; a rumor of the discontent is filtered through to the head by a medium. But whereas previously these agitations were misreported as it were by an inebriated ambassador, they are now mis*represented* by a duplicitous charlatan, who gives a false report of *true* discontent. The latent *content* of the picture of the courtly conjuror is an allegory of the senses in the dream-state—not as intoxicated emissaries, but as opportunistic schemers. And the difference between "dreams" and true "visions" suddenly becomes patent: dreams are fictions that get *interpreted* by quacks, they are not unmediated "visions." Visions are *realized,* but are *not interpreted beforehand*; dreams are *mis-interpreted* and then *fail to be borne out by history.* Nashe gives examples of three emperors whose dreams did *not* come true: Louis XI, who dreamt he "swam in blood on the toppe of the *Alpes*" a dream falsely interpreted by "Father *Robert* (a holy Hermit of his time)" (F1ᵛ/1:371); Charles V, who refused Cornelius Agrippa's offer of supernatural succour after the magician had "expounded" an apparently ominous dream he had dreamt, but who then went on nevertheless to triumph in spite of premonitions; and "*Alphonso* King of *Naples,*" a *self*-interpreter who saw in his night vision before the "rumor of the French Kings comming into *Italy*" an omen of the peaceful outcome of their contention,

> but far otherwise it fell out; for the French King came indeed, and he [Alphonsus] was driuen thereby into such a melancholy extasie, that he thought the verie fowles of the ayre would snatch his Crowne from him; and no bough or arbour that ouershadowd him, but enclosed him, and tooke him prisoner; and that not so much but the stones of the street sought to iustle him out of his Throne. (F2/1:372).

Nashe informs us that the misinterpretation attached to whatever proceeds "from anie vapourous dreggie parts of our blood or our braines" is the reason that "Learning" has been banished by the Turks: "because it is euerie daye setting men together by the eares, mouing straunge contentions and alterations, and making his professors fainthearted and effeminate" (F2ᵛ/1:372). It serves no purpose, in Nashe's mind, to amplify the "disordered skirmishing and conflicting of our sensitiue faculties" in the dream-state with waking analyses and "too busie examining of our paines ouer-passed" (F2ᵛ/1:373). In a series of interconnecting analogies, Nashe compares discoursing on the apparition to a master's tormentive preaching at a boy waiting for his breeching "a long time all law and no Gospel, ere he proceed to execution," or to the slow death of consumption, worse than death itself, and to "long depending hope friuolously defeated, than which there is no greater miserie on earth; & so *per consequens* no men in earth more miserable than courtiers" (F3/1:374). Such a person is only progressively weakened and oversensitized to misery through his desperate attachment to illusions spawned by the double-dealingness of possibility; eventually "anie terror, the least illusion in the earth, is a *Cacodæmon* vnto him. His soule hath left his bodie; for why, it is flying after these ayrie incorporeate Courtly promises, and glittring painted allurements; which when they vanish to nothing, it lykewise vanisheth with them" (G1/1:376-77). All of these lingerings—hope, disease, lecturing, interpretation—are fates worse than death, in that they simply postpone the fatal event in agonizing consciousness; they are finally like dying of a broken heart: "hee whom greefe vndertakes to bring to his end, hath his hart gnawen in sunder by little & little with vultures, like Prometheus" (G1/1:377).

As an extenuation and amplification of an unhappy and in some sense false consciousness, melancholy is indeed the sickness unto death, and Nashe's way out, fleetingly glimpsed through *The Terrors of the Night*, in fact demands a reappropriation of one's consciousness and one's responsibility for it: "Euerie one shapes his owne feares and fancies as he list" (G1ᵛ/1:377). Indeed, Nashe's keen sense of the economics of consciousness suggests to him a deliberate administration of unhappy consciousness not at all unlike the "anti-selfconsciousness" which Geoffrey Hartman claims to have been developed by the late Romantics to combat their own romantic anxiety (cf. Hartman 1970). As a form of melancholy, such anxiety was after all a commonplace in the Elizabethan age, apparently brought on by the breakdown of a hegemonic episteme caused by the explosion in learning, voyages of discovery, religious schizophrenia, unprecedented social mobility, and so on. Small wonder in such a situation if "ouermuch agitation of the mynd" led to atrabilious attacks upon "Magistrates and Officers in the Commonwealth, or Studentes which at vnseasonable times sit at their Bookes & Studies" (Lemnius 1576, 136ᵛ). Some Elizabethans, like the postromantics, recognized a possible source of melancholy in excessive contemplation and battled it with their own anti-melancholics, as exemplified in the constantly repeated advice Gabriel Harvey gives himself in his commonplace book to "post on to practis" (Harvey MS.b, 16/89): "He is A uery swadd, & sott that, dullith, or bluntith ether witt, or boddy with any lumpish, or Malácholy buzzing abowt this, or that" (7/87). Self-absorption is only a lingering disease, uncertainty and hesitation cancers of the stomach to which death would be preferable.

But the interest of Nashe's own pamphlet has rested on the anxious "fantastic realism" he has maintained throughout, the hesitation and doubt as to whether sources of trouble are within or without, natural or supernatural, real or imagined, to be interpreted or ignored. Such "fantastic realism," as Todorov suspected, *depends on* uncertainty; and there can be no sense of the *real* without it:

> If certain events in the universe of a book are put forward as imaginary, they thereby contest the imaginary nature of the rest of the book. If this or that apparition is only the product of an overexcited imagination, it is because everything that surrounds it is real. Far from being a glorification of the imaginary, fantastic literature posits the majority of a text as belonging to the real, or more precisely, as motivated by it, like a name given to a pre-existing thing. (Todorov 1970, 176).

Nashe maintains the dichotomy between real visions and unreal dreams; but it is often not clear which "things" in his text he is positing as real and which as imaginary. This is especially true of the long set piece near the end of the pamphlet, which he introduces on the heels of his insistence that we fashion our own fancies:

> I write not this, for that I thinke there are no true apparitiõs or prodigies, but to shew how easily we may be flouted if we take not great heed, with our own anticke suppositions. I will tell you a strange tale tending to this nature: whether of true melancholy or true apparition, I will not take vpon me to determine. (Nashe 1594c, G1ᵛ/1:378).

It is here that Nashe relates the mysterious deathbed discourse of "a Gentleman of good worship and credit" who had fallen sick at his home where Nashe had been staying "in Februarie last . . . in the Countrey some threescore myle off from London," and who had "pretended to haue miraculous waking visions" which before he died he "avouched" to "a great Man of this Land" who had then subsequently reported them to Nashe, or so it would seem (G1ᵛ-G2/1:378).

The series of apparitions had begun the first day of his illness, when the gentleman "visibly saw (as he affirmed) al his chamber hung with silken nets and siluer hookes, the diuell (as it should seeme) comming thether a fishing . . . with the nets he feard to be strangled or smothred, & with the hooks to haue his throat scracht out, and his flesh rent and mangled" (G2/1:378). This vision is replaced by one of "a cōpanie of lusty sailers . . . carousing and quaffing in large siluer kans to his helth. Fellowes they were that had good big pop mouths to crie Port a helme Saint George, and knew as well as the best what belongs to haling of bolings yare, and falling on the star-boord buttocke." These big pop mouths and star-board buttockses are apparently seen as a temptation, but the invalid refuses their "drunken proffers" and "sayd hee highly scorned and detested both them and their hellish disguisings" (G2/1:378-79). The "third course" follows, "stately diuels" in bravery and jewelry, "louely youths and full of fauour" who deck the room with treasure and set up a "Princely royall Tent" into which Lucifer makes an imperial entrance, sending to the sick man "a gallant Embassadour, signifying thus much, that if hee would serue him, hee should haue all the rich treasure that he saw there or anie farther wealth hee would desire" (G2ᵛ/1:379). The gentleman piously declines and the Satanic regalia departs. Here there is a strange lapsus in Nashe's account; the vision of the devil's pavillion had been served up as the "third course," but the next is introduced as follows: "Then did ther, for the *third* pageant present themselues vnto him, an inueigling troupe of naked Virgins" (emphasis added). This bizarre misnumbering opens the longest of Nashe's "amplifications" of the gentleman's visions, retailing the dancing and lascivious offers of these naked maids and continually spinning off into out-of-control hypotyposis. "Their daintie feete," for instance, "in their tender birdlike trippings, enameld (as it were) the dustie ground; and their odiferous breath more perfumed the aire, than Ordinance would, that is charged with Amomum, Muske, Cyuet, and Amber-greece" (G3/ 1:380). The sick man's "vision" here has even suddenly given way to olfactory detail, and we assume such details must be Nashe's. The "fourth Act" features "sober attyred Matrones" who offer to pray for the man. To this he acquiesces, and they kneel around his bed praying for him half an hour (G3ᵛ/1:381) until the vision is broken off by what is undoubtedly the most uncanny passage in Nashe's account:

> Rising vp agayne on the right hand of his bed, there appeared a cleare light, and with that he might perceiue a naked slender foote offring to steale betwixt the sheets to him.
>
> At which instant, entred a messenger from a Knight of great honour thereabouts, who sent him a most precious extract quintessence to drinke: which no sooner he tasted, but he thought hee saw all the fore-named Enterluders at once hand ouer head leap,

plunge, & drowne themselues in puddles and ditches hard by, and hee felt perfect ease. (G4/1:381)

But the ease does not last long: "within fowre houres after, hauing not fully settled his estate in order, hee grewe to trifling dotage, and rauing dyde within two daies following" (G4/1:381-82). "God is my witnesse," as Nashe ironically puts it,

> in all this relation, I borrowe no essential part from stretcht out inuention, nor haue I one iot abusde my informations; onely for the recreation of my Readers, whom loath to tyre with a course home-spunne tale, that should dull them woorse than Holland cheese, heere and there I welt and garde it with allusiue exornations & comparisons: and yet me thinks it comes off too goutie and lumbring. (G4/1:382)

Nashe's amplification of detail—authorized because "Truth is euer drawne and painted naked, and I haue lent her but a leathern patcht cloake at most to keepe her from the cold" (G4-G4ᵛ/1:382)—calls into question just whose visions and dreams we are actually talking about here. The second part of Nashe's pamphlet has featured more uneasy rulers, fraudulent seers, rumors and humors. The birds have been turned back into our persecutors (Alphonso's "fowles," the vultures on Prometheus), and we by implication have now become fish for whom the devil spreads his silken nets. "Are there anie doubts which remaine in your mynde vndigested?" Nashe asks the reader (G4ᵛ/1:382), and indeed we may respond that the material with which he has glutted us is beginning to whee borborygmically for the digestive action of a unifying reading. The picture as read is certainly unstomachably grotesque, just as Horace had promised would be a book

> . . . cuius, velut aegri somnia, vanae
> fingentur species, ut nec pes nec caput uni
> reddatur formae.
> [. . . whose idle fancies, like the dreams of a sick man, are fashioned so that neither head nor foot can be put down to a single shape] (*Ars poetica*, 7-9)

Such a scrambled picture of things, like a rebus, needs to have its material repieced together to make sense. We would seem now to have enough of that material in front of us to make a few tentative attempts at interpretation. But an obstacle is placed in our way by our uncertainty about whose dream we are in fact discussing. The voices we hear there in the dark, which, like the discourse of apparitions, may be God's, the devil's, or our own, themselves urgently pose the fundamental *question de conscience* of psychoanalysis, and of the prosaic as well: "*qui parle?*" But just as important in interpretation is the complementary query: "*qui écoute?*" (cf. Genette's precisions: 1983, 43). Whose dreams are we interpreting here, and what do the dreams really augur?

The answer to the second question will be inextricably caught up in our answer to the first. One such answer which a learned tradition will effortlessly produce is that the dream-material of Nashe's pamphlet wells up from a bottomless collective unconscious of intertextuality: the dreams are the dreams of the text. But it is difficult to be certain of this because the corroborative evidence is strangely lacking here. Nashe's infallible editor McKerrow was unusually embarrasssed in a search for sources, and even C.G. Harlow, who found an inspiration for a number of passages in Henry Howard's *Defensatiue against the Posion of Supposed Prophesies* (1583), suspected that Nashe had "invented the dreams," and pointed out that in the case of the three unfulfilled dreams of princes, where only that of Alphonso seems to find even a slight inspiration in Howard's text, "the further Nashe goes from Howard, the more confused the historical framework of each becomes" (Harlow 1965, 43). Harlow faithfully observes how textual sources existed from which the dreams could have partially been "built up," but his argument nevertheless involves a recurrence to *Nashe's* personality, his "fascination," for instance, with "[s]tories about Agrippa" (44). At least in a certain sense, then, for Harlow the dreams we are talking about are essentially Nashe's own. This is much more the argument, predictably, in the interpretation offered by Nashe's biographer, Charles Nicholl, who senses in the pamphlet a foreboding of a religious crisis to come, and the product of a "decidedly unsettled" period Nashe spent in the country, where he supposedly wrote it: "Deprived of the bustle and business of literary London, he turned in on himself, his voluble fidgety temper bottled up, his inquisitive mind aggravated into neurotic self-doubt" (Nicholl 1984, 153). In the fenny, foggy melancholy-producing damp of a country house at Conington, Nicholl suggests, something was rotten in the state of dream-work: "One hopes, but doubts, he slept well" (Ibid.). A similar concentration on Nashe's personality leads Stephen Hilliard to suppose that "*The Terrors of the Night* is an effort at exorcism, not in the disallowed medieval manner, but in the new rationalistic fashion that culminates for us in psychoanalysis" (Hilliard 1986, 101).

Tracing these dreams back to Nashe's stay in the country, and in fact to the specific incident of the dying man's visions, does not exceed the bounds of a naturalistic explanation of the text under analysis. In the pamphlet itself, Nashe asserts that it had as its "accidentall occasion . . . this dreame or apparition (call or miscall it as you will, for it is yours as freely as anie wast paper that euer you had in your liues)" (G4^v/1:382). The dying man's visions recounted near the end, then, served as the stimulus or external motivation for all the material in the pamphlet. But this does not necessarily lend support to the view that the dreams in it are Nashe's. Harlow had gone to considerable effort to prove that this mysterious country house at which Nashe was staying was "at Conington, near Huntington, in the house of the wealthy antiquary Robert Cotton" (Harlow 1961, 9), where Thomas Cotton, Robert's father, had in fact died in 1592. If we accept Harlow's theory (as scholars have), we can allow ourselves to trace all of the dreams back to the visions of Thomas Cotton. But this ignores the status of those visions as *pretexts*. For the other half of Harlow's argument is that *The Terrors of the Night* was only *written* in February 1593, when Nashe finally heard of Cotton's death (which, however, had occurred the previous May). Following up Nashe's opening remark that "[a] litle to beguile time idely discontented, and satisfie some of my solitarie friends heere in the Countrey, I haue hastily vndertooke to write of the wearie fancies of the Night" (B1/1:345), Harlow suggests that the pamphlet was in fact written for the dead man's *son*, Robert Cotton, and his circle of antiquaries. This becomes much more persuasive after Harlow has offered evidence that Robert Cotton was "ill or depressed in spirits a few months after his father's death in 1592, and that his affliction was due to melancholy" (Harlow 1961, 18). Harlow suggests that Cotton's melancholy was the source of the pamphlet, and that it was perhaps meant to serve as one of the "short papers on a set subject" by which the "discussions of the Society of Antiquaries were regularly opened" (20).

Here we would seem to have a textually and historically plausible, if still hypothetical, answer to the query, whose dreams are these anyway? But a further consideration must enter into our analysis. The pamphlet may have been largely *written* in February 1593 for Robert Cotton, and occasioned by interest in the circumstances of his father's death and his own subsequent melancholy, but it was not *published* until 1594, when Nashe had come under the protection of Sir George Carey, and had been staying with him in the Isle of Wight, of which Sir George was the governor (*The Terrors* is somewhat grotesquely dedicated to his daughter Elizabeth, a "cleare Lampe of Virginitie," and "cleare (if anie liuing) from the originall sin of thought" [Nashe 1594c, A2/1:341]). The dreams are actually Carey's, then, and support is once again lent to our hypothesizing by the historical sense of Harlow:

Nashe need not have had a special occasion for finishing and publishing *The Terrors of the Night* in 1594, but a suitable occasion did arrive that year from events with which Nashe was clearly connected. On 16 April Fernando, Earl of Derby, died after ten days' illness during which he was subject to dreams and hallucinations. . . . There were several suspicious circumstances, and some attributed the death to witchcraft. (Harlow 1961, 22)

Harlow adds that Nashe's present patron Carey soon heard of the death, "believed the accusations of witchcraft, and was taking steps to apprehend one of the suspects" (22-23). What's more, dead Fernando Stanley, when he had still been Lord Strange, "had been (by the most acceptable identification) the *Amyntas* who was Nashe's patron in 1592 and the *Lord S.* to whom he dedicated *The Choice of Valentines*" (23).

Thus, *The Terrors of the Night* would in fact be Carey's, and their publication would have been facilitated by the death of the one-time Lord Strange. This would have served as the accidental occasion upon which the opportunistic manifold of the more or less pre-formed discourse of apparitions would have seized as a pretext for coming forth, in much the same way as Maury's "wish-fulfillment" dream of execution made use of the fallen headboard in Freud's account. That the dream was finally Carey's is supported by what is generally taken to be a late insertion in the pamphlet. Directly on the heels of Nashe's comparison of melancholy to lingering hope unrequited, he tells of his own journey to "a fortunate blessed Iland, nere those pinnacle rocks called the Needles" (i.e. Carey's Isle of Wight; Nashe 1594c, F3/1:374). Nashe spends considerable effort on praise of the island, "a fertill plot fit to seat another Paradize, where, or in no place, the image of ancient hospitalitie is to be found" (Ibid.). He is eager to disassociate his enthusiasm for his newfound patron from the unhealthy expectation of the courtier that he has just diagnosed as a lingering disease: those who do not know his patron may be tempted to see his encomium as "words idly begotten with good lookes, and in an ouer-ioyed humour of vaine hope slipt from me by chance," i.e., as illusions nursed by sanguine melancholy. But Nashe insists that on the contrary it is only to Carey that he owes his spiritual well-being:

Thus I conclude with this chance-medley Parenthesis, that whatsoeuer minutes intermission I haue of calmed content, or least respite to call my wits together, principall and immediate proceedeth from him.

Through him my tender wainscot Studie door is deliuered

from much assault and battrie: through him I looke into, and am
lookt on in the world; from whence otherwise I were a wretched
exile. Through him all my good (as by a conduit head) is
conueighed vnto me; and to him all my endeauours (like riuers)
shall pay tribute as to the Ocean. (F4/1:375)

Nashe seems to insist here that the transactions between him and
Carey are commensal. But the metaphor, a conventional one for the
reciprocity of patronage relationships, has its source in Ecclesiastes, where
the theme is precisely the impossibility of satisfaction: "Vanitie of
vanities" (Eccl. 1:2; Geneva Bible). Submerged in the aquatic image is yet
another allegory of the tedium of pointless effort that Nashe has connected with the unhappy and diseased consciousness: "All the riuers go
into the sea, yet the sea is not ful: *for* the riuers go vnto the place, whence
thei returne, and go" (1:7). The choice of this commensurating image of
discursive exchange of goods (also, for example, used by Spenser with regard to himself and Elizabeth [*Faerie Queene*, 6.pr.7]) allows our pos-
tulation that there may be undercurrents to Nashe's dream-work which
would indeed rely for their psychic force on Nashe's *resistance* to
interpretation. Ecclesiastes immediately continues: "All things are ful of
labour: man can not vtter it: the eye is not satisfied with seing, nor the
eare filled with hearing" (Eccl. 1:8), and the end of the chapter, of course,
runs: "For in ye multitude of wisdome *is* much grief: & he that encreaseth
knowledge, encreaseth sorowe" (1:18). One recalls Nashe's claim that the
Turks banish "Learning, because it is euerie daye setting men together by
the eares" (Nashe 1594c, F2^v/1:372).

Assuming that the rest of the pamphlet was already pre-fabricated,
just waiting around for the death of Stanley and the patronage of Carey
to provide external stimulation for publication could actually facilitate an
interpretation that would unite otherwise disparate elements of the
dream-material. But to arrive at such an interpretation it would be
necessary to make use of that halieutics of suspicion, to trawl for the
source of such material, as we have been eerily inkling, in a *political* unconscious, and to recognize that Nashe has taken this chance opportunity
as an occasion to pour his fluvial discourse of apparitions collyrium-like
into the waiting ear of his knightly succourer.

Nicholl suggests that in his portrait of conjuring courtiers Nashe
wished to *warn* Carey about the dangers of patronizing a magician like
his familiar Simon Forman, alluding to the tragic fate of Fernando Stanley, who had been similarly involved with Edward Kelley, and was implicated in more than one quasi-Catholic plot to overthrow the throne
(Nicholl 1984, 197-201). This may be so, but the dream-pamphlet is eerier

than that. As with an actual dream, wish-fulfillments can suddenly turn to dread, roles and positions can shift without warning.

Take for example the leaden standish from which Nashe would expiscate silver-mouthed fish: the fish are patrons, but the bottomless inkpot, like Lake Vether, contains nought but devils; yet Nashe as fisherman is connected with the net-spreading devil himself, whose silver hooks will scratch out the throat and mangle the flesh of the bedridden gentleman. Are patrons the angling devils, or is Nashe?

Perhaps the most astonishing hermeneutic recuperation which a focalization on Carey makes possible, is that of the seeemingly *non sequitur* material relating to the stygian domain of Iceland, which now neatly fills the role of demonic double of Carey's Isle of Wight ("another Paradize"). Wight Nashe has seen, Iceland only heard of, but what he has heard could have had an eerie relevance for Carey, the draconian ruler of an island "realm" (cf. Nicholl 1984, 181f) and dabbler in the occult. Carey's interest in ghosts could have been fed by Nashe's stories of "spirites like rogues," who are "destitute of all dwelling and habitation, and they chillingly complayne if a Constable aske them *Cheuala* in the night, that they are going vnto *Hecla* to warme them" (D2/1:359). Carey was particularly obsessed with witchcraft, and in Iceland they have witches aplenty: "Farre cheaper maye you buy wind amongst them, than you can buy wind or faire words in the Courte" (D2ᵛ/1:359). This latter wind is the favor which Nashe later calls "ayrie incorporeate Courtly promises" that "vanish to nothing" (G1/1:377). It would be easier to pay witches for an ill wind that blows no good than it is to get advancement.

But let us stop right there, before these fowkins become any more embarrassing and we foist ourselves with our own petard. For it just about at this point that the credibility of such a reading has a tendency to start to break down: when one starts to bring in things to be adduced as evidence. "Evidence" is what can be seen; what is right there before one's eyes: the obvious. But the things offered up as exhibits never add up on their own to what we are *told*. It is at this point that the traditional historicist produces from up his sleeve the two passages in Carey's correspondence where the queen's "Knight Marshall" alludes to his fear of an insurrection on the part of the fishermen in the island, or mayhap the cryptic lines from a forgotten poem dedicated to the knight where something about silver-mouthed patrons is mentioned; while the new historicists, who go in for more extravagant effects, produce simultaneously from three apparently transparent repositories, statistical correlations between witch-hunts and vagabondage in sixteenth-century France, a capsule history of the Isle of Wight until the Revolution, and selected allusions to fishing in the dedicatory epistles of Jacobean revenge tragedies. The bathos of such moments must be familiar to us all; the more disconcerting in that we are probably firmly persuaded of the desirability, sensibility, and political appropriateness of such historical approaches to interpretation. But the readings thus produced are often still all too similar to those of Freud or Harold Bloom; it all sounds fairly reasonable and plausible as theory until the evidence is brought forth; the things that are supposed to support it are rushed together in a reading. The methodology makes sense, but the *things* do not add up. They are somehow hopelessly pathetic and intractable, and they seem inevitably to be held teeteringly in place by hypotheses, qualifications, adaptations, equivocations, ifs, ands and buts; or else held artily aloft by sheer illusions, conjurings. This is what it *really* means to be living within a hermeneutics of suspicion—for, as we know, it is no longer the things themselves that are doubtful, but the interpretations. As Paul Ricoeur succinctly put it: "The philosopher brought up in the school of Descartes is aware that things are uncertain, but he has no doubt that consciousness is as it appears to itself. . . . After uncertainty about the thing we have entered into uncertainty about consciousness" (Ricoeur 1965, 41). If that uncertainty authorizes our looking behind the appearances for an unconscious, personal or political, it also breeds an inability to trust in any evidence of any interpretation of any *thing* presented to us in corroboration of a reading. For we know that there is always a conjuring medium between us and the real, that the real has always been read, and that that conjuring medium may even be ourselves, misrepresenting what is really the matter as a wish-fulfilling dream.

In the epistle to the readers in *Strange Newes*, Nashe compares such interpretations to the hypnagogic visions of his "welwillers," who "pretending to see in the darke, talke of strange obiectes by them discouered in the night, when in truth they are nothing else but the glimmering of their eies" (Nashe 1592c, A4ᵛ/1:259). "Poore *Pierce Pennilesse*," he complains, "they haue turned to a coniuring booke, for there is not that line in it, with which they do not seeke to raise vp a Ghost" (B1/1:259). He quotes Aretino to the effect that "vpstart Commenters, with their Annotations and gloses had extorted that sense and Morall out of *Petrarch*" which the poet would never have acknowledged. Nashe had not heard of the intentional fallacy, and the unconscious irony of the freudy-cat interpretation one could put on his own subsequent denial is consequently lost on him: "So may I complaine that rash heads, vpstart Interpreters, haue extorted & rakte that vnreuerent meaning out of my lines, which a thousand deaths cannot make mee ere grant that I dreamd off" (B1/1:260). We now assume that Nashe is not too likely to be in a position to know *what* he may have dreamt of. But with that knowledge comes an awareness that what *we* have been dreaming may not be manifest to *us* either.

Still, it is not our *unconscious* interpretational bias that we should be worrying about, so much as that of the extortionate or embezzling kind; for we all know what we can do with a little juggling of the figures, a bit of legerdemain in the ledger domain, the seductive fortune-telling fabulation of doing "readings" where the medium is the misusage. Nashe insists on the diabolicalness of such a dealing with things: "What sense is there that the yoalke of an egge should signifie gold, or dreaming of Beares, or fire, or water, debate and anger, that euerie thing must be interpreted backward as Witches say their Pater-noster, good being the character of bad, and bad of good?" (D3ᵛ/1:361). But this cannot scare us; we know that there is a great deal of "sense" in it indeed, and no*thing* else, since we are living in the crapulous morning after Newton's sleep, Nietzsche's dawn, when we are aware that "there are no facts, but only interpretations," and that even the most lucid of empirical "realists" is "still the most passionate and melancholic of creatures in comparison to a fish, and still all too like to a love-sick artist":

> Your love of "truth," for instance—now there's an old, age-old "love." In every feeling, in every sense impression there is a bit of this old love: and in the same way, a kind of freakishness, prejudice, irrationality, unwittingness, fear and I don't know what all else! has been worked and woven into it. That mountain there! That cloud! What is "real" about it? Take away the imaginary and the human *ingredient*, you abstemious ones! Yes, if you *can*! If you could forget your descent, your past, your abc's—the whole of your humanity and animality! There is no "reality" for us—nor for you either, my abstainers—we are not so very unlike one another as you suppose, and perhaps our good intention of climbing out of intoxication is just as praiseworthy as your own belief that you are incapable of doing so. (Nietzsche 1882, 97-98)

We now "know" that the "real things" are only the hallucinations in a drunkard's or a sick person's stupor. And yet the things *will* come back to haunt us; the standing pool of a leaden standish breeds monsters; the screaming blocks of ice breaking up in a pseudo-Icelandic lake awaken us; in the night we hear the voices, no longer sure if they are ourselves, our patrons, God, the devil, or the nearing cries of a disillusioned populace, finally coming to get us. There is no doubt about it: uneasy lies the head that interprets. *Ja, ja,* I can hear Nietzsche chortling: uneasy *lies*.

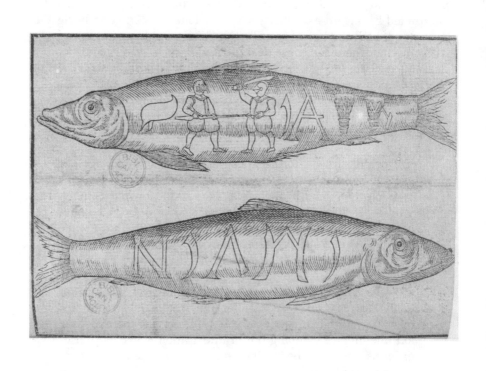

A
MOST STRANGE
and wonderfull Herring, taken on

the 26. day of Nouember 1597. neere vnto
Drenton sometime the old and chiefe
Cittie of the kingdome of
Norway.

Hauing on the one side the picture of two
armed men fighting, and on the other most
strange Characters, as in the picture
is here expressed.

First printed in Dutch at Roterdam by *Ian van*
Doetecum. And now translated into
English.

¶ Repent, for the kingdome of God
is at hand.

[Device: McKerrow 294]

LONDON
Imprinted by Iohn Wolfe.
1598.

A most strange &
wonderfull Herring taken on the
26. day of Nouember 1597. neere vnto Drenton, sometime the old and chiefe Cittie of the kingdome of Norway, hauing on the one side the picture of two armed men fighting, & on the other most strange characters: as in the picture is here expressed.

Repent for the kingdome of God is at hand.

The Lord God of heauen, the most righteous and mightie iudge of the world, neuer intends to inflict plagues or punishmentes on any Countrey, Cittie, or nation, but first it pleaseth him of his vnspeakeable mercie, to forewarne the same countrey, cittie, or nation thereof, by the mouthes of his Prophets, and other ministers of his worde, or else by his wonderfull signes and tokens shewed in the heauens, the earth, or other his creatures, that thereby the people may be induced to forsake their former wickednesse, and to learne amendment and newnesse of life. Examples hereof we haue in Genesis, how many tokens of his wrath did the Lord shew vnto *Pharao*, before his destruction in the red sea? Likewise before Sodome was consumde with the fire from heauen, it is written that *Abraham* had knowledge thereof, and intreated the Lord to spare it: but such were the sinnes of that cursed Cittie, that his prayers could not preuaile. Againe, more then the space of an hundred yeares before the waters drownd the worlde, had *Noah* warning to build ye Arke, and long it was ere hee finished that worke, insomuch that the children of men made a scorne thereof, and so farre were they from grace, that no warning at all they tooke thereby. The Niniuites hauing warning repented at the preaching of *Ionas*: but *Ierusalem* was nothing moued though Christ Iesus himselfe foretold their destruction: for which cause sorrow came vpon them as vpon a woman when she trauelleth. The signs and tokens which the Lord sent ouer that Cittie before their fall were many and maruellous, notwithstanding they persisted in their sinnes, and flattering themselues in their owne follies, made false interpretations of those prodigious wonders. Seeing then that as the Apostle saith, that what-soeuer is written, is written for our learning, let all Christians take warning hereby, not iestingly to ioyne themselues together (as they did in the old world) to deride or falsely to interpret the dreadfull tokens sent among vs, lest with them of *Ierusalem* destruction do suddenly come vpon vs. I haue here to shew you a strange and wonderfull token of Gods wrath figured forth in a silly Herring, in which smal fish he doth demonstrate great and dreadfull matters as by the picture you may perceive: on the one side whereof you may plainely behold the perfect shape of two armed men, the one hauing in his hand a launce, the other a sword, close buckled in their corslets, with burganets on their heades, standing as it were in their defence, threatning and assayling one another. I know that many will giue as small credit hereunto, and as sleightly esteeme thereof as *Pharao* did of the flies, and the Iewes of Christs miracles: notwithstanding the Lord hath chosen the foolish thinges of this world to confound the wise, and the weake to ouercome the mighty, as he himselfe hath expressed in his holy Gospell. Moreouer there was toward the taile of this Herring the right portraiture of two rods, the one farre bigger then the other, seeming to bee bound together with two strong bandes apeece, which euery man must confesse to bee the vndoubted signe of dreadfull correction: according as the Psalmist speaketh, saying: *Thou shalt bruse them with a rod of Iron, and breake them in peeces like a Potters vessell.* In scripture sword and pestilence is said to be the scourges of the Lord: and therefore that cruel and bloody tyrant *Tamberlaine* did iustly call himselfe the scourge of God, by whom he corrected the proud, rebellious and wicked world: bringing by bloody wars many kingdomes into his subiection. If we enter then into due consideration hereof, and with the eyes of grace behold the same, we cannot but confesse, that the righteous Lord hath sent these signes vnto vs, to forewarne vs of our wickednesse, least by the sharpe correcting rods of Gods wrath wee be most iustly punished with sword and famine. But now behold on the other side of this Herring, were fiue Characters most perfectly ingrauen, some of them vsual, and wel knowne among vs at this day, others strange and not vnderstood: but what the God of all power and might will giue hereby to be known is left to better iudgement, notwithstanding let vs remember, that as it once pleased God by the finger of his power to write on the wall a heauie sentence against *Balthasar*, so hath it pleased him at this present to write on this Herring vndoubtedly a heauie sentence against the sinnes of this age, thereby to call this drowsie worlde out of the damnable sleepe of sinne and wickednes, wherein it hath slugged so long time. Then what is he that seeing the same, and dreading the hot vengeance of the Lord, will not be inforced with *Balthasar* to shake and tremble at the grieuous iudgements which is therby likely to bee threatned: if *Balthasar* being a heathen King, shooke so sore at the handwriting on the wall, wel may all Christians harts shake to see, and therewithall to consider what fearfull sentence may vpon the Herring be engrauen. When our Sauiour Christ did write vpon the ground, before those that accused the woman of adulterie, her accusers were therby so confounded in conscience, that for very shame they slipt away out of his sight: how much more then may we be confounded at the sight & interpretation of these strange characters which the Lord hath not written on the ground in the dust of the earth, but in the very meat which we should eat, thereby (as it were) laying his iudgements in our dishes, at euery meale to be remembred. For who is ignorant that among the fishes of the sea, there is none so common at our table as the Herring, no fish more vsed in any land, nor better knowne among all sorts of people: whereby it is iustly to be gathered, that the Lord hath sent it for a generall warning vnto his people: the Lord grant our heartes may be moued thereby. Moreouer, this Herring was full fourteene inches in length: importing (as I coniecture) that this iudgement threatned against the world for sinne is an extraordinarie and no vsuall iudgement, but such as the eyes of men haue seldome or neuer seene: besides, the markes were all of red and bloody colour. The Lord for Christes sake be merciful vnto vs, & giue vs grace with such repenting harts to turne from our sinnes, that he may turne his iust wrath from vs. This Herring among a number of others was taken on the 26. day of Novemb. 1597. neer vnto *Drenton*, sometime the ancient and chiefe Cittie of the kingdome of *Norway*. And after it was shewen to diuers of the nobility, & magistrates of that countrey. The portraiture thereof & admonition was first printed in *Roterdam*, by *Iohn van Doetecum* in the Dutch tongue, & out of the same language translated into English, for the profite and instruction of our countrey people. The Lord God Almighty giue vs grace to watch and waite for the comming of the heauenly brydegroome, that being decked and attired in the true wedding garment of Christes righteousnes, we may enter with him to the heauenly banket, there to raigne in his glorious kingdome for euermore, Amen.

FINIS.

Stuff and Nonsense

PRAYSE OF THE RED HERRING

Wann und wie kommen Dinge als Dinge? Sie kommen nicht *durch* die Machenschaft des Menschen. Sie kommen aber auch nicht *ohne* die Wachsamkeit der Sterblichen. Der erste Schritt zu solcher Wachsamkeit ist der Schritt zurück aus dem nur vor-stellenden, d. h. erklärenden Denken in das andenkende Denken.
Martin Heidegger, *Das Ding*

. . . howsoeuer I haue toyed, and trifled heretofore, I am now taught, and I truste I shall shortly learne, (no remedie, I must of meere necessitie giue you ouer in the playne fielde) to employ my trauayle, and tyme wholly, or chiefely on those studies and practizes, that carrie as they saye, meate in their mouth . . .
Harvey, Letter to Spenser, 23 April 1579

Nashes Lenten Stuffe was written in 1598, when both Nashe and the sixteenth century were, equally unmindfully, broaching their demise; both of them were mysteriously gone by 1601, and no one can now tell where either of them is buried. *Lenten Stuffe* was the last great prose work of the century and the end of the decade's "literature of things." For already with the first years of the seventeenth century we seem to be present at the baleful reinterment of human subjectivities in what Bakhtin, or rather his translators, once beautifully termed "the plots that contain them" (1981, 35). By a "literature of things," incidentally, I mean a literature which, for all of its playing out of the self-conscious rhetorics developed in the previous generation, was clearly the most concretely palpable and thing-cluttered corpus of the English Renaissance.

Nashe's pamphlets in general have appeared to offer puzzling examples of this "thingfulness," since they seem so often to brink on the content-free, the *purely* rhetorical or "performative." Almost all critical attempts to grapple with this pure performativeness begin with the things and then pull the rug out from under them. David Margolies, for instance, opens his discussion of Nashe in *Novel and Society in Elizabethan England* by proclaiming that Nashe's "power in the medium of language is such that the medium seems superfluous and, endowing abstractions with physicality and conjuring up the solid texture of the material world, Nashe appears to present, not mere word pictures of reality, but reality itself"; but like all critics, Margolies must then go on to scruple that "[f]or all his linguistic virtuosity, Nashe has very little to say and his interest, now as in the sixteenth century, lies almost entirely in his style (to which he himself directs the reader)" (Margolies 1985, 85). As Margolies sees things, "with neither originality of intellect nor a critical attitude toward the assumptions of his society, style was the only area in which he could make his mark" (102) and, as a result of his attempt to reconcile his commercial interests with the official humanistic and courtly apologies for rhetoric, Nashe's "work becomes self-referential" (103).

Yet I would counter that, surprisingly enough, if one actually reads Nashe's books, one will find that those *things* which one would assume to be mere pretexts in such a self-referential rhetorical runaround are somehow much more *there* there (critics can never quite—no matter how intellectualist or politically committed their responses—*ignore* this) than is a lot of the ostensibly weightier and more inflated matter one encounters in rhetorically (or even politically) more "substantial" pieces. *Lenten Stuffe* for its part purports to harbor a guided tour of the town of Yarmouth—the author's haven in a ticklish moment—and a quasi-commercial encomium of that city's unsung benefactor, the red herring. The tour is *de force*, and the "encomium," at least in some sense, mock. Nashe's lexiphanic antics were never bolder, and have led some to see *Lenten Stuffe* as a kind of sixteenth-century *Finnegans Wake*. It is not in fact unusual for critics to become distracted from "content" when confronted with such a hell of words and stylisms; the meaning is the massage—and there for many's the rub. But personally, at least, I still find it impossible to ignore all the *stuff* that Nashe's virtuosity drags along in its intricate nets. To grasp the substance of Nashe's pamphlet, I suggest, we need to work toward what I will perfidiously be calling an "extra-rhetorical" reading.

There has been *nothing but* talk of Nashe's "nihilism" and "themelessness." This goes back at least to an influential statement made by C.S.

Lewis: "Paradoxically, though Nashe's pamphlets are commercial literature, they come very close to being, in another way, 'pure' literature:
literature which is, as nearly as possible, without a subject. In a certain
sense of the verb 'say', if asked what Nashe 'says', we should have to
reply, Nothing" (Lewis 1954, 416). This view has been elaborated and
darkened by a whole despondent slough of critics (cul-de-sic) who,
concentrating on *The Vnfortunate Traueller*, have come up with a kind of
"Nashe Our Contemporary" reading. It was especially prevalent in the
sixties (e.g. Leech 1963; Lanham 1967; Davis 1969), but has gained a
certain popular currency, and was even faintly urged by as historically
and classically situated a reader as Mihoko Suzuki (1984), for whom
Nashe's perpetual recursion to violence and chaos in his attempts to
reflect actuality drive him toward a postmodern "silence." This "nihilism"
is tied up with Nashe's "themelessness," again as exemplified for various
critics in *The Vnfortunate Traueller*. He is considered a nihilist because his
multiplicity of rhetorical gestures will not jibe, leaving no totalizing
authorial meaning schemes or unifying thematics but only the incoherent
brute realism of endless action and violence abetted by wordplay.

There is some truth to this in speaking of *The Vnfortunate Traueller*,
I think, whose meaningful moments are transient and for the most part
the work of structuring or associative mechanisms. But the book is not
really themeless, but rather heterothematic in a way which is unsatisfying
for the modernist, though not perhaps for the pre- or the post-modernist.
Most of Nashe's other pamphlets have relatively discernible "themes": the
Montaignesque meditation on dreams in the *Terrors of the Night*, the
admonitory civic similitudes of the Rev. Gnashe in *Christs Teares*, or the
flippant pantsing of Harvey by Tom Panache in *Haue with You*, for
example. *Lenten Stuffe* seems to be excluded because its themes cannot be
taken seriously by a sophisticated reader. Yet like the *Moriæ Encomium*
and other mock encomia of the Renaissance, it is really only half-
unserious. The history of Yarmouth it offers is, as G.R. Hibbard avowed,
"coherent as well as lively" (1962, 243), and C.S. Lewis was led wistfully
to sigh that it "is a relief after the somewhat feverish unsubstantiability
of his other pamphlets, in so far as it at last brings our mind to bear on
things like walls, sand, ships, and tides" (Lewis 1954, 415). I think, as I
have said, that *Lenten Stuffe* is indeed the Nashe work with the most
concrete sense of "presence," and that it is wrong to consider it devoid
of content. The finest critics *see* the content, but nevertheless fail to
reconcile it with their own mixed feelings about Nashe's curious collapse
of form and *dis*content. Neil Rhodes, looking, like Margolies, in the mid-
eighties for political excuses for Nashe's texts that he can't honestly find,
tries to supercede Crewe's attempt to read Nashe's texts as dramatizing

the strain between rhetoric and logic by showing that they are actually *prose*lytizing the tension between rhetoric and *satire*. Rhodes agrees with Crewe that "Nashe's work displays, or seems to display, the qualities which contemporary literary theory has celebrated in modernist and post-modernist texts, and has sought in earlier literature" (Rhodes 1985, 26), but Rhodes clearly sees this as indicative of a political conservatism. In the end, it must be noted though, Rhodes simply cannot stop himself from reaffirming the very visceral power of Nashe's politically unexcused rhetoric (so well accounted for in his earlier *Elizabethan Grotesque*): "From the froth and surge of Nashe's prose, at its most 'boysterous' in *Lenten Stuffe*, comes a vivid sense of the materiality of language, and it is the satirical edge which also produces the plastic, quasi-physical quality of his writing and saves it from mere wind-baggery" (41). Yet the body of Rhodes's essay is nevertheless there to expose how Nashe's wild, self-referential rhetoric recedes from engagement with *political* realities, so that, as the critic is forced to admit, the move in Dekker and the following generation "away from Nashe" and toward a simpler prose style in satirical writing is "a move toward effective social criticism" (31). This lack of *political* content (i.e. *dis*content) is what ultimately leads Rhodes—for all his clarity about the mate*reality* of Nashe's writing—to join everyone from Lewis to Crewe in disowning the idea of any "content" in the Nashean corpus: "The first thing to say is that it is futile to look in Nashe for consistent points of view or characteristic themes; in fact, we can discard the notion of content altogether" (25). The *notion*, if you like; but please: *not the content!* (We must be careful not to throw the bathwater out with the baby.) All of these critics, whether for or agin him, seem to be resigned to bringing Nashe and his style into line with "the Academicks opinion, who absolutely conclude, that nothing is to be affirmed" (Nashe 1594b, *4^v/2:179). No-thing *"affirmed,"* I dunno. But in my reading Nashe's "pure performativeness" actually *leads* to an un-paralleled—and a *firm* if "unaffirmed"—*thingfulness*.

In attempting to get to the bottom of this seeming incongruency, it will be helpful to return once again to Jonathan Crewe's *defense* of Nashe's dis-contented rhetoricity in what is probably still the most souped-up work on Nashe to date, the yet provocatively titled, *Unre-deemed Rhetoric*. Taking cues from French deconstructionists, as you will recall, Crewe wished to expose the ritual excommunication of literature which approaches "pure performance" or "unredeemed rhetoric" from a metaphysical humanistic great tradition. Thus, he was aiming at a re-evaluation of the characteristic features of Nashe's prose without attempting to redefine those features; he tacitly accepts the received view of *Lenten Stuffe* as "pure style" which "says nothing," admitting that here

"Nashe elevates 'themelessness' to a conscious principle" (Crewe 1982, 92). As I have said, I am somewhat at odds with this whole conception of Nashe's work, and there *have* in fact been a few attempts to move away from it in subsequent criticism. Though Stephen Hilliard was to supplement Crewe's sentiments by remarking that "[r]hetoric often overwhelms substance," he had already insisted that in *Lenten Stuffe* Nashe's irony for once "does not undercut the praise of Yarmouth. . . . Nashe has found an ideal to set against his satiric vision in a fishing port, not in a humanistic tract. His utopia has a geographical location, flesh-and-blood inhabitants, and a prosperity based on the most mundane of foodstuffs" (Hilliard 1986, 230; 225). Michael D. Bristol had earlier gone so far as to view Nashe's analysis of the market economy of Yarmouth as legitimate and even canny, if still rather utopian, commentary that "shows a society a way to achieve independence from the land as the exclusive source of subsistence and thus to break the hegemony of propriety ownership" (Bristol 1985, 103). And, most recently, while Lorna Hutson ultimately feels obliged to valorize the pamphlet's "linguistic substance," she deals with its theme in words which hardly suggest that she thinks it can't stick to a point: "The 'poverty' of *Lenten Stuffe*, as all critics, and indeed the work itself, would agree, is its continual harping on the same subject" (Hutson 1989, 248). But even if we agree that such thematic content is absent or nugatory or downplayed or impoverished, can we really ignore the rawer and more obvious (too obvious?) content? It is this crude content which the extra-rhetorical reading still hopes to disinter(pret?).

But Crewe's discussion remains useful because he was the first to really make explicit the dichotomy lurkingly underriding practically all previous (and perhaps even subsequent) Nashe criticism: that of rhetoric vs. logic (with the tired old megrim of "Truth" preventing any intercourse between them). As soon as we recognize that it is in these terms that the critical community tends to do its cogitating, it becomes much clearer why Nashe is perennially accused of (and now and then extolled for) "themelessness" and lack of content. As Crewe has it, the "problem" with the existing body of Nashe criticism is that "'theme' or 'content' are taken to be primary, while 'writing' is taken to be secondary" (Crewe 1982, 1); but in truth Nashe calls attention to writing or rhetoric or style[1] through the minimalization of "content" or logical development: "*style* becomes not merely the antithesis of *content*, but that which discloses itself in the absence of content" (12). We now see, however, why all of

[1]Terms by no means so equatable in the Derridean discussions which are Crewe's springboards. But we now have other fish to fry—unless they are the same?

Nashe's critics, Crewe included, insist upon his lack of content or "themelessness," compensated (or not) by an overdose of "writing"—it is because by "content" they mean logical argument, fully articulated plenitude of sense, or unifying meaning schemes.

What this implied dichotomy of rhetoric vs. logic actually discloses is a pervasive litcritical belief in the power of systematic form in general, be it logical *or* rhetorical, to *intend*, or do anything else, without extratextual interference or reference—the pervasive ignorance of the fundamental (yet *freilich* still mental) power of *things* to overcome the meanings that would embrace them, and the complicitous infidelity of words to the designs of systematic order, as to their own supposedly autotelic interests. The real content of any text is not just or even mainly meanings (messages), but above all words and names of things; and words are not necesssarily so inimical to things as we have come unself-consciously to suppose. There is another level beyond the logical *or* rhetorical; there is diversion from the literal text to an extratext, whether or not that extratext is ultimately in some sense a "text" itself. *Things* are there through the words, behind the words, and the *things* remain there *regardless* or even *in spite of* the claims of rhetorical or logical formalities. Rhetoric has no more priority than logic here. Crewe, however, insists that "[q]uestions of priority (of rhetoric or logic) are always involved, an ultimate power of representation remains at stake, and no equilibrium is possible while the opposing, but also mutually constitutive, terms may each lay claim to ultimate exclusiveness" (89). But there is a third factor beyond this aporetic antinomy (and the Truth it ain't). Ignoring rhetorical or logical schemes, *we* may read Nashe's text literally—by which I now mean, of course, *extra-literally*. This, and I hope the reader is already halfway over the levee, is where my extra-*rhetorical* reading leads: to a reading that is both more rhetorical than usual and in some ways beyond rhetoric.

But let us luxuriate a moment in the pungent salt air of the merely rhetorical and literal before we head back. Breathe in: those gusts dig deep into your guts and cut out a gusto for the honest kerseyest stuff. Soft and fair, as Nashe tells his readers, "[s]oft and faire my maisters, you must walke and talke before dinner an houre or two, the better to whet your appetites to taste of such a dainty dish as the redde Herring, and that you may not thinke the time tedious, I care not if I beare you company, and leade you a sound walke round about Yarmouth, and shew the length and bredth of it" (Nashe 1599, B4/3:159). What I am groping towards is really not reading literally or rhetorically, but (and this, of course, is a distinction which can only be conveyed in the literally ineluctible modality of the visible): reading *littorally*. Amble with me along this slippery shoreline for a moment (which would not be so slippery were it not for the eddying breakwater that separates the literal from the oral), and for chrissake don't be afraid for the nonce of getting your feet wet! Things will no doubt dry out again soon enough.

The thingfulness of Nashe's prose *can* then admittedly in part be accounted for by "mere" rhetoric. Lorna Hutson nicely points out how Nashe stresses the "material resourcefulness" of his *language* itself, and its "capacity to create further substance, to increase his material, to 'turne mole-hills into mountaines'" (sic: more literally h-i-single toothpick "mole-*hils*"; cf. Nashe 1599, A4ᵛ/3:151 [emphasis added]):

> One of the ways in which the illusion of substance and plenty is achieved is by the rich and diverse associations which images accrete within the self-referring confines of pamphlet [sic 'em]. The conventional definition of paradox as means of inflating the trivial, making 'mountains out of mole-hills', is thus associated in this context with Yarmouth's geological and commercial increase, which is in turn made analagous to Nashe's oratorical recovery and the procreativity which he attributes to metaphor. (Hutson 1989, 260)

Though considered intratextual ("self-referring") and "metaphorical," this illusion is apparently really broadly mimological and "auricular," and Hutson points out such examples as when "[t]he profits of the net-weaving industry come alive in the verbal relationships generated by image and assonance; nets appear to transform themselves into clothes as *braiding* miraculously produces *bread*" (264).

Earlier, Neil Rhodes, in his then essentially stylistic analysis in *Elizabethan Grotesque*, had pointed out in some detail elements of style that could account for a more boldly referential concreteness peppering Nashe's fiercely intertextual writing. Discussing similarities in style between Aretino and Nashe, Rhodes drew attention to onomatopoeia or sound effects devices ("as in an earth-quake the ground should open, and a blinde man come feeling pad pad ouer the open Gulph with his staffe" [Nashe 1594d, K2/2:303]), an overall "feeling for the texture of things," and an unparalleled sense for apt physical metaphors ("Pulpit-men" who "writhe Texts lyke waxe" [1593, R1/2:127]). These physical metaphors sometimes overstep their jurisdiction, roughing up the abstract, and Rhodes points out that the author is padpaddingly aware of that void that is "the no-man's land of the non-existent" and that "many of Nashe's coinages and images are designed, like the word 'ploddinger,' to fill that void by rendering in solid terms what was previously a purely abstract concept, and to make that concept comically palpable. Indeed it is one of Nashe's coinages—'palpabrize' ('they cannot grosslie palpabrize or feele God with their bodily fingers')—which perfectly articulates Nashe's transmutation of the verbal into the physical" (Rhodes 1980, 26; cf. Nashe 1593, P2ᵛ/2:115).

In *Lenten Stuffe*, the transmutation Rhodes describes is accompanied and finally occulted by the reverse operation: as the ascendancy of the herring and the fishing trade and the folk of Yarmouth comes to the fore, more metaphysical matter falls away pretty entirely. Nashe *really means it* when he extols the goodness of lusty Humphrey King, the morrice-dancing "tobacconist's" patron, or proclaims the "priority and pre-ualence" (Nashe 1599, D3/3:174) of the herring and the overall pre-eminence of the plain and simple in those rhapsodic potshots of his. Thus, I am only half in accord with Rhodes's statement: "Characterizing literary style itself Nashe makes comically palpable phenomena which are essentially mental" (Rhodes 1980, 41). This is surely one of the charms of Nashe's style, but in *Lenten Stuffe* I think he is moving even "beyond" this anti-abstract agenda. Rhodes does, on the other hand, make a remark which I think leaves Crewe's subsequent "unredeemedly rhetorical" construal always already padpaddingly supplemented: "Stylistically self-conscious he is, but the expression is physical, and his tireless manipulation of stylistic effects is intimately connected with his exploration of the stranger realms of physical activity" (Ibid.). Here all that might be cavilled with is "stranger." Rhodes comes very close to pointing out the distinction that I would make to those who see Nashe's writing as devoid of "content" when he admits that "[t]o say that there are themes of high seriousness in Nashe's writing is to suggest an explicit moral and philosophical concern which he plainly does not have to any great degree" (43). He has no unifying *philosophical* content. But even if we preferred to cavil with this and concur with Hutson's more intention-alist view of Nashe's materialistic style, there would *still* be a hell of a lot of essentially needless stuff there, politically or epistemologically authorized or not, cluttering up the "writing" and splashing us awake when the spiel begins to pall.

Much of Nashe's pamphlet, most of his critics on all sides would agree, is mere stuff and nonsense; and it is precisely where there is the least *sense*, the most nonsense, I would finally argue, that we have a sense of the most *stuff*. At the limits of rhetorical and logical, or even dialogical, overdetermination the things themselves once more begin to emerge. At the upper verges of noncompossible rhetoricity—whap! well, I'll be damned: there's a herring in your lap (or are you just happy to see me?). It is naive to suggest that it is the *Ding an sich* that is served up at such an odd moment—Mussyour Hair Professor Doctor von Herring in poison—but at least it would seem to be the *Ding an mich* or the *Ding für mich*, the thing as it is for me. Style has chased its flapping tail out of existence; rhetoric and logic have shown themselves to be the two faces of the coin with which writing would cozen us, and the "things" in *Lenten Stuffe* confess themselves to be lenten stuff indeed, stuff which reality has lent, and which can never belong to writing.

To the extent that rhetoric in *Lenten Stuffe* successfully directs us back to *things* it constitutes what I would call a *rhetoric of mentions*. To Nashe's pamphlet and to other highly sophisticated "hetero-rhetorical lyricism" (as we might call it) I find I have much the same reaction that I have to works at the other extreme, would-be monological works with a single, all too obvious rhetoric (the pop song): I get next to nothing in terms of message—I get the things themselves, together with little more than whatever "meanings" they have for me. Works with rhetoric that is either too ineffectual or too exploded must rely on a rhetoric of mentions for their force, and I think that this rhetoric can have a great deal of force indeed. For when rhetoric (or logic, or meaning) is either too poor *or* too rich there opens a chasm and the *reader's* meaning drive, "the pressure of sense," as Gérard Genette has called it, "the semantic horror of a vacuum that is a natural disposition of the mind" (1976, 371), rushes with no critical padpadding of that Joycean ashplant to fill the void with *my* themes; and incidentally (caveat pre-emptor), as Lichtenberg put it, "such works are mirrors: if an ape peers in, no apostle can look back out at him."

Nashe naturally was ever repining his readers' readiness to impose extrinsic interpretations onto his text ("My readers peraduenture may see more into it then I can" [Nashe 1599, K3/3:220], etc.), but the heightened disorder presented by his gallimaufry of stylisms and "themes" (or things) invites precisely this kind of readerly provision; the text takes on the characteristics of what Umberto Eco used to call the "open work," and into that open work the verbally intoxicated reader, like the drunk in Dekker's *Wonderfull Yeare*, is bound to tumble face first. In my experience the rhetoric of mentions can thus be an extraordinarily "persuasive" rhetoric, though perhaps it persuades to nothing we do not already "know."

To suggest that Nashe makes *premeditated* use of such a rhetoric would perhaps be to grasp stupidly at some insubstantial fallacy or heresy once again, proclaiming him nihilist or worse (or better). My point here, since at the end of the day I still have to subscribe to what Hilliard calls "the unintentional fallacy" (1986, 122), is that the singularity of Nashe's writerly performance leads to such a rhetorical superfluity that whatever Nashe might have persuaded us to is practically irrelevant. In the last analysis (for now), Nashe's work manifests nothing but a rhetoric of mentions, and for me, *für mich*, therein lies its greatness, "as small a hoppe on my thumbe as hee seemeth" (Nashe 1599, E4^v/3:186). May*be* it "nothing *affirmeth*," but it is gorgeously loose, lusciously fast and loose with no end of unaffirméd *things*.

Morally and commercially unprofitable, epistemologically and aesthetically incoherent, the stylistic excess and copia of the quotidian which I cannot help but admire may of course finally betoken a less politically correct materialism (by either Elizabethan *or* twentieth-century humanist standards) than the utopian ones of Bristol or Hilliard or Hutson. Indeed, Nashe's *extra*-rhetoricity may have been what the mysterious "Gentleman" whose conversation suggested to Harvey the title of his massive tome *against* Nashe meant when he spoke of "Pierce's Supererogation."[2] In his book of the same name, Harvey tells how someone "this other day very soberlie commended some extraordinary giftes in Nashe" (Harvey 1593b, D1/2:61), and then quotes from the discourse of this other person at length. Frances Yates was confident in her identification of the reported speaker as John Eliot, author of the mock language manual *Ortho-epia Gallica* (which appeared from John Wolfe the same year) and theoretically Nashe's ally against Harvey and John Florio *et al.* But it seems more likely to me that we have here an example of Harvey's *own*

---

[2]Technically, "works of supererogation" were, in Roman Catholicism, works performed beyond those God demanded, whose spiritual surplus value could then be reallocated by the Church to others deficient in good works. But the phrase was probably heard by Protestant ears with Harvey's extremely negative ring of super-"arrogance" (the *OED* quotes from *Articles agreed on by Bishoppes 1552*: "Voluntarie woorkes besides, ouer, and aboue Goddes commaundementes, which thei cal woorkes of Supererogation, cannot be taught without arrogancie, and iniquitie"). Those who would argue a crypto-catholicism in Nashe (e.g., Nicholl 1984) might point to his many affirmations of good works (particularly throughout *Christs Teares*), and will find that it is from Nashe that Harvey, or his unnamed "Gentleman" friend, actually picked up the term "supererogation," a word employed by Nashe with a more positive accent. He had used it in the opening of his address "to the Gentlemen *Readers*" in *Strange Newes*: "The strong fayth you haue conceiu'd, that I would do workes of supererogation in answering the Doctor, hath made mee breake my daye with other important busines I had, and stand darting of quils a while like the Porpentine" (1592c, A4^v/1:259). The phrase had been used by Harvey, on the other hand, with its heavily censuring connotations in a passage from his commonplace book, probably written in the 1580s: "when you haue doñ yor uttermost by witt, & Trauayle, you shall haue fewe workes of Supererogation, to spare for other" (Harvey MS.b, 7^v-8/88).

pretersarcastic "wit" at its most excruciating, a piece of dramatic irony whose rhetoric is actually for its own part so "supererogatory" as to cancel itself. The speaker shrilly opines that Nashe's *"Sanguine witt"* will put *"Melancholly Arte* [by implication Harvey's] *to bedd. I had almost said, all the figures of Rhetorique must abate me an ace of Pierces Supererogation"* (D1^v/2:63). This praise is meant to fall flat, I think, the rhetoric to undercut itself with ostensibly unintentional connotations ("abate me an ace") of roguery: *"Penniles hath a certayne nimble and climbinge reach of Inuention, as good as a long pole, and a hooke, that neuer fayleth at a pinch"* (Ibid.). But, in what seems to be an uncontrollable ironic runaway, the same one—basically—that almost all of Nashe's subsequent critics have at least briefly succumbed to, the sarcasm finally undercuts *itself* and what comes through is genuine admiration for Nashe's lively response to "Melancholy Arte": *"Life is a gaming, a iugling, a scoulding, a lawing, a skirmishing, a warre; a Comedie, a Tragedy: the sturring witt, a quintessence of quicksiluer; and there is noe deade fleshe in affection, or courage"* (D1^v/2:62). Like real life, the extrarhetorical finally has no excuse for itself, and only incidentally serves the profit motive of discursive resourcefulness still tenuously prized in the institutional settlement at the end of the century; but it carries on all the same. Its "material" *can* be exploited by that profit motive through the usual processing, but this is gilding a lily: *"Coosen not your selues with the gay-nothings of children, & schollers: no priuitie of learning, or inspiration of witt, or reuelation of misteryes, or Arte Notory, counteruayleable with Pierces Supererogation: which hauing none of them, hath them all, and can make them all Asses at his pleasure"* (D2/2:64). "Pierces Supererogation" (Nashe's "singular" brand of "rhetorical excess") may be only the accidental creation of a disordered psyche or, on the contrary (as Harvey's grudgingly admirative "Gentleman" implies), an ambition-fueled product of the most highly sophisticated of meta-rhetorical strategies, strategies that Nashe fell upon and exploited in his desperate attempt to be a writer, even though he had "nothing to say." But those who have nothing to say may sometimes give us the most, the "walls, sand, ships and tides" we forgo when we enter the text, or find it hard to put aside for a moment our ongoing exegesis of the prose of the world.

So "[d]ismissing this fruitles annotation *pro et contra*" (Nashe 1594d, D4^v/2:245), *"Ad rem"* (1599, D4/3:176), for "logique hath nought to say in a true cause" (1600, G3^v/3:279) in any case. Rhetoric is truth; truth, rhetoric: that is all you know and all you need to know. And the only "counterpoison" or *contrepoisson* to rhetoric is, of course, more rhetoric. But there are still those works that invite us to read beyond the lines, beyond truth and logic, but also beyond rhetoric. *Nashes Lenten Stuffe* by this reading is not "self-referring" after all, just *self-reef-herring*: "in its Falstaffian way," it gives itself and us, if we still want it, the world. The net result of an extra-rhetorical reading of *Lenten Stuffe* is not Crewe's reading of Derridean *erring* but Nashe's actual writing of an always all-ruddy red *herring*. Keep the err-ogatory rhetoric, then, and give me some supererogatory *unredeemed redherring*; that, as Nashe said of unwatered-down wine, "begets good bloud, and heates the brain thorowly" (1599, A4ᵛ/3:152).

That poor old crumpled academic foil, Gabriel Harvey, used to try to discount the force of Nashe's rhetoric with remarks such as: "There is Logicke inough, to aunsweare Carters Logicke" (Harvey 1592, F3/1:214). Harvey, like all of Nashe's critics since, could only envision the vanquisher of unredeemed rhetoric to be logic. Perhaps I am only in a sense pathetic myself then if I applaud Harvey for phrasing it, at least once, in a somewhat more prosaic manner: "it is not the Affirmatiue, or Negatiue of the writer, but the trueth of the matter written, that carryeth meat in the mouth, and victory in the hande" (1593b, B4/2:47).

FINIS.

Works Cited

Although in the arguments I have put forward it may sometimes have seemed as though I was following some variant of the maxim of the makers of costume dramas—"modern hair for the stars, authentic hair for the extra[s]" (Hollander 1978, 310, VI.45 caption)—I have in fact *literally* made every exertion to ensure realistic costuming for the stars, while much less effort has been spent on the textual authenticity of those in the supporting roles. For the works of Nashe, and also those of Robert Greene and Gabriel Harvey, I have thus, so far as possible, referred to the original editions, followed by corresponding page references in the most reliable modern editions. In adopting the readings of the original editions I have, both for my own convenience and that of readers, generally followed the exemplars reproduced in readily accessible facsimiles such as those from Scolar Press (where they were available) or else the copies reproduced by University Microfilms International in the collection *Early English Books, 1475-1640*. I have not been able to reproduce all font variations, and have been obliged to replace long *s* with its modern allograph and ligatures with discrete letters, but I have otherwise made every effort to conform to the copy text indicated below.

In citing other Elizabethan works I have for the most part been content to make reference to modern editions when they were available, but I have made an effort to give the citation date as that of the original edition adopted as copytext by the editor of the modern edition cited. If not otherwise stated, the place of publication of Elizabethan texts is London. Classical works, the Bible, and a few "standard" Renaissance texts such as *The Faerie Queene*, are cited according to their conventional titles and divisions. For quotations from Shakespeare's plays I have followed the reading of the first folio as represented in the Norton facsimile *(The First Folio of Shakespeare*, prepared by Charlton Hinman [New York: Norton, 1968]), citing by traditional act and scene divisions and "through line number" (TLN) in the Norton text. Except where otherwise indicated, translations from works not in English are my own, even if they were not in my "best" languages. As Stanisław Lem says, "Nie kupuję ich, zapewne, wszędzie, lecz człowiek wykształcony może domyślić się sensów w hiszpańskim nawet, choć nie włada tym językiem" (1971, 22).

Adams, Carol J. (1990) *The Sexual Politics of Meat: A Feminist-Vegetarian Critical Theory.* New York: Continuum.

Agnew, Jean-Christophe. (1986) *Worlds Apart: The Market and the Theater in Anglo-American Thought, 1550-1750.* Cambridge: Cambridge University Press.

Albertini, Stefania. (1985) "Personaggi a confronto: Lazarillo de Tormes e Jack Wilton." *Quaderni di filologia e lingue romanze* n.s. 1: 33-51.

Allison, A. F. (1975) *Robert Greene, 1558-1592, A Bibliographical Catalogue of the Early Editions in English (to 1640).* Folkestone, Kent: Dawson.

Anselment, Raymond A. (1979) *"Betwixt Jest and Earnest": Marprelate, Milton, Marvell, Swift and the Decorum of Religious Ridicule.* Toronto: University of Toronto Press.

Ascham, Roger. (1570) *The Scholemaster.* John Day.

Atwood, Margaret. (1969) *The Edible Woman.* Toronto: McClelland and Stewart, 1973.

Babcock, Barbara A. (1978) "'Liberty's a Whore': Inversions, Marginalia, and Picaresque Narrative." *The Reversible World: Symbolic Inversion in Art and Society,* ed. Barbara A. Babcock. Ithaca: Cornell University Press.

Bacon, Francis. (1605) *The Tvvoo Bookes of Francis Bacon. Of the Proficiencie and Aduancement of Learning, Diuine and Humane.* H. Tomes.

Bakhtin, M. M. (1965) Творчество франсуа Рабле и народная култура средневековья и ренесанса. Moscow: Художественная литература. / *Rabelais and His World,* tr. Hélène Iswolsky. Cambridge, Mass.: MIT Press, 1968.

Bakhtin, M. M. (1970) *L'œuvre de François Rabelais et la culture populaire au Moyen Age et sous la Renaissance,* tr. Andrée Robel. Paris: Gallimard.

Bakhtin, M. M. (1979) Эстетика словесного творчества. Moscow: Искусство.

Bakhtin, M. M. (1981) *The Dialogic Imagination,* ed. Michael Holquist, tr. Caryl Emerson and Michael Holquist. Austin: University of Texas Press.

Bakhtin, M.M. (1984) *Speech Genres and Other Late Essays,* ed. Caryl Emerson and Michael Holquist, tr. Vern McGee. Austin: University of Texas Press.

Banfield, Ann. (1982) *Unspeakable Sentences: Narration and Representation in the Language of Fiction*. Boston: Routledge and Kegan Paul.

Barker, Francis. (1984) *The Tremulous Private Body: Essays on Subjection*. London: Methuen.

Barthes, Roland. (1966a) *Critique et vérité*. Paris: Seuil.

Barthes, Roland. (1966b) "L'effet du réel." *Le bruissement de la langue*. Paris: Seuil, 1984.

Barthes, Roland. (1970) *S/Z*. Paris: Seuil.

Belsey, Catherine. (1985) *The Subject of Tragedy: Identity and Difference in Renaissance Drama*. London: Methuen.

Benjamin, Walter. (1924) "Goethes Wahlverwandtschaften." *Gesammelte Schriften* 1.1, ed. Rolf Tiedemann and Hermann Schweppenhäuser. Frankfurt: Suhrkamp, 1974.

Berlioz, Marc. (1985) *Rabelais restitué: II - Gargantua, Tome I: Du prologue au chapître xxiv*. Paris: Didier.

Berrong, Richard M. (1986) *Rabelais and Bakhtin: Popular Culture in Gargantua and Pantagruel*. Lincoln: University of Nebraska Press.

Berryman, John. (1960) Introduction to Thomas Nashe, *The Unfortunate Traveller, or the Life of Jack Wilton*, ed. John Berryman. New York, Putnam.

Bowers, Fredson T. (1941) "Nashe and the Picaresque Novel." *Humanistic Studies in Honor of John Calvin Metcalf*. Charlottesville: University of Virginia Studies.

Bowlby, Rachel. (1988) *Virginia Woolf: Feminist Destinations*. Oxford: Basil Blackwell.

Bradbrook, M. C. (1936) *The School of Night: A Study in the Literary Relationships of Sir Walter Ralegh*. Cambridge: Cambridge University Press.

Bristol, Michael D. (1985) *Carnival and Theater: Plebian Culture and the Structure of Authority in Renaissance England*. London: Methuen.

Bristol, Michael D. (1989) *Shakespeare's America, America's Shakespeare: Literature, Institution, Ideology in America*. London: Routledge.

Burgess, Anthony. (1973) *The Clockwork Testament; or, Enderby's End*. New York: Knopf.

Calvino, Italo. (1972) *Le città invisibili*. Torino: Einaudi.

Carey, John. (1970) "Sixteenth- and Seventeenth-Century Prose." *English Poetry and Prose, 1540-1674*, ed. Christopher Ricks. London: Sphere.

Carlson, Leland H. (1981) *Martin Maprelate, Gentleman: Master Job Throckmorton Laid Open in His Colors*. San Marino: Huntington Library.

Carroll, William. (1974) "Nabokov's Signs and Symbols." *A Book of Things About Vladimir Nabokov*, ed. Carl Proffer. Ann Arbor: Ardis.

Cashion, Tim. (1991) "Rorty, Freud, and Bloom: The Limits of Communication." M.A. thesis, McGill University.

Cixous, Hélène. (1979) "L'approche de Clarice Lispector." *Poétique* 40: 408-19.

Cloud, Random. (1990) "from Tranceformations in the Text of 'Orlando Furioso.'" *Library Chronicle of the University of Texas at Austin* 20 (1/2): 61-85.

Coleman, Robert. (1977) *Introduction and Commentary to Vergil's Eclogues.* Cambridge: Cambridge University Press.

Compagnon, Antoine. (1979) *La seconde main, ou le travail de la citation.* Paris: Seuil.

"Cony-Catcher, Cuthbert." (1592) *The Defence of Conny-catching or a Confutation of Those Two Iniurious Pamphlets Published by R.G.* A. Jeffes for T. Gubbins, sold by J. Busbie. / *The Defence of Conny-catching* (1592), ed. G. B. Harrison. London: The Bodley Head, 1924.

Crewe, Jonathon. (1982) *Unredeemed Rhetoric: Thomas Nashe and the Scandal of Authorship.* Baltimore: Johns Hopkins University Press.

Croston, A. K. (1948) "The Use of Imagery in Nashe's Unfortunate Traveller." *Review of English Studies* 24: 90-101.

Curtius, E. R. (1953) *Europäische Literatur und Lateinisches Mittelalter.* 2nd. ed. Bern: Francke.

Cuvelier, Eliane. (1981) "Horror and Cruelty in the Works of Three Elizabethan Novelists." *Cahiers Elisabéthains* 19: 39-51.

Cuvelier, Eliane. (1986) "Le voyageur malchanceux de Thomas Nashe, ou la satire absolu." *La satire au temps de la Renaissance,* ed. M. T. Jones-Davies. Paris: Jean Touzot.

Davis, Walter R. (1969) *Idea and Act in Elizabethan Fiction.* Princeton: Princeton University Press.

Deleuze, Gilles, and Félix Guattari. (1975) *Kafka: pour une littérature mineure.* Paris: Minuit.

Demadre, Antoine. (1986) *Essais sur Thomas Nashe.* 2 vols. Salzburg: Institut für Anglistik und Amerikanistik, Universität Salzburg.

de Man, Paul. (1979a) *Allegories of Reading.* New Haven: Yale University Press.

de Man, Paul. (1979b) "Epistemology of Metaphor." *On Metaphor,* ed. Sheldon Sacks. Chicago: University of Chicago Press.

Derrida, Jacques. (1967a) *De la grammatologie.* Paris: Minuit.

Derrida, Jacques. (1967b) *La voix et le phénomène.* Paris: Presses universitaires de France.

Derrida, Jacques. (1971) "La mythologie blanche." *Poétique* 5: 1-52.

Derrida, Jacques. (1972a) *La dissémination.* Paris: Seuil.

Derrida, Jacques. (1972b) *Positions.* Paris: Minuit.

Derrida, Jacques. (1978) "The Retrait of Metaphor." *Enclitic* 2 (2): 5-33.

Derrida, Jacques. (1979) *Eperons: Les styles de Nietzsche.* Paris: Flammarion.

Dickenson, John. (1598) *Greene in conceipt. New Raised from his Graue to Write the Tragique Historie of Faire Valeria of London.* R. Bradocke for W. Jones.

Du Bartas, Guillaume de Salluste, Sieur. (1605) *Bartas His Devine Weeks and Works,* tr. Josuah Sylvester, ed. Susan Snyder. 2 vols. Oxford: Clarendon, 1979.

Duncan-Jones, Katherine. (1968) "Nashe and Sidney: the Tournament in *The Unfortunate Traveller.*" *Modern Language Review* 63: 3-6.

Eco, Umberto. (1984) *Semiotics and the Philosophy of Language.* Bloomington: Indiana University Press.

Edwards, Philip. (1987) "Unfortunate Travellers: Fiction and Reality." *Huntington Library Quarterly* 50: 295-301.

Emerson, Caryl. (1988) "Problems with Baxtin's Poetics." *Slavic and East European Journal* 32: 503-525.

Ferguson, Margaret. (1981) "Nashe's *The Unfortunate Traveller*: The 'Newes of the Maker' Game." *English Literary Renaissance* 11: 165-82.

Fish, Stanley. (1984) "Fear of Fish: A Reply to Walter Davis." *Critical Inquiry* 10: 695-705.

Fraunce, Abraham. (1592) *The Third Part of the Countesse of Pembrookes Yuychurch. Entituled, Amintas Dale,* ed. Gerald Snare. Northridge, Cal.: California State University Press, 1975.

Freud, Sigmund. (1900) *Die Traumdeutung. Gesammelte Werke* 2/3. London: Imago, 1942. / *The Interpretation of Dreams. The Standard Edition of the Complete Psychological Works* 4, 5. Rev. ed. London: Hogarth Press, 1958.

Friederich, Reinhard H. (1975) "Verbal Tensions in Thomas Nashe's *The Unfortunate Traveller.*" *Language and Style* 8: 211-219.

Frye, Northrop. (1957) *The Anatomy of Criticism: Four Essays.* Princeton: Princeton University Press.

Garber, Marjorie. (1987) *Shakespeare's Ghost Writers: Literature as Uncanny Causality.* New York: Methuen.

Gascoigne, George. (1575) *Posies,* ed. John W. Cunliffe. Cambridge: Cambridge University Press, 1907.

Genette, Gérard. (1972) *Figures III.* Paris: Seuil.

Genette, Gérard. (1976) *Mimologiques: Voyage en Cratylie.* Paris: Seuil.

Genette, Gérard. (1979) *Introduction à l'architexte.* Paris: Seuil.

Genette, Gérard. (1983) *Nouveau discours du récit.* Paris: Seuil.

Genette, Gérard. (1987) *Seuils.* Paris: Seuil.

Gibbons, Brian. (1980) *Jacobean City Comedy: A Study of Satiric Plays by Jonson, Marston and Middleton.* Rev. ed. London: Methuen.

Gibbons, Sister Marina. (1964) "Polemic, the Rhetorical Tradition, and *The Unfortunate Traveller." Journal of English and Germanic Philology* 63: 408-21.

Gohlke, Madelon S. (1976) "Wits Wantonesse: *The Unfortunate Traveller* as Picaresque." *Studies in Philology* 73: 397-413.

Goldberg, Jonathan. (1992) *Sodometries: Renaissance Texts, Modern Sexualities*. Stanford: Stanford University Press.

Greene, Robert. (1591a) *A Notable Discouery of Coosenage*. John Wolfe for T. Nelson. / Greene 1881-86, vol. 10. / *A Notable Discovery of Coosnage* (1591), ed. G. B. Harrison. London: The Bodley Head, 1923.

Greene, Robert. (1591b) *The Second Part of Conny-catching*. J. Wolfe for W. Wright. / Greene 1881-86, vol. 10. / *The Second Part of Conny-catching* (1592), ed. G. B. Harrison. London: The Bodley Head, 1923.

Greene, Robert. (1592a) *The Black Bookes Messenger Laying Open the Life and Death of Ned Brown One of the Most Notable Cutpurses*. J. Danter for T. Nelson. / Greene 1881-86, vol. 10. / *The Blacke Bookes Messenger* (1592), ed. G. B. Harrison. London: The Bodley Head, 1924.

Greene, Robert. (1592b) *A Disputation betweene a Hee Conny-catcher and a Shee Conny-catcher*. [Init. R. G.] A Jeffes for T. Gubbin. / Greene 1881-86, vol. 10. / *A Disputation betweene a Hee Conny-catcher and a Shee Conny-catcher* (1592), ed. G. B. Harrison. London: The Bodley Head, 1923.

Greene, Robert. (1592c) *Greenes Groats-worth of Witte, ... Written before His Death*. [J. Wolfe and J. Danter] for W. Wright / Greene 1881-86, vol. 12. / *Groats-vvorth of Witte* (1592), ed. G. B. Harrison. London: The Bodley Head, 1923.

Greene, Robert. (1592d) *Greenes Vision: Written at the Instant of his Death*. E. Allde for T. Newman. / Greene 1881-86, vol. 12.

Greene, Robert. (1592e) *A Quip for an Vpstart Courtier: or, a Quaint Dispute. Wherein Is Plainely Set Downe the Disorders in All Estates and Trades*. J. Wolfe.

Greene, Robert. (1592f) *The Repentance of Robert Greene*. J. Danter for C. Burbie. / Greene 1881-86, vol. 12. / *The Repentance of Robert Greene* (1592), ed. G. B. Harrison. London: The Bodley Head, 1923.

Greene, Robert. (1592g) *The Thirde and Last Part of Conny-catching*. T. Scarlet for C. Burbie. / Greene 1881-86, vol. 10. / *The Thirde & Last Part of Conny-catching* (1592), ed. G. B. Harrison. London: The Bodley Head, 1923.

Greene, Robert. (1881-86) *The Life and Complete Writings of Robert Greene, M. A.*, ed. Alexander B. Grosart. 15 vols. London: The Huth Library. Reprt. New York: Russell & Russell, 1964.

Harlow, C. G. (1961) "Nashe, Robert Cotton the Antiquary, and *The Terrors of the Night.*" *Review of English Studies* n.s. 12: 7-23.

Harlow, C. G. (1965) "A Source for Nashe's *Terrors of the Night* and the Authorship of 1 Henry VI." *Studies in English Literature* 5:31-47; 269-81.

Harrington, Susan Marie and Michal Nahor Bond. (1987) "'Good Sir, Be Ruld by Me': Patterns of Domination and Manipulation in Thomas Nashe's *The Unfortunate Traveller.*" *Studies in Short Fiction* 24: 243-50.

Hartman, Geoffrey. (1970) "Romanticism and Anti-Self-Consciousness." *Romanticism and Consciousness*, ed. Harold Bloom. New York: Norton.

Harvey, Gabriel. (MS.a) British Library Sloane MS. 93. / *The Letter-book of Gabriel Harvey, A.D. 1573-1580*, ed. Edward John Long Scott. London: Camden Society, 1884.

Harvey, Gabriel. (MS.b) British Library Additional MS. 32,494. / *Gabriel Harvey's Marginalia*, ed. C.G. Moore Smith. Stratford-upon-Avon: The Shakespeare Head, 1913.

Harvey, Gabriel. (1592) *Foure Letters and Certeine Sonnets, Especially Touching Robert Greene*. J. Wolfe. / Harvey 1884, vol. 1. / *Foure Letters and Certeine Sonnets*, ed. G. B. Harrison. London: The Bodley Head, 1922.

Harvey, Gabriel. (1593a) *A New Letter of Notable Contents. With a Straunge Sonet, Intituled Gorgon*. J. Wolfe. / Harvey 1884, vol. 1.

Harvey, Gabriel. (1593b) *Pierces Supererogation or New Prayse of the Old Asse*. J. Wolfe. / Harvey 1884, vol. 2.

Harvey, Gabriel. (1884) *The Works of Gabriel Harvey*, ed. Alexander B. Grosart. 3 vols. London: "Privately Printed."

Haworth, R. G. (1956) *Two Elizabethan Writers of Fiction: Thomas Nashe and Thomas Deloney*. Capetown: University of Capetown Press.

Hayman, David. (1983) "Toward a Mechanics of Mode: Beyond Bakhtin." *Novel* 16: 101-20.

Heidegger, Martin. (1950) "Das Ding." *Vorträge und Aufsätze, Teil II.* Tübingen: Neske, 1953.

Helgerson, Richard. (1977) *The Elizabethan Prodigals*. Berkeley: University of California Press.

Hibbard, G. R. (1962) *Thomas Nashe: A Critical Introduction*. Cambridge, Mass.: Harvard University Press.

Hilliard, Stephen S. (1986) *The Singularity of Thomas Nashe*. Lincoln, Neb.: University of Nebraska Press.

Hobbes, Thomas. (1651) *Leviathan*, ed. C. B. Macpherson. Harmondsworth: Penguin, 1968.

Hollander, Anne. (1978) *Seeing Through Clothes*. New York: Viking Penguin.

Holquist, Michael. (1983) "Answering as Authoring: Mikhail Bakhtin's Trans-linguistics." *Critical Inquiry* 10: 307-319.

Hutson, Lorna. (1989) *Thomas Nashe in Context.* Oxford: University of Oxford Press.

Irigaray, Luce. (1974) *Speculum de l'autre femme.* Paris: Minuit.

Jameson, Frederic. (1983) "Pleasure: A Political Issue." *Ideologies of Theory: Essays 1971-1986, Volume 2: Syntax of History.* Minneapolis: University of Minnesota Press, 1988.

Jameson, Frederic. (1984) "Periodizing the 60s." *Ideologies of Theory: Essays 1971-1986, Volume 2: Syntax of History.* Minneapolis: University of Minnesota Press, 1988.

Jones, Ann Rosalind. (1983) "Inside the Outsider: Nashe's Unfortunate Traveller and Bakhtin's Polyphonic Novel." *ELH* 50: 61-81.

Jones, Dorothy. (1971) "An Example of Anti-Petrarchan Satire in Nashe's *The Unfortunate Traveller.*" *Yearbook of English Studies* 1: 48-54.

Jordan, John Clark. (1915) *Robert Greene.* New York: Columbia University Press. Reprt. New York: Octagon Books, 1965.

Kaula, David. (1966) "The Low Style in Nashe's The Unfortunate Traveler." *Studies in English Literature* 6: 43-57.

Kierkegaard, Søren. (1955) *On Authority and Revelation: The Book on Adler, or a Cycle of Ethico-Religious Essays,* ed. and tr. Walter Lowrie. Princeton: Princeton University Press.

Kierkegaard, Søren. (1968-70) *Søren Kierkegaards Papirer.* 13 vols. Copenhagen: Gyldendal.

Kilgour, Maggie. (1990) *From Communion to Cannibalism: An Anatomy of Metaphors of Incorporation.* Princeton: Princeton University Press.

Kinney, Arthur E. (1986) *Humanist Poetics: Thought, Rhetoric, and Fiction in Sixteenth-Century England.* Amherst: University of Massachusetts Press.

Kittay, Jeffrey and Wlad Godzich. (1986) *The Emergence of Prose: An Essay in Prosaics.* Minneapolis: University of Minnesota Press.

Kofman, Sarah. (1971) "Nietzsche et la métaphore." *Poétique* 5: 77-98.

Kristeva, Julia. (1977) *Polylogue.* Paris: Seuil.

Kristeva, Julia. (1979) "Le vréel." *La folle vérité: vérité et vraisemblance du texte psychotique,* ed. Jean-Michel Ribettes. Paris: Seuil.

Lacan, Jacques. (1966) *Ecrits.* Paris: Seuil.

Lacan, Jacques. (1986) *Le séminaire, livre VII: L'éthique de la psychanalyse.* Paris: Seuil.

Lanham, Richard A. (1967) "Tom Nashe and Jack Wilton: Personality as Structure in *The Unfortunate Traveller.*" *Studies in Short Fiction* 4: 201-216.

Larson, Charles. (1975) "The Comedy of Violence in Nashe's *The Unfortunate Traveller.*" *Cahiers Elisabéthains* 8: 15-29.

Latham, Agnes M. C. (1948) "Satire on Literary Themes and Modes in Nashe's 'Unfortunate Traveller.'" *English Studies* n.s. 1: 85-100.

Leech, Clifford. (1963) "Recent Studies in Elizabethan and Jacobean Drama." *Studies in English Literature* 3: 269-85.

Leggatt, Alexander. (1974) "Artistic Coherence in *The Unfortunate Traveller.*" *Studies in English Literature* 14: 31-46.

Leishman, J. B., ed. (1949) *The Three Parnassus Plays (1598-1601).* London: Ivor Nicholson & Watson.

Lem, Stanisław. (1971) *Bezsenność.* Cracow: Wydawnictwo literackie.

Lemnius, Levinus. (1576) *A Touchstone of Complexions,* tr. T. Newton. T. Marsh.

Levin, Richard. (1979) *Old Plays vs. New Readings.* Chicago: University of Chicago Press.

Lewis, C. S. (1954) *English Literature in the Sixteenth Century, Excluding Drama.* London: Oxford University Press.

Lichfield, Richard. (1597) *The Trimming of Thomas Nashe, Gentleman.* E. Allde for Philip Scarlet. / Harvey 1884a, vol. 3.

Lovatelli, Rosamaria. (1984) *Di picaro a picaro: le trasformazioni di un genere letterario dalla Spagna all'Inghilterra.* Rome: Bulzoni.

Lubin, Peter. (1970) "Kickshaws and Motley." *Nabokov: Criticism, Reminiscences, Translations and Tributes,* ed. Alfred Appel, Jr. and Charles Newman. Evanston, Ill.: Northwestern University Press.

M., I. (1598) *A Health to the Gentlemanly Profession of Seruingmen: or, The Seruingmans Comfort.* W. White.

Macdonald, Virginia L. (1981) "Robert Greene's Innovative Contributions to Prose Fiction in *A Notable Discovery.*" *Shakespeare-Jahrbuch* (Weimar) 117: 127-37.

Macdonald, Virginia L. (1983) "The Complex Moral View of Robert Greene's *A Disputation.*" *Shakespeare-Jahrbuch* 119: 122-36.

Macdonald, Virginia L. (1984) "Robert Greene's Courtesan: A Renaissance Perception of a Medieval Tale." *Zeitschrift für Anglistik und Amerikanistik* 32: 211-19.

MacKenzie, Scott. (1992) "The Cadaver's Pulse: Film Theory's Construction of the Viewer and the Real." M.A. thesis, McGill University.

Mackerness, E. D. (1947) "A Note on Thomas Nashe and 'Style.'" *English* 6: 198-200.

Maguin, J.M. (1983) "Nashe's Lenten Stuffe: The Relevance of the Author's Name," *Cahiers Elisabéthains* 24: 73-74.

Marcus, Leah S. (1988) *Puzzling Shakespeare: Local Reading and its Discontents*. Berkeley: University of California.

Margolies, David. (1985) *Novel and Society in Elizabethan England*. London: Croom Helm.

Marin, Louis. (1986) *La parole mangée et autres essais théologico-politiques*. Montréal: Boréal.

"Marprelate, Martin." (1588a) *Oh Read ouer D. John Bridges*. Printed ouersea, in Europe, within two furlongs of a bounsing priest, at the cost and charges of M. Marprelate, gent. [East Mortesey: R. Waldgrove.]

"Marprelate, Martin." (1588b) *Oh Read ouer D. John Bridges*. Printed on the other hand of some priests. [Fawsely: R. Waldgrove.]

"Marprelate, Martin." (1589) *Hay Any Worke for Cooper: or a Briefe Pistle Directed to the Reuerende Byshops*. Printed in Europe, not farre from some of the bounsing priestes. [Coventry: R. Waldgrove.]

"Marprelate, Martin," et al. (1911) *The Marprelate Tracts*, ed. William Pierce. London: James Clark.

McGinn, Donald J. (1944) "Nashe's Share in the Marprelate Controversy." *PMLA* 59: 952-84.

McGinn, Donald J. (1946) "The Allegory of the 'Beare' and the 'Foxe' in *Pierce Penniless*." *PMLA* 61: 431-53.

McGinn, Donald J. (1981) *Thomas Nashe*. Boston: Twayne.

McKerrow, R. B. (1908) "Commentary," in Nashe 1958, vol 4.

McKerrow, R. B. (1910) "Introduction," in Nashe 1958, vol 5.

Migliorini, Bruno. (1957) *Saggi linguistici*. Florence: F. le Monnier.

Millard, Barbara C. (1978) "Thomas Nashe and the Functional Grotesque in Elizabethan Prose Fiction." *Studies in Short Fiction* 15: 39-48.

Miller, Edwin Haviland. (1954) "The Relationship of Robert Greene and Thomas Nashe (1588-1592)." *Philological Quarterly* 33: 353-67.

Montaigne, Michel de. (1588) *Essais*, ed. Maurice Rat. 2 vols. Paris: Garnier, 1962.

Morin, Edgar. (1980) *La méthode 2: La vie de la vie*. Paris: Seuil.

Morrow, Patrick. (1975) "The Brazen World of Thomas Nashe and *The Unfortunate Traveller*." *Journal of Popular Culture* 9: 638-44.

Mullaney, Steven. (1988) *The Place of the Stage: License, Play, and Power in Renaissance England*. Chicago: University of Chicago Press.

Nabokov, Vladimir. (1967a) "Vladimir Nabokov: An Interview" [conducted by Herbert Gold]. *Paris Review* 41: 99-111.

Nabokov, Vladimir. (1967b) "An Interview with Vladimir Nabokov" [conducted by Alfred Appel, Jr.]. *Nabokov: The Man and His Work*, ed. L. S. Dembo. Madison, Wisconsin: University of Wisconsin Press.

Nashe, Thomas. (1589a) *The Anatomie of Absurditie: Contayning a Breefe Confutation of the Slender Imputed Prayses to Feminine Perfection.* J. Charlewood for T. Hacket. / Nashe 1958, vol. 1.

Nashe, Thomas. (1589b) Preface to Robert Greene, *Menaphon Camillas Alarum to Slumbering Euphues.* T. Orwin for S. Clarke. / Nashe 1958, vol. 3.

Nashe, Thomas. (1592a) Epistle to the Printer, *Pierce Pennilesse His Svpplication to the Diuell.* (2nd ed.) A. Jeffes for J. Busbie. / Nashe 1958, vol. 2.

Nashe, Thomas. (1592b) *Pierce Penilesse His Supplication to the Diuell.* J. Charlewood for R. Jhones. / Nashe 1958, vol. 1.

Nashe, Thomas. (1592c) *Strange Newes, of the Intercepting Certaine Letters.* J. Danter. / Nashe 1958, vol. 1.

Nashe, Thomas. (1593) *Christs Teares ouer Ierusalem.* J. Roberts, solde by A. Wise. / Nashe 1958, vol. 2.

Nashe, Thomas. (1594a) Dedicatory epistle, *The Vnfortunate Traueller.* (1st ed.) T. Scarlet for C. Burby. / Nashe 1958, vol. 2.

Nashe, Thomas. (1594b) Epistle to the Reader, *Christs Teares ouer Ierusalem.* (2nd. ed.) For A. Wise. / Nashe 1958, vol. 2.

Nashe, Thomas. (1594c) *The Terrors of the Night or, a Discourse of Apparitions.* J. Danter for W. Jones. / Nashe 1958, vol. 1.

Nashe, Thomas. (1594d) *The Vnfortunate Traueller. Or, the Life of Iacke Wilton.* (2nd ed.) T. Scarlet for C. Burby. / Nashe 1958, vol. 2.

Nashe, Thomas. (1596) *Haue with You to Saffron-Walden.* J. Danter. / Nashe 1958, vol. 3.

Nashe, Thomas. (1599) *Nashes Lenten Stuffe, Containing, the Description of Great Yarmouth. With a New Play of the Praise of the Red Herring.* T. Judson and V. Simmes for N. Ling and C. Burbie. / Nashe 1958, vol. 3.

Nashe, Thomas. (1600) *A Pleasant Comedie, Called Summers Last Will and Testament.* S. Stafford for W. Burre. / Nashe 1958, vol. 3.

Nashe, Thomas. (1958) *The Works of Thomas Nashe,* ed. Ronald B. McKerrow, with corrections and supplementary notes by F.P. Wilson. 5 vols. Oxford: Basil Blackwell.

Nicholl, Charles. (1984) *A Cup of News: The Life of Thomas Nashe.* London: Routledge and Kegan Paul.

Nietzsche, Friedrich. (1873) "Über Wahrheit und Lüge im aussermoralischen Sinne," in *Werke Kritische Gesamtausgabe* 3.2, ed. Giorgio Colli and Mazzino Montinari. Berlin: Walter de Gruyter, 1973.

Nietzsche, Friedrich. (1874) "Rhetorik," in *Gesammelte Werke,* Musarionausgabe, vol. 5. Munich: Musarion, 1922.

Nietzsche, Friedrich. (1881) *Morgenröthe*, in *Werke Kritische Gesamtausgabe* 5.1, ed. Giorgio Colli and Mazzino Montinari. Berlin: Walter de Gruyter, 1971.

Nietzsche, Friedrich. (1882) *Die fröhliche Wissenschaft*, in *Werke Kritische Gesamtausgabe* 5.2, ed. Giorgio Colli and Mazzino Montinari. Berlin: Walter de Gruyter, 1973.

Nietzsche, Friedrich. (1886) *Jenseits von Gute und Böse*, in *Werke Kritische Gesamtausgabe*, 6.2, ed. Giorgio Colli and Mazzino Montinari. Berlin: Walter de Gruyter, 1968.

Nietzsche, Friedrich. (1887) *Zur Genealogie der Moral*, in *Werke Kritische Gesamtausgabe* 6.2, ed. Giorgio Colli and Mazzino Montinari. Berlin: Walter de Gruyter, 1968.

Ortega y Gasset, José. (1910) "Una primera vista sobre Baroja." *Obras completas*, t. 2. Madrid: Revista de Occidente, 1950.

Parker, Patricia. (1987) *Literary Fat Ladies: Rhetoric, Gender, Property*. London: Methuen.

Patterson, Annabel. (1984) *Censorship and Interpretation: The Conditions of Writing and Reading in Early Modern England*. Madison: University of Wisconsin Press.

Peñuelas, Marcelino C. (1954) "Algo más sobre la picaresca: Lázaro y Jack Wilton." *Hispania* 37: 443-45.

Pierce, William. (1908) *An Historical Introduction to the Marprelate Tracts: A Chapter in the Evolution of Religious and Civil Liberty in England*. London: Archibald Constable.

Pil. (1599) *A Pil to Purge Melancholie*. W. White.

Puttenham, George. (1589) *The Arte of English Poetrie*, ed. Gladys Doidge Willcock and Alice Walker. Cambridge: Cambridge University Press, 1936.

Quiller-Couch, Sir Arthur and John Dover Wilson. (1923) Introduction to *Love's Labour's Lost*. Cambridge: Cambridge University Press, 1923.

R., B. (1593) *Greenes Newes Both from Heauen and Hell. Commended to the Presse by B. R.* Widow Charlewood. / *Greenes Newes Both from Heaven and Hell* (1593), ed. R. B. McKerrow. Stratford-upon-Avon: The Shakespeare Head, 1922.

Ralegh, Sir Walter. (1951) *The Poems*, ed. Agnes M. C. Latham. London: Routledge and Kegan Paul.

Relihan, Constance C. (1990) "The Narrative Strategies of Robert Greene's Cony-Catching Pamphlets." *Cahiers Elisabéthains* 37: 9-15.

Rhodes, Neil. (1980) *Elizabethan Grotesque*. London: Routledge and Kegan Paul.

Rhodes, Neil. (1988) "Nashe, Rhetoric and Satire." *Jacobean Poetry and Prose: Rhetoric, Representation and the Popular Imagination,* ed. Clive Bloom. New York: St. Martin's Press, 1988.

Richards, I. A. (1934) *Coleridge on Imagination.* 3rd ed. London: Routledge and Kegan Paul, 1962.

Ricoeur, Paul. (1965) *De l'interpretation.* Paris: Seuil.

Rilke, Rainer Maria. (1910) *Die Aufzeichnungen des Malte Laurids Brigge. Sämtliche Werke.* Frankfurt: Insel, 1966.

Ryan, Kiernan. (1985) "The Extemporal Vein: Thomas Nashe and the Invention of Modern Narrative." *Narrative: from Malory to Motion Pictures,* ed. Jeremy Hawthorn. London: Edward Arnold.

Schlauch, Margaret. (1963) *Antecedents of the English Novel 1400-1600 (from Chaucer to Deloney).* London: Oxford.

Schor, Naomi. (1987) *Reading in Detail: Aesthetics and the Feminine.* London: Methuen.

Scoufos, Alice Lyle. (1968) "Nashe, Jonson and the Oldcastle Problem." *Modern Philology* 65: 307-24.

Schrickx, W. (1956) *Shakespeare's Early Contemporaries: The Background of the Harvey-Nashe Polemic and Love's Labour's Lost.* Antwerp: Nederlandsche Boekhandler.

Serres, Michel. (1980) *Le passage du nord-ouest.* Paris: Minuit.

Serres, Michel. (1982) *Génèse.* Paris: Grasset.

Sidney, Sir Philip. (1590) *The Covntesse of Pembroke's Arcadia,* in Sidney 1912, vol 1.

Sidney, Sir Philip. (1595) *The Defence of Poesie.* W. Ponsonby. / *A Defence of Poetry,* ed. J. A. Van Dorsten. Oxford: Oxford University Press, 1966.

Sidney, Sir Philip. (1912) *Prose Works,* ed. Albert Feuillerat. 3 vols. Cambridge: Cambridge University Press.

Simons, Louise. (1988) "Rerouting *The Unfortunate Traveller*: Strategies for Coherence and Direction." *Studies in English Literature* 28: 17-38.

Smith, John Dale. (1968) "Narrative Technique in the Realistic Prose Fiction of Greene, Nashe, and Deloney." Ph.D. Dissertation, University of Wisconsin.

Sontag, Susan. (1964) "Against Interpretation." *Against Interpretation.* New York: Farrar, Straus and Giroux, 1966.

Steane, J. B. (1972) Introduction to Thomas Nashe, *The Unfortunate Traveller and Other Works.* Harmondsworth: Penguin, 1972.

Stephanson, Raymond. (1983) "The Epistemological Challenge of Nashe's *The Unfortunate Traveller.*" *Studies in English Literature* 23: 21-36.

Stevenson, Ruth M. (1980) "The Roman Banketting House: Nashe's Forsaken Image of Art." *Studies in Short Fiction* 17: 291-306.

Stow, John. (1603) *A Suruay of London*, ed. Charles Lethbridge Kingsford. 2 vols. Oxford: Clarendon, 1908.

Sulfridge, Cynthia. (1980) "*The Unfortunate Traveller*: Nashe's Narrative in a 'Cleane Different Vaine.'" *Journal of Narrative Technique* 10: 1-15.

Summersgill, Travis L. (1951) "The Influence of the Marprelate Controversy upon the Style of Thomas Nashe." *Studies in Philology* 48: 145-60.

Suzuki, Mihoko. (1984) "'Signiorie Ouer the Pages': The Crisis of Authority in Nashe's *The Unfortunate Traveller*." *Studies in Philology* 81 (3): 348-71.

Tilley, Morris Palmer. (1950) *A Dictionary of the Proverbs in England in the Sixteenth and Seventeenth Centuries*. Ann Arbor: University of Michigan Press.

Todorov, Tzvetan. (1970) *Introduction à la littérature fantastique*. Paris: Seuil.

Turler, Jerome. (1975) *The Traveiler*. W. How for A. Veale.

"Tyro, T." (1598) *Tyros Roring Megge. Planted against the Walles of Melancholy*. V. Simmes.

Valéry, Paul. (1960) *Œuvres, t. 2*. Paris: Gallimard.

Vološinov, V. N. (1926) "Discourse in Life and Discourse in Art (Concerning Sociological Poetics)." *Freudianism: A Marxist Critique*, tr. I. R. Titunik, ed. in coll. with Neal H. Bruss. Bloomington: Indiana University Press, 1987.

von Koppenfels, Werner. (1971) "Two Notes on Imprese in Elizabethan Literature: Daniel's Additions to *The Worthy Tract of Paulus Iouius*; Sidney's *Arcadia* and the Tournament Scene in *The Unfortunate Traveller*." *Renaissance Quarterly* 24: 13-25.

von Koppenfels, Werner. (1976) "Zur zeitgenössischen Aufnahme des elisabethaneschen 'Romans': Nashes Unfortunate Traveller in der Literatur des Shakespeare-Epoche." *Anglia* 94: 361-87.

Vonnegut, Kurt, Jr. (1968) *Slaughterhouse-Five*. New York: Laurel, 1988.

Weimann, Robert. (1970) "'Jest-book' und Ich-Erzählung in *The Unfortunate Traveller*: Zum Problem des 'point of view' in der Renaissance-Prosa." *Zeitschrift für Anglistik und Amerikanistik* 18: 11-29.

Weimann, Robert, ed. (1977) *Realismus in der Renaissance: Aneignung der Welt in der erzählenden Prosa*. Berlin: Aufbau-Verlag.

Weimann, Robert. (1983) "'Appropriation' and Modern History in Renaissance Prose Narrative." *New Literary History* 14(3): 459-96.

Weimann, Robert. (1984) "Fabula and Historia: The Crisis of the 'Universall Consideration' in *The Unfortunate Traveller*." *Representations* 8: 14-28.

Wells, Stanley. (1964) Introduction to *Thomas Nashe: Selected Works.* London: E. Arnold.

Wenke, John. (1981) "The Moral Aesthetic of Thomas Nashe's The Unfortunate Traveller," *Renascence* 34: 26-27.

Whetstone, George. (1584) *A Mirour for Magestrates of Cyties.* R. Jones.

White, Hayden. (1966) "The Burden of History." *Tropics of Discourse.* Baltimore: Johns Hopkins University Press, 1978.

Woodbridge, Linda. (1986) *Women and the English Renaissance: Literature and the Nature of Womanhood, 1540-1620.* Urbana, Ill.: University of Illinois Press.

Yates, Frances. (1934) *John Florio: The Life of an Italian in Shakespeare's England.* Cambridge: Cambridge University Press.

Yates, Frances A. (1979) *The Occult Philosophy in the Elizabethan Age.* London: Routledge and Kegan Paul.

Index

Renaissance and Baroque Studies and Texts

This series deals with various aspects of the European Renaissance and Baroque. Studies on the history, literature, philosophy and the visual arts of these periods are welcome. The series will also consider translations of important works, especially from Latin into English. These translations should, however, include a substantial introduction and notes. Books in the series will include original monographs as well as revised or reconceived dissertations. The series editor is:

Eckhard Bernstein
Department of Modern Languages
and Literatures
College of the Holy Cross
Worcester, MA 01610